8/97

 St. Louis Community College

Forest Park
Florissant Valley
Meramec

Instructional Resources
St. Louis, Missouri

GAYLORD

Oscar Wilde was a major influence on the culture of his time, and remains relevant today, as a model of wit and style, a sexual icon, and a moral example. In a sequence of detailed and imaginative chapters on Wilde and his times, John Stokes shows how in the 1880s and 1890s Wilde played a vital part in the development of modern culture, inspiring others to carry his ideas on into the twentieth century. Stokes offers studies of Wilde's place in the Romantic tradition, and of his relationships with such legendary figures of the *fin de siècle* as Aubrey Beardsley, Alfred Jarry, and Arthur Symons. And always, as part of the process of historical inquiry, Stokes considers those who came after: humanitarian disciples who kept Wilde's memory sacred, performers in his plays, actors who impersonated the man himself. *Oscar Wilde: Myths, Miracles, and Imitations* explains why Wilde, a "material ghost," haunts us still.

OSCAR WILDE: MYTHS, MIRACLES, AND IMITATIONS

OSCAR WILDE: MYTHS MIRACLES, AND IMITATIONS

JOHN STOKES
University of Warwick

CAMBRIDGE UNIVERSITY PRESS

Published by the Press Syndicate of the University of Cambridge
The Pitt Building, Trumpington Street, Cambridge CB2 RP
40 West 20th Street, New York, NY 10011–4211, USA
10 Stamford Road, Oakleigh, Melbourne 3166, Australia

First published 1996

Printed in Great Britain at the University Press, Cambridge

A catalogue record for this book is abailable from the British Library

Library of Congress cataloguing in publication data
Stokes, John, 1943–
Oscar Wilde: myths, miracles, and imitations / John Stokes.
p.   cm.
Includes bibliographical references and index.
ISBN 0 521 47537 6 (hardback)
1. Wilde, Oscar, 1854–1900.   2. Homosexuality and literature –
Great Britain – History – 19th century.   3. Authors, Irish – 19th
century – Biography.   4. Wilde, Oscar, 1854–1900 – Influence.   5. Gay
men – Great Britain – Biography.   6. Romanticism – Great Britain.
1. Title.
PR5823.S68 1996
828'.809 – dc20   95–32382   CIP

ISBN 0 521 47537 6 hardback

For Richard Ellmann
1918–1987

Contents

Illustrations

Acknowledgments

My own involvement with Oscar Wilde began when I played the role of Gwendolen Fairfax, not accurately but with wonderful expression, in a school production in the mid-fifties. Like many of the men and women I write about in this book, I felt liberated by my contact with notoriety. In the early 1960s good fortune took me to Reading University. There I encountered Ian Fletcher, who knew more about the *fin de siècle* than anyone else alive. In the 1970s Ian and I ransacked libraries on both sides of the Atlantic for all traces of Wilde and compiled two long bibliographical essays.

In the 1980s I began to realize the paradox of Wilde's reputation. As his historical moment grows ever more distant he is increasingly recognized as an ally in all quarters. This is because he occupied a complicated historical space: the son of an Irish Republican who was at home with the Prince of Wales; a socialist Oxonian who embraced boulevard theater; a radical thinker accused of effeminacy as well as of feminism; a sometimes loving husband and a constantly devoted father who was deeply and proudly homosexual. His cultural permanence depends on his multiple personality – the double life not so much the alternative life as the mirroring life, because all lives involve love, fidelity, betrayal.

These days he's everywhere. As I write this, in the summer of 1994, three events take place in rapid succession. First it is announced that Wilde is to be commemorated in Poets' Corner in Westminster Abbey. The Dean of Westminster counters any objections by insisting that he was "someone who is likely to be remembered a hundred years after his death and someone who is not a militant atheist...basically a religious man" (*Independent*, 21 July 1994). Meanwhile a group of theatrical admirers proposes a scheme to have a statue erected to his memory, perhaps in the Strand, and "Outrage", the gay rights association, continues to press for a pardon in time for the centenary of his arrest in 1995. It is precisely at this moment that the Perrier-Jouet company (which long ago benefited from product placement in *The Importance of Being Earnest*) opts for the advertising slogan, "When Oscar Wilde called for the Champagne waiter he was only after one thing."

"The evolution of man is slow," as Wilde was obliged to conclude in *The Soul of Man under Socialism*.

Over the years my researches have been greatly aided by the expertise and courtesy of library staff. Thanks to the British Library; the William Andrews Clark Memorial Library, University of California at Los Angeles; the London Library; the Miller Library, Colby College, Waterville, Maine; the Harry Ransom Humanities Research Center, University of Texas at Austin, Texas; the Theatre Museum, London; Warwick University Library.

My final chapter, on Wilde in performance, involves special debts. I am much obliged to Joel Kaplan for supplying me with copies of the major reviews of recent productions. The picture of Wilde as member of the audience by Maurice Greiffenhagen first appeared as an illustration to George Moore's *Vain Fortune* in 1891. I owe its reproduction here to Russell Jackson who originally drew my attention to its existence.

Many other individuals have helped me along the way. Thanks to Karl Beckson, Carol Ann Duffy, Claude Féron, Sir Rupert Hart-Davis, Merlin Holland, Nicholas Horsfield, Tony Howard, Robert Langenfeld, Etrenne Lymberry, Paul Raven, Anthony Reid, Ian Small, Julie Speedie, Kelsey Thornton, Doreen Vincent, Jeffrey Weeks, John Willett, Erika Wilson. And to Faith Evans.

With the exception of "The Magic Ball," which was delivered as a paper at the International Wilde Conference at the University of Birmingham in April 1993, all the chapters have appeared previously. In every case I have expanded, sometimes greatly, and updated to take account of more recent research. I am grateful to the editor of the *Times Literary Supplement* and to the editors of the following publications for permission to reprint material:

"*Some Gentle Criticisms of British Justice*: J. H. Wilson's Defence of Oscar Wilde," in *Journal of the Eighteen Nineties Society*, 12–13, 18–23.

"Wilde at Bay: The Diaries of George Ives," in *English Literature in Transition*, 26, 175–86.

"Arthur Symons's 'Romantic Movement': Transitional Attitudes and the Victorian Precedent," in *English Literature in Transition*, 31, 133–50.

"Beardsley/Jarry: The Art of Deformation," in *Mr. Aubrey Beardsley Reconsidered: Essays and An Annotated Secondary Bibliography*, ed. by Robert Langenfeld (UMI Research Press, 1989), pp. 55–69.

"Dieppe: 1895," in *English Literature in Transition*, Special Series Number 4: Essays and Poems in Memory of Ian Fletcher, 11–23.

"Wilde Interpretations," *Modern Drama*, 37, 156–74.

Extracts from Wilde's letters appear by permission of Oxford University Press and Merlin Holland; extracts from *De Profundis* © Estate of Oscar Wilde 1962 appear by permission of Merlin Holland.

Figures 1 and 4 are reproduced by permission of the British Library; figures 5, 6, 8 by permission of Rétrocadres, Méru, France. Figure 9 was supplied by Ivan Kyncl, figure 10 by John Haynes, figures 11–12 by Catherine Ashmore and are reproduced by their permission. Figure 13 is reproduced by permission of the Trustees of the Victoria and Albert Museum.

Abbreviations

The following abbreviations are used throughout:

Ellmann Richard Ellmann, *Oscar Wilde* (London: Hamish Hamilton, 1987).
Letters *The Letters of Oscar Wilde* ed. by Rupert Hart-Davis (London: Hart-Davis, 1962).
Works *The Complete Works of Oscar Wilde* (Glasgow: HarperCollins, 1994).

Unless otherwise stated all translations are my own.

Introduction

A few years ago I was sent a posthumous poem said to have been written by Oscar Wilde and communicated to the world via a spiritualist medium. My name had been mentioned, or so the accompanying letter said, as someone who might be able to help with authentication. Before I had even read the poem I was livid, and once I had done so (it was, of course, the inevitable mush) I sent off a short, sharp reply in which I made it plain what I feel about people who thrive upon the gullibility of others.

Only much later did it occur to me that in being true to myself I was betraying Wilde, who would undoubtedly have found the situation of considerable interest and some amusement. Wilde was fascinated by mysteries of all kinds. He was happy to take part when Dr. Onofroff of Paris gave a public demonstration of his extraordinary skills in "thought-reading" in London in 1889;[1] he visited Mrs. Robinson, a Society fortune-teller, in 1894 (and was impressed by what she had to tell him); and he even employed a palmist, the fashionable "Cheiro" who, in later life, was able to boast of his contact with a famously doomed man. Premonitions, prophecies, and strange coincidences are, as many critics have noticed, a constant thread in Wilde's work, at least from *Lord Arthur Saville's Crime* and *The Canterville Ghost* through *The Importance of Being Earnest*.

This concern with the paranormal bears an obvious but disturbing relationship to the curiosity about more orthodox beliefs that would eventually allow Wilde's death-bed entry into the Catholic church. He seems to have turned toward Rome on

I

at least two previous occasions: as an Oxford undergraduate, when his friends were surprised and perturbed by his apparent fervor; immediately after his release from Reading Gaol in 1897, when he applied for six months' retreat among the Jesuits at Farm Street, and was refused. Only on a third occasion, when he was beyond speech, was he admitted.

It is a pattern that suggests sporadic desperation rather than a long-delayed homecoming. Catholicism was only another option; and only occasionally, at times of great personal crisis, was it attractive. In Wilde's mind there were many possibilities for belief, and they coexisted. So, for instance, whereas the long prison letter that came to be known as *De Profundis* may look on the surface to be his most Christian statement, in fact it offers a radically different dispensation, based on outright agnosticism.

The faith that others give to what is unseen, I give to what one can touch, and look at. My Gods dwell in temples made with hands, and within the circle of actual experience is my creed made perfect and complete: too complete it may be, for like many or all of those who have placed their Heaven in this earth, I found in it not merely the beauty of Heaven, but the horror of Hell also. When I think about religion at all, I feel as if I would like to found an order for those who cannot believe: the Confraternity of the Fatherless one might call it, where on an altar, on which no taper burned, a priest, in whose heart peace had no dwelling, might celebrate with unblessed bread and a chalice empty of wine. Everything to be true must become a religion. And agnosticism should have its ritual no less than faith...Its symbols must be of my own creating. (*Works*, 1019–20)

The eclectic appeal of agnosticism made it quite different from most versions of Christianity, with their stress on atonement and the afterlife, their essential dreariness. As Vivian complains in *The Decay of Lying*, despite the fact that priests are "men whose duty it is to believe in the supernatural, to perform daily miracles," in the Church of England "a man succeeds, not through his capacity for belief, but through his capacity for disbelief" (*Works*, 1089). Wilde was always on the side of belief, of acceptance, of making the impossible real, and recognizing the material world as a marvelous place.

My own instinctive preference is for the more straightforwardly materialist Wilde, but I now realize that in order to get in touch with that side of him, it is sometimes necessary to engage with his double, the seemingly superstitious man. Together they form the whole. The rationalist was no sceptic, nor was the adept simply naive. Like many of his contemporaries – W. T. Stead, Arthur Conan Doyle, W. B. Yeats among them – Wilde was drawn to manifestations of the supposedly supernatural because he could see there what the feminist historian of spiritualism Alex Owen has called "the unfolding of a vision of human fulfilment."[2] Yet always he looked for signs of that human fulfillment within the phenomenal world. "It is only shallow people who do not judge by appearances. The mystery of the world is the visible, not the invisible," he wrote in "Cheiro's" visitor's book – slightly mis-quoting Lord Henry Wotton's unacknowledged borrowing from Gautier.[3]

The reason why Wilde loved mystery so much is, paradoxi-cally, that he was at heart a rationalist, willing to accept that scientific discovery could offer an increasingly adequate account of the visible world. One of the "Phrases and Philosophies for the Use of the Young" proposes that "religions die when they are proved to be true. Science is the record of dead religions" (*Works*, 1244). Questioned about this by Edward Carson at the Queens-berry libel trial in 1895, he described it as "a suggestion towards a philosophy of the absorption of religions by science" though that, naturally enough, was "too big a question to go into now."[4]

It was, though, a question that had interested him for many years.[5] In the short story *The Canterville Ghost*, written in the 1880s, the ghost is first defied, and then made afraid by mortals. It is finally relieved of its obligation to haunt because of an unnamed act of charity carried out by a living girl. "The mystery of love is greater than the mystery of death": that principle is reasserted again and again throughout Wilde's works (*Works*, 198, 604).

It is not surprising then that no sooner was Wilde dead than he began to reappear in the visions of those who had known and, sometimes, loved him. Lord Alfred Douglas's poem "The Dead Poet", written in Paris in 1901, is only the most famous instance:

I dreamed of him last night, I saw his face
All radiant and unshadowed of distress,
And as of old, in music measureless,
I heard his golden voice and marked him trace
Under the common thing the hidden grace,
And conjure wonder out of emptiness,
Till mean things put on beauty like a dress
And all the world was an enchanted place.[6]

Douglas had the advantage of having known the face, having heard the voice, though lack of direct contact never deterred others from dreaming of Wilde, from pretending to be him and, in a few cases, from claiming to have seen him after his death. Wilde was glimpsed in New York in 1905[7] and, as late as 1934, the then occupant of his rooms in Magdalen College, "an Australian who plays ice-hockey for the University – not a man given to aesthetic fancies," saw him standing by the window: "a tall man, with a long jacket, very old-fashioned, with rows of buttons and very short lapels. His tie was loose, and tied in a big knot."[8] The phantom left through a wall, uncharacteristically silent.

It is more common for such ghosts to speak. The strangest report, by far, is the one given by Wilde's nephew, the poet "Arthur Cravan." Cravan's real name was Fabian Avenatius Lloyd: born in 1887,[9] he was the son of Otho Holland, Constance Wilde's brother. In 1912 Cravan founded in Paris a literary magazine called *Maintenant*, and it is in the third issue, under the title "Oscar Wilde est vivant," that the visitation is described.

Wilde arrives at Cravan's Paris flat one dark rainy night. Old, wrinkled, gray, and bald, he is nevertheless "beautiful," as an elephant is "beautiful"; his rear overwhelms the seat upon which he sits; he has enormous arms and legs, but small, flat feet give him the dreamy and rhythmic allure of a "pachyderm." Cravan loves him for this, imagines him "in the green madness of Africa, amid the music of the flies making mountains of excrement" (56).

The two men compare notes and Cravan offers to put his uncle on the music hall, but then, after a great deal of drink, Cravan turns abusive: "Get out of it! You bum, you good for nothing, with your rotting face, you shovel-load of shit, water-cress from a urinal, you faker, old queen, great cow!" (61). As Wilde leaves, his nephew is suddenly overcome by pity: remembering that the old man has no overcoat, he runs after him, shouting his name. When he realizes that Wilde has gone for ever he slowly returns – a desolate man.

"Oscar Wilde est vivant" is offered as fiction, though a previous issue of *Maintenant* has a piece entitled "Document inédit," attributed to "W. Cooper" (one of Cravan's pseudonyms), which is presumably factual. Here Cravan gives Wilde more conventional but still exotic features: Greek profile, aristocratic nose, and a sculptured mouth curved like an antique mask, which gave him "a sort of cruelty in repose" (30). When Wilde entered a room he was like a French king, full of "elegant nonchalance" (42); his presence seemed to reverberate, to carry on rolling and shining like a luminous ball. He was, says Cravan, both radiant and intangible.

This more sober though still dazzling description may bear some relation to the impression given by the real Wilde, but the Paris sighting is certainly true to Cravan, a famously cantankerous man – modernist poet of sorts, acquaintance of Apollinaire and Blaise Cendrars, husband of the poet Mina Loy, an amateur boxer who fought the great black heavyweight Jack Johnson in 1916 (and lost). When Cravan disappeared in South America in 1918 he left behind him a vision of Wilde unrivalled for its *bizarrerie* yet curiously lacking in aura. As Sigmund Freud was to say about *The Canterville Ghost*, an apparition "loses all power of at least arousing *gruesome* feelings in us as soon as the author begins to amuse himself by being ironical about it and allows liberties to be taken with it."[10]

It is precisely for this reason that most Wildean visitations tend to avoid outright comedy, though they, too, often involve a high degree of self-projection. The reasons for reappearance given by the spirit who communicated with Mrs. Hester Travers Smith in 1923 was that he needed to correct rumors that he was still alive:

Men are ever interested, my dear lady, in the remains of those who have had the audacity to be distinguished, and when, added to this, the corpse has the flavour of crime, the carrion birds are eager to light on it. In my case the corpse was taken from the humble place where it was cast off by my mental portion and conveyed to a retreat where it might decay quietly and in peace. It had none of the gaudy obsequies which would have fitted such as I was.[11]

If the reality of the discarnate Wilde were to be established then it was essential to maintain that he died in the first place. All questions of authenticity of manner would follow upon that premise. Mrs. Smith was a well-known medium who communicated with Wilde in the best professional way, with the help of automatic writing, ouija boards, and an intermediary or "control." On this occasion, however, her most recognizable control is *De Profundis*, since the visitation comes after its partial revelations as well as after several informative books: two by Robert Sherard (1902 and 1906); Arthur Ransome's *Oscar Wilde: A Critical Study* (1912), which prompted famous lawsuits; and Frank Harris's *Oscar Wilde: His Life and Confessions* (1916). It is inevitable then that Mrs. Smith should produce an inspirational Wilde who brings a message of comfort: "I wither here in twilight, but I know that I shall rise from it again to ecstasy. That thought is given to us to help to endure," the voice pronounces. "The human spirit must pierce to the innermost retreats of good and evil before its consummation is complete" (55). In the "dimness" of another world Wilde reenacts the purgatorial experiences prefigured in *De Profundis*. For this is also a repentant Wilde (quite why is never made clear), who makes the unlikely confession that he adores rustic people because "they are at least near to nature, and, besides, they remind me of all the simple pleasures I somehow missed in life." Nevertheless he remains poetic, anxious to replace the solecism of his "control," who describes the moon as "like a great golden cheese," with "like a great golden pumpkin hanging in the blue night" (7).

This, too, is Wilde the critic, prepared to pronounce even upon those who have survived or come after him. Arnold Bennett and H. G. Wells, for instance, "believe they are fit for the company of the gods who drink the nectar of pure mind" (21). Shaw "cannot analyse, he is merely trying to overturn the furniture and laughs with delight when he sees the canvas bottoms of the chairs he has flung over" (22). Galsworthy, rather surprisingly, is "the only mind I have entered into which appeals to my literary sense" (23), while Joyce's *Ulysses* is castigated because "the creatures he gives birth to leap from him in shapeless masses of hideousness, as dragons might, which in their foulsome birth contaminate their parent" (39). Hardy and Meredith are briefly dismissed and the Sitwells passed by altogether: "I do not spend my precious hours in catching tadpoles" (46).

With some of these judgments Mrs. Smith concurs, with others she parts company, providing incidental evidence of the separate reality of the spirit Wilde. Should there be any lingering doubts about the quality of the witticisms, Mrs. Smith is on hand with excuses, pointing out that after all he had been through, Wilde could hardly be expected to maintain his old standards.

But Mrs. Smith didn't really need an excuse, because her Wilde's inability to imitate his own inimitable style neatly coincided with the widespread belief, which she repeats, that the great *mots* were always prepared well in advance (107). Smith's Wilde, speaking from his "place of dimness," makes his entry with such awesome promise that his failure to touch the heights gains an alternative authenticity from the evidence of Wilde's later years (95), reproducing the pattern of the earliest biographies: a tragic life cut down at its peak.

The issue, as usual, is not so much authenticity as appropriateness. Mrs. Smith's Wilde represents an act of biographical reinterpretation that, however much she would deny it, reflects her own involvement in current debates about the reality of the spirit world.

That said, by the side of Mrs. Smith's effusions, *The Ghost-Epigrams of Oscar Wilde as Taken Down through Automatic Writing by Lazar*, which appeared in print in New York in 1929, seem even less Wildean.[12] "Wrinkles are the deathbed wherein women bury their illusions"; "Out of a love affair a man emerges bored to death; woman completely exhausted"; "All works of art are the autobiographies of liars"; "Nothing kills love like an overdose of it"; "Infidelity in woman is a masculine trait." These contain superfluous words, rarely reverse the familiar, and are often deeply misogynistic. They are also inexplicably American: "Bachelors are the bootleggers of love," and "People who live in glass

houses try to sublet their apartments." Whoever he may have
been professionally, all that "Lazar" produces here are the leaden
quips of a mediocre stand-up comedian.

As time went by, memories of Wilde became stronger – which
is no paradox because the facts of his life had become increasingly
available through such widely read books as Hesketh Pearson's
biography (1946) and H. Montgomery Hyde's account of the
trials (1948). John Furnell's *The Stringed Lute*, "An Evocation in
Dialogue" of 1955, opens with "a massive and somewhat corpu-
lent gentleman," appearing in a dream to the author, who
currently occupies Wilde's Tite Street house:

> He wore an overcoat and seemed to be about to set out on some
> journey for there was a bundle of rugs beside him fastened with a
> leather strap. There was an extraordinary dignity and kindliness about
> him which gave him the appearance of a benevolent but rather
> dissipated Roman Emperor, and I at once recognised him as Oscar
> Wilde, the Wilde whom Toulouse-Lautrec had painted. . .[13]

What follows is, in fact, a drama, its dialogue based on actual
quotes, mainly from Wilde, but also from Douglas, Ada Leverson,
and others. At the end the narrator awakes, depressed to realize
that Wilde has been nothing but a figment of his own imagination. As he does so, a violet falls to the floor: "Reverently I placed
the flower between two folded sheets of paper, and as I did so I
knew that it had been no dream; that although my friend was
already far away on his travels, yet something of him remained
with me here, in this room" (191).

Strange, perhaps, to think of Wilde as a guardian angel,
though this is what he has been for so many, right up until today.
In his extraordinary meditation *Who Was That Man?*, published in
1988,[14] the actor and theatre director Neil Bartlett is again
stalked by a spectral Wilde. Bartlett's book is, at one and the
same time, a quest for gay lives in the past, and his own
autobiography. Setting out to discover "our" history, he finds
that Wilde's words "began to ghost his writing" (26). This is a
reversal of what is normally meant by the term, since Wilde
becomes the "ghost-writer" whose story Bartlett must tell in order
to tell his own. And in the process he discovers that he is by no

means the first gay man to be hooked on history, to pursue the idea "that one man's experience may be a repetition of another's" (199).

"What if I rounded the corner of Villiers Street at midnight," Bartlett speculates, "and suddenly found myself walking by gas-light, and the man looking over his shoulder at me as he passed had the same moustache, but different clothes, the well-cut black and white evening dress of the summer of 1891 – would we recognise each other?" (xx). But this is a Wilde who haunts a gay man of the 1980s, after "liberation" and the coming of AIDS, and although Bartlett is led to conclude that "we have a common identity, common interests," simply to exclaim "he's just like us" would be to abolish time, distance and difference altogether, "to refuse the task (and pleasure) of identifying where he is like us, where he differs" (217). Nor are these the questions that only an author need address. As Bartlett asks his own readers: "When you are old, who will ghost your memoirs?" (208).

ACTING THE PART

Just as ghosts play parts in the lives of the living, so actors may take on the character of the dead. There have been many theatrical impersonations of Wilde, and even more imitations of a verbal style often described though never recorded. What did he sound like, really? How to embody that legendary voice?

When the English première of *Salome* took place in 1905 the role of Herod was played by a young actor who appeared under the name of Robert Farquarson, though his real name (he was of Spanish descent) was Robin de la Condamine. Both Robert Ross and Max Beerbohm were greatly impressed,[15] and it was on the basis of this performance that Farquarson was cast as Forgael in Yeats's *The Shadowy Waters* in the same year. Yeats, though, was bitterly disappointed, complaining that "he is over-emphatic and shoots his voice up and down the scale in a perfectly accidental way."[16] Farquarson went on to play Duke Ferdinand in *The Duchess of Malfi* (1919), Count Francesco in *The Cenci* (1922 – cast by Lewis Casson because his voice could reach three octaves),[17] Iachimo in a futurist *Cymbeline* (1923), Lenin in Hugh Griffith's *Red*

Sunday (1929), and a number of roles in innovative productions of Chekhov. When he died in 1966, both Sir John Gielgud and Sir Donald Wolfit found time to add their own memories to *The Times* obituary.[18] As by all accounts he had an impressive physical and vocal presence, it is riveting to learn that Farquarson was said to have based his vocal delivery upon that of Wilde himself.[19]

Mythic truth or mimicry merely? Farquarson's style links him, apostolically at least, with the man in whose play he had first made his name, and he certainly carried forward, long into the twentieth century, a distinctive manner that came to stand for one version of the Wildean: an imperious hauteur coupled with an ultimately deflationary tendency to excess. Farquarson, in short, was "camp."[20]

On stage, what Gielgud in his obituary note described as a "powerful and witty, though somewhat malevolent stage person-ality" gave Farquarson a career. Offstage, he seems to have been able to get away with much the same manner because he operated in the relatively closed and knowing worlds of the theater, of Chelsea, and of expatriate Italy, where Reggie Turner, for another, was renowned for his uncanny ability to mimic Wilde. When Reggie reminisced, "his voice descended to the depths of an imaginary corpulence, his gestures became sculp-tured and hieratic and his fingers sprouted scarab rings." "It was as if Oscar's spirit had taken possession of him," recalled Harold Acton.[21]

In certain circles Wilde lived on as a private memory, but in 1936 the chance came to imitate him on stage before a wider public. The actor was Robert Morley, the play was *Oscar Wilde* by Leslie and Sewell Stokes, and the opportunity did not come easily, because the play was initially refused a license by the Lord Chamberlain's Office on the grounds of its representation of homosexuality. *Oscar Wilde* eventually opened as a club perform-ance at the Gate Theatre on 29 September 1936 where it was, in general, positively received. One critic noted that "the jokes remain good because Wilde had several practical things to say, and said them extremely well. And the British public, which was his butt, has not so changed that these jokes have lost their truth today."[22]

The printed text of the Stokeses' play carries a preface by Alfred Douglas in which he complains about an earlier drama about the trials by the French writer Maurice Rostand, suggesting that Douglas had had no dealings with Wilde after his imprisonment. In deliberate contrast the Stokes play makes Douglas's loyalty a major theme and culminates with a scene in Paris in which Douglas is seen providing a drunken Wilde with the winnings of one of his racehorses. Douglas's own justification for certain inaccuracies in the play-text is that it tells "an historically true story, allowing, of course, for dramatic licence."[23] So, for instance, Wilde returns to Tite Street after prison, and characters who seem to be based on Gide and Ross compete for Wilde's attention.

The most striking misrepresentation, however, lies in the fact that this is a totally male play (no Constance, no Ada Leverson) which refers only to the most familiar of Wilde's works, mainly to *The Importance*. As the authors make clear in their initial description, their aim is to seduce the audience: "Most people dislike him at first, but they are quickly won over by his charm of manner, his exceptionally fine speaking voice, his genial gaiety and vivacity of expression" (24). By all accounts Morley fulfilled this to the letter with his impeccable delivery of the famous witticisms and parables, as well as of dramatic moments from the trials.

Twenty years later John Furnell's "dialogue", *The Stringed Lute*, did have a number of female characters: Constance and Ada Leverson appear together; Douglas, Sherard and Ross make up a chorus of male admirers; Lady Wilde and Willie Wilde feature along with Toulouse-Lautrec and an assortment of cockney maids and French youths. The relationship between Wilde and Douglas is clearly modeled upon that between Lord Henry Wotton and Dorian Gray, the stress is on the "affected and the effeminate," and the coverall word "sin" does service for sexual detail – even though the great speech on the "love that dare not speak its name" is delivered at length with both passion and poise: "His eyes sweep contemptuously over the rows of his listeners, and there is a ring of absolute sincerity in his voice…" (73). As for Bosie, "however much he stirs our disapproval, we are forced to admit that he is a thing of breath-taking beauty" (157).

Charisma counts for a great deal. At the first night of *The Importance* Wilde towers above his companions, "one hand on hip, the other dangling his white gloves, as from his lips issues a non-stop stream of wit and epigrams. But his attitude is in no way irritating, since it is belied by the gay and friendly twinkle in his eyes, which shows that he is enjoying the game every bit as much as they are" (48). Given the opportunities that this portrait opens up, it seems a shame that Furnell's drama seems never to have been given a major professional performance.

For those who experienced it (and there were many, for the production toured the world, was seen on television and preserved on a long-playing record), the most charismatic Wilde of modern times was created by the actor Michéal MacLiammoir.

Together with the director Hilton Edwards, MacLiammoir had made the Gate in Dublin one of the hotbeds of Irish theater for some forty years.[24] In 1960, stuck for a filler in their programme, the two men came up with a one-man show based on Wilde which they called *The Importance of Being Oscar*. The production was brilliantly economical in its resources. MacLiammoir wore a dinner jacket, bow tie, and green carnation, and the set consisted of a few props, a carpet of violet and gold, and a vase of lilies which turned in the second half to autumn leaves. In the course of the following decade, the show visited London, Paris, and the USA. It even managed to clinch Wilde's rehabilitation in the land of his birth.

A discriminating balance of narration to quotation, recitation to commentary, brought out the variety within the *œuvre*. Portions of *Salome* were delivered in French and there were excerpts from *The Importance*. After the interval Gide's memoirs, *The Ballad of Reading Gaol* and *De Profundis* took the story through to Wilde's death, marked not by the last words most commonly attributed to him, but by his touching promise to Ross that when they were both dead, and the last trumpet was about to sound, he would turn and whisper to his companion, "Robbie, dear boy, let us pretend we do not hear it."[25]

The trials are assumed to have taken place during the interval. Though Wilde's offense isn't detailed, neither is it concealed. MacLiammoir's comment on the refusal of Mr.

Justice Wills to allow Wilde a final statement was unmistakably heartfelt:

And yet one cannot help wondering if Oscar Wilde had been allowed to speak at that moment what would have happened? Would he have delivered some speech comparable in eloquence and in power to that of the Irish rebel, Robert Emmet: a speech that, independently of his own fate, might have revealed the strange and uniquely Anglo-Saxon quality of the law that has sentenced him? (39)

Orotund yct confiding, equipped with a velvety brogue and a glossy wig, MacLiammoir's Wilde had a deep patina that seemed both richly Irish and glamorously cosmopolitan. "Now, the Hôtel d'Alsace in the rue des Beaux Arts – it is still there, you may see it any day in Paris – was the first place in the world to honour the still dishonoured poet by a plaque upon its outer walls," MacLiammoir informed his audience, adding for those who cared to know: "It is, in fact, a modest, completely unpretentious but by no means unattractive hotel" (64).

Though, like Wilde, MacLiammoir was certainly well traveled, he was not in fact Irish at all. Born in 1899 of English parents, his real name was Alfred Willmore, and he had been raised in Kensal Green, London. The Irish name, considerable fluency in the Irish language, and an entirely fabricated Irish background (he claimed to have been born in Cork) came later. In 1927 MacLiammoir met Hilton Edwards when both men were members of Andrew MacMaster's company, and their homosexual partnership seems to have been happily accepted as a familiar part of the Dublin scene for many years.

MacLiammoir's identification with Wilde was psychological, romantic, and intellectual. Like Wilde, he had a deep and formative friendship with a young woman and, like Wilde, he was much concerned with appearance and with youthfulness, dyeing his hair and using makeup and a toupee long before they were necessary.

As both the narrator and the leading character in his one-man show MacLiammoir was effectively two men, neither of them quite himself. Edwards's director's notes insist that "impersonation" is to be avoided:

At no moment should the actor *play*, that is to say impersonate Wilde. He could identify himself with Wilde's theories and emotions; he could temporarily become the characters of Wilde's creation, but he must never attempt to *be* Wilde but must remain always himself. Stepping, as it were, in and out of the picture as occasion demanded he yet must always maintain an attitude aloof and ultimately objective; that of the Teller of the story, of the *Seanchai*. (xii)

In such ways MacLiammoir could weave his own story into the story he was telling, much as Bartlett was to do decades later. This duality resulted in a magisterial stage presence of a third kind, "camp" in the important sense that MacLiammoir was entirely and visibly in control of his own creation.

"Camp" in its more startling manifestations is precisely what many respectable modern representations of Wilde have tended to play down, substituting sincerity for sex and style for subversion. When two rival films of Wilde's life were made in the early 1960s, the tell-tale demeanor was displaced by romantic sensitivity in the case of Peter Finch, sybaritic girth in the case of Robert Morley.

The Trials of Oscar Wilde, which starred Finch and was directed by Ken Hughes, was based in part upon John Furnell's *The Stringed Lute* and in part upon Montgomery Hyde's account of the trials.[26] "I don't say that you look like one," remarks Lionel Jeffries's scene-stealing Queensberry to Finch's Wilde. In terms of homophobic caricature there is some truth in this, as Hughes later confirmed when he said: "What I felt about Finch was that he would level out any suggestion of the camp faggot because he was basically heterosexual."[27] Nor, despite Wilde's several protestations that he is "an Irish gentleman," is there much trace of brogue in Finch's delivery, and there are few of those special emphases, delays, and pauses that his contemporaries remember as being so characteristic.

This time the roles are fairly evenly distributed between the sexes, though Bosie, the male lover as tempter, is finally seen off by two women: Leverson, the understanding female friend, and Constance, the long-suffering wife. What the film offers, following the liberal ideology of the moment – it came out soon after the Wolfenden report of 1957 and just before the film *Victim* of 1961,

1. Advertisement for *Oscar Wilde*, starring Robert Morley, in the
Evening Standard, 20 May 1960

in which Dirk Bogarde plays a gay barrister soothed by a loving wife – is the "human tragedy" of homosexuality. Wilde's declaration, "Constance I only loved you and I only will," suggests that if anyone has killed the thing he loves it is Douglas.

The Trials of Oscar Wilde is full of historical color (quite literally: purple, pink, and puce in the reconstructions of the Café Royal and the foyer of the St. James's Theatre), whereas the Robert Morley film, simply entitled *Oscar Wilde*, is in stark black and white. Although based on the play Morley had premiered in London and New York in the 1930s, the film is clearly a post-Hyde courtroom drama and that, by and large, is how it was valued by the critics.[28]

Twenty-five years later the world had changed yet again, and Wilde with it. John Hawkesworth's three-part television drama *Oscar*, shown on BBC TV in 1985, had full-frontal male nudity, same-sex kissing, and the odd sexually explicit phrase. This was, beyond all doubt, to be the story of a great love affair. "They cannot understand that I can't live without you," Douglas promises Wilde. "They can do nothing to stop me loving you. There is nothing I wouldn't do for you." The degree of feeling is, in fact, a measure of the comparative sophistication of the adaptation, and it is matched by a generous display of Wilde's writings, ranging from a rehearsal of *A Woman of No Importance* with Beerbohm Tree to a version of *The Happy Prince* improvised to please Wilde's sons, Cyril and Vivian. Nevertheless the guiding presence remains, to a great extent, that of Montgomery Hyde, whose *Oscar Wilde: The Aftermath* had appeared in 1963, to be followed by a full biography in 1976. It must have been Hyde's influence, too, that encouraged yet another rerun of the trials, much legal detail, and an emphasis upon the later years.

Oscar is kind to virtually everyone: to Constance, who is commonsensical and understanding almost to the end, to the rent-boys, and, harder task, to Douglas, who is shown to have been outwitted by his rival, Ross. In the closing moments Wilde's invitation to Ross to ignore the last trump is followed by a reading of Douglas's "I dreamed of him last night." When voice-over readings from *De Profundis* are heard during the long prison sequences, and flashbacks are shown which confirm Wilde's mental recollections rather than the complicated set of relationships we have actually seen, the effect, perhaps intentionally, is of conflicting evidence.

For the most part, though, it is *The Ballad of Reading Gaol* that dominates the final episode, turning Wilde's suffering into a fictional documentary that matches the poem's particulars with poetic use of television's capacity for realism. The title credits show the two leading actors in sepia mock-ups of Victorian photographs, offering the authenticity of intimacy rather than the overpersuasive spectacle of period colour.

Michael Gambon's Oscar, an aging man determined to stay true to a self he is even now in the process of shaping, is large but still handsome, with an instinctive appreciation of masculine beauty. He delivers "The love that dare not speak its name" as if slightly drunk, in a tone both wistful and fervent. Although Gambon himself has Irish origins (and once worked for Mac-Liammoir), his brogue is very slight in comparison with the actors playing Carson and Shaw. Quite slow to reply, ever thoughtful, even his most lurid sexual exploits have a gentle, exploratory air.

If *Oscar* lacks a sense of danger and therefore doesn't quite add up historically, that may, in 1985, have been its strength. Only four years later Terry Eagleton's *Saint Oscar* would present Wilde as far too camp for comfort, a Bakhtinian Lord of Misrule, an Irish socialist (albeit a rather reluctant one) who penetrates the Establishment and exposes its sexual mayhem. Most previous narratives of the life, from the Stokeses to Hawkesworth, had been skeletal frames to be filled with Wilde's own words according to the preferences of the writer. This convention, which still persists in some biographical treatments, is directly flouted by Eagleton – as it is by Peter Ackroyd in his novel *The Last Testament of Oscar Wilde* (1983). Both devise accounts of Wilde's life using as few of Wilde's own words as possible. In such instances the dead author is a blatant vehicle to express the allegiances of the living: for Terry Eagleton, Wilde is a radical intellectual; for Peter Ackroyd, a connoisseur of the shifting boundaries between fact and fiction.

FAKING IT

As Neil Bartlett says of "The Portrait of Mr. W.H.," "the fake and true are indistinguishable" (209) – a paradox that often seems to be true of much of Wilde's life. The historical record is certainly littered with false trails.

A sound-recording purporting to be the author reciting portions of *The Ballad of Reading Gaol* into Edison's machine at the Paris Exhibition of 1900 has frequently been broadcast. Expert opinion now pronounces it to be a deliberate deception concocted decades after Wilde's death.[29] Similarly, the notorious photograph in Ellmann's biography captioned "Wilde in costume as Salome" has finally been proved not to be of Wilde at all, but of the opera singer Alice Guszalewicz.[30] The wrong identification here was most likely made in good faith. In both cases, recording and photograph, fake and mistake, the association was tempting because the circumstances seemed right, or could be made to seem so.

Willingness to believe that the recording really was made in Paris, really was of Wilde, depended not only upon long-established curiosity about how he sounded (how Irish? how "camp"?), but upon the force of the imaginary situation. Wilde was in the right place at the right moment. As Walter Benjamin reminds us, "Around 1900 technical reproduction had reached a standard that not only permitted it to reproduce all transmitted works of art and thus to cause the most profound change in their impact upon the public; it also had captured a place of its own among the artistic processes."[31] Wilde's voice, never forgotten by those who heard it, evoked with such care and admiration by his disciples, remains forever inaudible, but only by a matter of years, of months even. Repetition is written into the record.

Similarly the photograph tells a modern story, or rather allows for a number of competing stories. Alan Sinfield rightly objects to the readiness to identify Wilde with a picture of Salome, complaining that "it is part of the modern stereotype of the gay man that he should want to dress as a woman, especially a fatally gorgeous one."[32] Yet the first skirts that we see Wilde wearing in

Ellmann's book are entirely conventional: a dress of a style commonly worn by Victorian children, boys as well as girls, and then the uniform of a Greek soldier. Though the sequence of portraits may have been designed to persuade us of rather more, it is undoubtedly true that Wilde loved being photographed in costume.

He lives in his photographs still – another factor that makes him permanently immanent.[33] His career spanned the very cusp of the modern world and, to the degree that we still inhabit the conditions which made that career possible, we reproduce him according to circumstance, his and our own – even when that leads to confusion and error.

BEING THERE

The chapters of this book are haunted by Wilde's appearance and by his reappearance, by ghosts, by impersonations, and by copies, some of which turn out to be authentic, others false. They are linked by the idea that Wilde is available for reproduction. Not that it will do to leave him floating forever in hyper-real space. In the soil of the pre-modern lay the seeds of the post-modern. Wilde's behavior hinged on the ability to be recorded quickly and endlessly. His professional life begins with the assault on the gossip columns, the recognition, as recent critics have been able to demonstrate, of the implications for literature of a consumer world.[34] Because we see him in so many publicity pictures, almost hear him on commercial recordings, the impact continues long after his death.

Still so very visible, so almost audible, Wilde can be shaped into many different images: a sexual icon who, as Alan Sinfield claims in *The Wilde Century*, defined the "queer" for a hundred years, a model artist who blithely ignored the boundaries between high and low culture, and, my own particular concern, a humanitarian prophet who viewed the material world with religious passion.

My first chapter, "The Magic Ball," suggests that the true materialist is someone who believes in miracles, and that this truth is demonstrated by the artist-magician. The underlying argument is that what comes into being is always strongly determined, or overdetermined, by precedent, specifically by popular culture. Wilde responded to the entertainments of his time, and show business has paid tribute in return, from Mick Jagger dressing himself up as Wilde in a film made after his arrest on a drugs charge in 1967 to the devotion to Wilde's memory publicly professed by Morrissey of "The Smiths," the most stylish rock group of the 1980s.

He has certainly never lacked fans, even in the years immediately following his downfall. In July 1896 a touring production of *An Ideal Husband* reached Newcastle where, despite the fact that the author was not named in the advertisements, it did extremely well. Ada Leverson tells how Cosmo Gordon-Lennox, who played Lord Goring, recounted to her a "very curious incident" concerning "a man who called on him and was like a shadow of Oscar, an exact imitation and great likeness." This backstage visitor apparently "adores Oscar and always has his photograph in a silver frame covered with forget-me-nots. He kissed Cossie, once for Oscar's sake, once for Lord Goring's and once for his own."[35] Could this have been James Wilson, the obscure Newcastle poet who is the subject of my second chapter? In the absence of further evidence, the tempting thought must be resisted. How can we know how many other Newcastle men identified with Wilde's suffering?

James Wilson and George Ives, whose diary I describe in the third chapter, are examples of individuals whose lives were deeply affected by moving within Wilde's orbit and who, in their very different ways, tried to preserve that contact by protesting against the conditions that made it possible. Their case histories reveal some of the complexities of living under, and through, oppressive ideologies. In both instances we can see how the manipulation of class impeded the expression of sexuality, but how humanitarian principles could sometimes cut the knots. This is the inspirational force of Wilde, the secular moralist.

The fourth chapter, "Romantic Reincarnations," takes a very different tack and approaches Wilde by contrasting his readings of the Romantic poets with those of Arthur Symons. The aim is to show how the Romantic ambivalence towards revolution was continued and confronted by the late Victorian age. The search for Romantic "genius," though now bolstered by biological science, also remained, at heart, ideological. The comparison is between Wilde, who stayed faithful to a materialist, Paterian view of Romanticism and who decided to exploit the marketplace as best he could, and Symons, who had a highly developed sense of the commercial and artistic world yet became a virtual mystic. Here, as elsewhere, Wilde acts out roles, aware that live performance is a form of agency as well as of imitation.

Aubrey Beardsley and Alfred Jarry both knew Wilde directly. What they shared with him, as with each other, was a premonitory sense of new ways of thinking about art that would draw upon both scientific and aesthetic languages. At the very moment when reproduction through technological means became the norm, there emerged a countering perception of the irreducible essence of the unique particular. This realization determined the new science that Jarry was to name "pataphysics." Like Wilde, both Beardsley and Jarry knew that the best way to deal with cultural change was to overstep the mark. Lovers of excess, all three men recognized the burgeoning future with stylistic exaggeration and outrageous pretence.

Though Symons and Wilde were never close, their lives were contingent, sometimes literally, geographically so. As he monitored the holiday town of Dieppe in the summer of 1895 Symons, like many others, must have had Wilde's absence in mind. The final section of my chapter on Dieppe in the 1890s shows how later artists and writers have redrawn the town over and above a social space created at that time.

All the chapters are to do with reenactment, which is why they are about lives as much as about literature. They are interdisciplinary because Wilde's influence has embraced many media, and like Wilde himself they prefer not to denigrate one form of cultural expression in favor of another. My intention has always been to watch the ways in which ideas and images have taken shape, modified, and regrouped in relation to the changing times. Accordingly the last chapter, like the first, is about performance itself. "Wilde Interpretations" returns to the representation of the author in a study of recent productions of his plays. I trace Wilde's circumstances as they are made visible in subsequent interpretations of his work. On stage, as in life, he stalks us still.

CHAPTER I

The magic ball

There are stories that Wilde never wrote, but most certainly told. There is an oral Wilde, who is at least as well known as the written Wilde, and who even conditions the way we read him now. So there's an aural Wilde as well. Those who heard Wilde speak never forgot the experience and fragments of his conversation are scattered across the memoirs of Charles Ricketts, André Gide, W. B. Yeats, Laurence Housman,[1] and many others, and collected together in a chaotic compendium of apocrypha by the French aficionado, Guillot de Saix.[2]

Ricketts says that in the polish of Wilde's prose we miss not only the spontaneity of his speech, but the way in which he cued his audience into an understanding of what he was about to say with "a smile, a wave of the hand," a preceding laugh (13). And Ricketts adds that he would test a story by relating it to various listeners "till he found the definite form he felt it required" (15). When so much of his writing sounds like speech, and so much of his speech was apparently written down, Wildean authority may not be entirely beyond recovery. Richard Ellmann, that great scholar who could never resist quotation, knew this. With its stress on the spoken word Ellmann's is not only the best life, it's the most Wildean life.

Hearing the things Wilde said made people see things too. In the memoirs he is habitually described as a kind of verbal magician who could bring objects to life, a shaman, and several people claimed to have seen a halo around his head. The knowledge that this had to be an illusion, or delusion, did nothing to lessen the attractiveness of the idea.

So, for example, one of Wilde's auditors, reported by de Saix

(81), tells of hearing him recount his parables outside the Café de la Paix in Paris. Suddenly the vision of a huge golden angel appeared, slowly bearing down upon them. Wilde began to tremble, clasped her arm. A messenger come to announce the end of the world? An optical illusion, in fact, a refracted image, created by the play of mist and sunlight upon the great gilded statue of Apollo that crowns the Opéra. None the less, from this moment on the woman would always remember Wilde as accompanied by a golden angel. The mirage retained its potency even when scientifically explained, and her story is authentically Wildean for that very reason.

The role of secular prophet was one that greatly appealed to Wilde, and he loved to tell parables that expressed the power and the mystery of his humanistic vision. In one of his best-known stories, "The Master," a young man works miracles, but then complains that, unlike Jesus, he hasn't been crucified (*Works*, 901–2). This is typical in that by an ironical reversal it sets the possibilities for miracles in the worldly here-and-now against the Christian vision of suffering and the hereafter – and questions the need for the latter.

"The Gospel disturbed and tormented the pagan Wilde," said Gide in a passage that inspired a wonderful essay by Ellmann, "He did not forgive it its miracles."[3] Many of Wilde's spoken parables do turn out to be about miracles. It is as if by describing miracles he was re-performing them, compelling belief through the power of his personality and his narrative gift rather than through simple trust in the supernatural. In the nineties he even seems to have been thinking of compiling his own alternative gospel, which would have borne the title of "Useless Miracles";[4] "Useless" here presumably carrying the same positive charge that it does in the preface to *Dorian Gray* which declares that "All art is quite useless" (*Works*, 17).

Even as an undergraduate Wilde had been fascinated by the subject, eagerly refuting Hume's doubt. "Hume's argument from probability is essentially unsound," he wrote in one of the notebooks he compiled at Oxford:

It may be improbable that water ever turned into wine but it is not impossible or inconceivable.

a Law of nature is merely often verified experience

Upon the other hand the more a statement of facts conflicts with ordinary registered experience the more complete ought the evidence to be it is merely a question of *Evidence,*

To define a miracle as a violation of the Laws of Nature is absurd Nature is all which is: it is the series of phenomena of which the alleged miracle is one.[5]

Miracles appear too in his poem "The Garden of Eros":

> What profit if this scientific age
>   Burst through our gates with all its retinue
> Of modern miracles! Can it assuage
>   One lover's breaking heart?   (*Works*, 850)

Although Wilde's miracles may be both scientific and avowedly anti-Christian, they do not necessarily invite skepticism. Skepticism limits, and in the Wildean view all limitations are there to be breached, transgressed, in the name of life. Skepticism is quite literally deathly.

In another apocryphal fragment the Emperor Nero persecutes the early Christians because they are taking attention away from him, making him look ridiculous. "When I get up in the morning and look out of the window," Nero complains, "the first thing I see is a miracle going on in the back garden" (*Ellmann*, 531). In this respect Wilde's mad emperor seems to be a close cousin of Herodias, his commonsensical queen, who, in a cynical aside that is also a moment of acute self-betrayal, complains: "I do not believe in miracles. I have seen too many" (*Works*, 595).

Wilde's re-visions may come to us in multiple form – shadows of stories, ghostly paradigms, curtailed drafts, other people's memories – but in the wider context of nineteenth-century thought they can be related to the theological revisionism of David Friedrich Strauss and of Ernest Renan. Both deal with miracles. Renan, whose life of Christ Wilde requested when he was in Reading Gaol, and described as "that gracious Fifth Gospel, the Gospel according to St. Thomas" (*Works*, 1029), has a chapter entitled "Miracles."[6] Strauss has a similar chapter and devotes a whole section to the single miracle of the water and the wine.[7]

Because it appears only in St. John, and not in the synoptic gospels, this was a story that was particularly open to challenge. Strauss points out that the change from water to wine is qualitative, not just quantitative like the miracle of the loaves and fishes, and that it redresses the temptation (which Christ resists) of turning stones into bread. Nor can this be explained as simply "accelerated natural process" (519) since water can never become wine by itself, though Strauss supposes that grapes could perhaps do the trick. Morally he finds it odd that Christ might encourage drunkenness, might counter the water of baptism in this symbolic way. He even wonders if Jesus might not have planned the miracle in advance, warned Mary, brought in the wine and hidden it, though such behavior would conflict with "the straight-forwardness of character elsewhere ascribed to him" (525). Finally Strauss compares Jesus with Moses, who is said to have turned water into blood, a "retributive" (526) act quite at odds with the mild spirit of the Savior; he links him instead with the pagan Bacchus, who is also said to have turned water into wine.

In questioning traditional biblical scholarship, rational theology produced its own mirroring hermeneutics: the clash of rival interpretations opening up the road to an overall enlightenment and a renewed appreciation of the complex variety of earthly pleasures. This is also the way in which Wilde liked to reconsider the scriptures, since his miracles invariably involve riddling situations that threaten, but never finally defeat, the resources of rational explanation. In an early form the parable of "The Master" featured a god, presumably pagan, who "left his temple out of compassion for the world" and set about performing miracles. He too changed water into wine, but on this occasion the wedding guests refused to drink it, for they knew he could not taste joy, being a god.[8]

Divinity pays a high price, too high. Another miracle that, like the water and wine, cried out for re-vision involved the grim testimony of the stigmata. The final line of Wilde's early poem of religious doubt, "E Tenebris," rests on the unresolved antithesis: "The wounded hands, the weary human face" (*Works*, 773), just as "Humanitad" closes with "Staunch the red wounds – we shall be whole again, / That which is purely human, that is Godlike, that is God" (*Works*, 826). And at the end of *The Selfish Giant*, the Child's promise that the Giant will go to heaven is accompanied by a display of *his* wounded hands, at which point the Giant promptly dies. The ending is typically double: it endorses the Christian power of forgiveness, but at the same time it demonstrates precisely what those sacrificial "wounds of Love" (*Works*, 284) in fact proclaim.

Wilde's favorite stigmata parable has, as its main object, the same counterpointing between the Christian doctrine of love and the cruel demands that invariably accompany it. There are several versions. The French writer Georges Maurevert has Wilde improvise the story before an audience of writers in the back room of Bar Calisaya on the Boulevard des Italiens at midnight on Christmas Day 1899. "His half-closed eyelids were red and swollen," recalls Maurevert, morbidly setting the scene, "and between his gouty fingers he was twisting the fragile stem of a gin glass." In this version Joseph of Arimathea rescues Jesus from the cross by administering a drug that makes him only appear to be dead. Jesus retires to the country where he works, anonymously, as a carpenter. One day the apostle Paul arrives preaching the new religion and telling of the stigmata. Jesus's friends hear Paul and are converted, but Jesus still doesn't reveal his identity. On Jesus's death his colleagues discover the wounds upon his hands and feet and hail him as a saint, crying out in their ignorance, "It's a miracle. A great miracle."[9]

Frank Harris also heard this Wildean parable and, without any acknowledgment, wrote it up in the collection of short stories called *Unpath'd Waters* which he published in 1913.[10] In Harris's much extended version (it runs to nearly twenty-five pages) we are given a naturalistic portrayal of the main character, Joshua ("a middle-aged Jew, with features sharpened by suffering" [3]), and of his young wife Judith. Paul comes to Caesarea. Joshua declines to hear him preach, though he apparently knows something about the life of Jesus from an earlier time spent in Jerusalem. Judith, however, is overwhelmed by Paul and reports back to Joshua, who is deeply perturbed by what she and others have to say, insisting that Jesus's real message was of love. Here Harris introduces gospel texts: has

Joshua respond unfavorably to "He that is not with me is against me" (Matthew, xii, 30), but favorably to "He that is not against us is on our part" (Mark, ix, 40). Paul tells his followers that they must not associate with unbelievers and so Judith leaves Joshua. Eventually, when Joshua dies, she returns with her mother to prepare the body for burial. This reveals the stigmata which have, it seems, newly appeared on Joshua's body. Paul is consulted and pronounces a miracle: because of Joshua's unbelief, "and for a sign to the whole world, the Stigmata of Jesus the Crucified had been put upon him" (26).

Harris's expansion of the story drains it of the oracular quality that the implied echoes of delivery can convey. In contrast, a marvelously concise version of the same story in Yeats's *Auto-biographies* sets it as reported speech:

One day he began, "I have been inventing a Christian heresy," and he told a detailed story, in the style of some early Father, of how Christ recovered after the Crucifixion, and escaping from the tomb, lived on for many years, the one man upon earth who knew the falsehood of Christianity. Once Saint Paul visited his town and he alone in the carpenter's quarter did not go to hear him preach. Henceforth the other carpenters noticed that, for some unknown reason, he kept his hands covered.[11]

By merely alluding to the realistic detail of the story as it was originally recounted, Yeats is able to leave a space for Wilde's imagined voice. Textual absence is filled with oral presence.

Harris's *Unpath'd Waters* has another miracle story also taken from Wilde, and this time the source is acknowledged. Subtitled "After O.W.," *The Irony of Chance* is dated September 1901.

The narrator, whose name is Jack, tells the story of a man called Mortimer, a contemporary at Winchester and at Balliol. Mortimer is described as always having been "strangely proud and sensitive," with a "curious temperament" (61): at school, no games player, but a brilliant scientist. Mortimer goes up to Oxford in May 1883 to study chemistry, where Jack is reading Greats. Jack's interest in a newly discovered part of Euripides' *Bacchae*, a palimpsest, prompts Mortimer to speculate on what the scientific equivalent of a palimpsest would be:

I came on rather an interesting idea. Suppose strong sunshine beating on a rock. Every shadow of man or beast cast on the rock modifies the sun's influence, and so leaves an imprint, however faint, on the stone. Fancy if, in time to come, we were able to read such a palimpsest, and print off for you photographs of Plato and Sophocles from some rock on Colonus. (63)

After Oxford the two men lose touch. Jack enters the law while Mortimer goes into retirement in Wales, only to reemerge as a public lecturer with a message so startling that his pronouncements are reported in the daily papers. "Laws of nature and ideas in the mind are correlatives, and suppose each other as eyes suppose light," he pronounces. And "Spiritual forces are only mechanical forces raised to a higher power, and will yet be found more efficient – even in industries" (65).

"People thought Mortimer a little mad," Jack recalls. "He pretended to be able to work miracles, they said, and told wild stories about him." Sensation turns to scandal when it is reported that Mortimer has been discovered cheating and swindling. He turns up in Jack's chambers and recounts his life-story.

After Oxford, Mortimer had journeyed to Heidelberg where he worked with Bunsen, inventor of the spectroscope, the instrument which had enabled the discovery of the chemical composition of the stars. Inspired by Comte's edict that there were two secrets man would never unravel – the composition of the stars and the origin of life – Mortimer had set out to discover the latter.

Plato talks about the unity and universality of life; but Plato had no idea that plants are so much alive as men and women...And, just as there is no gap between vegetable and animal life, so there is no gap between organic and inorganic existence; the being of stones and gases and metals must be subject to the same law, swayed by the same force, moving to the same end; a thought in the mind of man is a law in the furthest star. (68)

Scientific experiment had led Mortimer to develop ways of fusing inanimate matter, of uniting gases without regard to their atomic weight. Finally he had reached the point where he believed that he had discovered a direct equivalent to the bonding process that human beings call love. By changing temperature it had become possible, for instance, to make gold interpenetrate lead. As Mortimer now explains it to Jack:

This simply means that the atoms of both metals are in a constant state of motion or vibration: there is no such thing in nature as stillness or death...You remember a story in the Bible how a woman touched the hem of Jesus' garment and he turned round to see who it was, for he felt that the virtue had gone out of him. (70)

Inspired by such insights Mortimer had, he says, made up his mind that by a combination of "electricity," of "virtue," and of "personal magnetism" he would prove the "unity and universality of life" so that men would "grow more pitiful and more kindly to all forms of being" (71). One of his mentors here was the philosopher Ernst Haeckel, whom he quotes to this effect: "Matter and ether are not dead, and moved only by extrinsic force; they are endowed with sensation and will; they experience an inclination for condensation, a dislike for strain" (72).

The result was a fusion of seven metals in a great sphere shaped like the earth. This ball turned out to have remarkable qualities: it sometimes responded to Mortimer's commands, as if he were God Himself, but not always. Sometimes it seemed that the ball had a mind of its own. "For weeks despair would lie on me, crushing me; and then a change would come, and I was master again and king" (75), Mortimer confesses. This unpredictability encouraged his futher realization that "just as there is no limit between what is possible and what is impossible, so there is no line between sanity and insanity...As soon as we think of our bodies, we are unwell; and as soon as we think of our minds we are on the verge of madness."

Mortimer had continued to give public lectures on his discovery that the laws of physics are the laws of thought, and, because he was now able to demonstrate his ideas with the great ball, he began to attract huge audiences. "It was the miracle, Jack, which they had come out to see" (77). Yet there were still those occasions when the ball didn't respond to his command and his whole teaching was threatened, since "the dull generation that wanted a sign was not easily satisfied." Prompted by an Edgar Allan Poe story Mortimer had then decided to cut open the ball and to insert a mechanism that could be operated by a small boy planted inside. He could now be sure that the ball would always move on command, though he swears to Jack that he was determined to resort to the trick only when the ball failed to respond.

Another factor now enters Mortimer's story. As he had continued giving lectures around the country he had gradually become aware that he was being followed by a "man with an evil face...envy and hatred in his eyes" (78). Matters came to a head when he appeared in Birmingham. At the first lecture the ball performed splendidly, but at the second its movements were feeble. Challenged by the man with the evil face, Mortimer had capitulated, and rather than have the crowd break open the ball, publicly admitted to his deception. The audience, as he later recalled to Jack, "jeered at me and spat upon the ground, and crowed that Birmingham was too wise to be taken in by my tricks, and demanded their money back, and went away sneering and triumphant" (82).

But then a true miracle occurred: the little boy appeared and confessed that he had spent the whole evening visiting his mother in Edgbaston. The ball had indeed obeyed Mortimer of its own accord.

It is with this unresolved mystery that Frank Harris's version of Wilde's story ends. We do, however, have several other variants. Louis Latourrette, an acquaintance of Wilde during the final years in Paris, claimed to have heard Wilde deliver the story when they were both drunk at the Bar Calisaya in 1898. The reminiscence in which this occasion is decribed first appeared in a short-lived periodical, *Paris Mondiale*, in 1901 but was then, according to de Saix, reprinted at least four times over the next two decades.

Latourrette describes the main character as "un savant célèbre" (215) who believes that he has discovered the secret of spontaneous movement. He arranges for a demonstration, in front of the King, parliament and academicians, of a great ball that he will make roll of its own accord. On the morning of the demonstration he is overcome with fear. What if his calculations are wrong? He sees a passing urchin and calls to him, offering sweets if he will hide inside the ball and make it move on command.

The boy agrees. The demonstration takes place, and is hailed as a "miracle." But the "savant," overcome by his scientific conscience, confesses his trick, and admits that he really doesn't know whether he has discovered spontaneous movement or not. The King, outraged, says that he has ridiculed the science of his country and condemns him to life imprisonment. On the way to the jail the "savant" passes a gang of children playing hopscotch, among them the street urchin who calls out that because he'd been enjoying the game so much he hadn't hidden in the ball after all, though he hopes he will still get the sweets. As Latourrette records it, the story ended with the "savant" giving the boy money for sweets and continuing on his way to prison, with an ineffable smile upon his face.

Then there's the version told to de Saix by Paul Poiret, who claimed in turn to have heard it from other friends of Wilde (305–8). Again it features a magician, an illusionist who travels England with his tricks, among them a magic ball which he claims to make move according to gestures with his cane. The magician is commanded to appear before the King. Thrilled, he tells his partner, a dwarf who is hidden within the ball and who actually causes it to roll. But the dwarf refuses to take part and says that having learnt the trick himself he is off to America to make his fortune.

The despairing magician then has the good luck to find another dwarf, a sad, scrofulous creature who lives with his impoverished grandmother. In return for a large sum this second dwarf agrees to participate in the deception and the magician instructs him to climb into the ball an hour before the show is due. The trick is a tremendous success. Appearing before the whole court in a great hall of mirrors the magician waves his cane to make the ball salute the King, his Queen, and Princes, each in turn, rolling towards them of its own accord. At the end the magician pronounces that he has been able to present the King with a symbol of absolute obedience. As a reward he is given a diamond cross, a ring, and a box of specially made royal cigars. He returns to his lodgings and is sitting back, enjoying one of these wonderful cigars, when the second dwarf appears, full of apologies. His grandmother had been so ill, he confesses, that he hadn't been able to carry out his task as instructed. Poiret's version ends with the magician never daring to repeat the performance again.

There may well be other versions of this story of the magic ball,[12] though these three are enough to allow a quasi-structuralist reading of variants. Motivation shifts and the mode is unpredictable: tragic, comic, or ironic. The only constant factor is that the ball moves of its own accord. It is this unassimilable premise that places the story of the magic ball in the genre of the "fantastic," as modern theoreticians such as Tzvetan Todorov and Rosemary Jackson would define it.[13] Either the movement of the ball is an illusion and the world continues to operate according to known rules, or it really did move, in which case it is an aspect of a reality hitherto unappreciated.

On the other hand, the multiplicity of texts might invite an inter-textual reading. After all Harris's version makes reference to many familiar names: Poe, Haeckel, Comte, Bunsen. An inter-textual reading would obviously have no trouble in placing the story within a nineteenth-century context. Wilde may well have been remembering William Beckford's *Vathek*, a work he certainly knew, which contains a celebrated episode when an Indian escapes his attackers by metamorphosing into a ball that bowls along like some self-sufficient universe.[14] The central character of the magic ball story certainly belongs in the line of Faustian mad scientists: Wells's Dr. Moreau and Edward Prendrick, Bram Stoker's Van Helsing. The important motif of the double draws on the tradition of Poe, of Hoffmann, of Wilde himself, of countless others. And there are many *fin-de-siècle* fictions that are likewise concerned with interactions between organic and inorganic worlds. There's Stevenson's *Dr. Jekyll and Mr. Hyde* (1886), for instance: when Henry Jekyll thinks of Hyde it is "as of something not only hellish but inorganic. This was the shocking thing – that the slime of the pit seemed to utter cries and voices; that the amorphous dust gesticulated and sinned; that what was dead, and had no shape, should usurp the offices of life."[15] In *Dracula* (1897), which displays an obsessive interest in materiality, human bodies are said to be made out of atoms of dust, a state to which they must eventually return. That thought haunts the science fiction of Arthur Machen as well. And there is Wilde's own *Dorian Gray*, with its hero's concern that there might be "some subtle affinity between the chemical atoms, that shaped themselves into form and colour on the canvas, and the soul that was within him," and his later interest in the "materialistic doctrines of the *Darwinismus* movement in Germany" (*Works*, 101). "We are part / Of every rock and bird and beast and hill," as Wilde had already put it in his early Tennysonian poem entitled *Panthea* (*Works*, 833).

This process of transference between mind and matter is at heart a deeply Romantic idea. Todorov has an interesting, a rather Wildean, comment on it. "The multiplication of personality, taken literally, is an immediate consequence of the possible transition between matter and mind: we are several persons mentally, we become so physically."[16] That tallies with Wilde's interest in multiple personality, though it omits the element of prophecy which accompanies the true Wildean miracle.

For the oddest, the most miraculous and yet the most Wildean aspect of the magic ball story is that it is to all intents and purposes true – or rather, that it came true. We easily forget, as we intone Wilde's edict that life imitates art, that in the context of *The Decay of Lying* this refers first to narrative, only secondly to pictures and landscapes. The magic ball is an example of a narrative that was lived out after it had been told, that came true though performance.

The fact is there really was a "magic ball": "una bolla misteriosa," "den globus mysteriosus," "un globe magique," a miraculous feat that astonished the world. The magic ball was a circus act and there was a certain amount of competition between its two main practitioners: a French clown called Lepère who introduced the trick in 1893 in Paris (where it is not impossible that Wilde saw him perform), and a Romanian contortionist named Léon LaRoche, who appeared all over Europe later in the same decade. LaRoche's story was first told in German by A. H. Kober in a book published in 1925, later translated into English as *Star Turns* in 1931.[17]

As a child in Romania LaRoche, Kober tells us, was alienated from his parents and his contemporaries. Disliking games, he developed "an almost morbid love of knowledge. He lived in and through books." When he was thirteen, he read the confessions of a saint which brought on a strange sensation:

He stood up in front of a large mirror. What he saw was a perfectly built young body with a beautiful radiant face, like those of the statues of saints he had seen. This lasted only an instant; with equal suddenness the blood started rushing again through his veins, he became aware of the weight of his limbs and all he saw in the looking-glass was the short and ill-shaped figure of an untidily dressed boy, with a thick and heavy head and a wild mop of dishevelled fair hair hanging over his forehead. Mechanically he made a gesture. He repeated it intentionally, and ran through the room under a strange compulsion. It was as though motion were the only salvation from rigidity or volatilisation. And on that night the Grammar School boy left his parents' house. (110–11)

LaRoche ran away for good, meeting up with a traveling magician who instructed him, and becoming a circus performer: "a sturdy jumper, an india-rubber man, a tight-rope dancer, an acrobat" (112). He walked to Budapest, joined the royal circus as an equestrian. He then had the second of his strange experiences. Performing on his horse one night, he sensed a reluctance in the animal and looking across the ring, had the same experience of glimpsing his double.

Again LaRoche fled. He joined other circuses, toured Eastern Romania. One night he observed outside the circus tent an extraordinarily popular gambling game which involved getting a ball to roll down a spiral about a foot high. He devised his own version, but this time the spiral was twelve feet high and the ball was six feet in diameter and it rolled of its own accord, slowly up the spiral, and then slowly down again, where it split apart to reveal LaRoche himself. The act was a phenomenon, hailed as "a miracle," "an unfathomable mystery, a sudden stroke of genius" (118), and its inventor became an international star.

There were still crises. In London (Kober says in 1893) the ball tipped over the side of the spiral and LaRoche was slightly injured. It seemed that "while inside the ball he had some kind of vision" (119). He joined Barnum and toured Europe, but his wife, a singer from the Alhambra music hall in London, left him when he exploded in an outburst of uncontrollable rage. He married again, this time a middle-class girl from Berlin. His first wife set up a rival ball act, but was injured. He had a daughter and determined that she should never enter the ring. In 1908 LaRoche himself twice had to be dragged from the ball "where he was crouching in a trance" (122). "I knew that 1908 would bring me bad luck," he said. "Just work it out: 1873 – 1883 – 1898 – 1908. Every ten or fifteen years something evil happens to me. At present I am only afraid of 1918 and 1923" (123).

These fears were borne out. In 1918 he lost all his money, which he had invested in German bonds. He retired from the ring, but returned in 1921 after thirteen years' absence and once again toured the world. Aged sixty-three he was thrown by a horse and injured his leg which prevented him from working for a time. Then, in 1923, while crossing the Equator on his way to perform in Spain, he suddenly threw himself overboard. His biographer has no doubt why: "He had seen his own image reflected by the waves; he had seen it as it had appeared to him when he was a boy of thirteen in the house of his parents" (124).

That seems to be as much as is generally known about Léon LaRoche. Most accounts are heavily dependent on Kober, including an English novel *The Golden Ball* by R. M. Manning-Sanders, which though published in 1954 still describes the act in classic terms:

As if one of those universal atoms had become miraculously magnified, and were demonstrating its latent powers to incredulous eyes, so does that golden ball take to itself life, mount heavenwards and roll to earth again – to lie once more motionless, lifeless, impercipient on the sawdust.[18]

At the end of this novel the artist commits suicide by drowning, just like Léon LaRoche. Yet despite that awful warning, the tradition of the act has lived on. In the 1920s a performer called Jim Burns met LaRoche's daughter Geri in Russia and later created his own version. Performing at Tom Arnold's circus at Harringay Arena in 1949 Burns was seen by hundreds of young spectators, including myself.[19]

This seems like a miracle to me: a Wildean miracle. It feels fated, but it's undeniable, entirely explicable, and even common-place. It's the kind of coincidence that makes history real. Lady Bracknell says that "in families of high position strange coinci-dences are not supposed to occur. They are hardly considered the thing" (*Works*, 404). No matter. Even if I know that the scientific miracle of the magic ball, that mind can control matter, is an illusion, and must have known it at the time when the ball fell open, the artistic miracle of the circus performance remains in my memory.

Wilde's miracles are always of this kind. They draw upon a level of collective experience in which we all participate. That is why we respond to them and remember them as we do. Life imitates art because art draws on life in the first place, not life as nature, but life as culture, popular culture, so "popular" as to be unspoken, invisible much of the time: the rich bedrock of farce that produced *The Importance of Being Earnest*,[20] the bottomless pile of Gothic stories that supports *Dorian Gray*, the powerful tradition of prison protest that validates *The Ballad of Reading Gaol* and, of course, the vestigial echoes of the scriptures to be heard every-where in Wilde's work. This cultural heritage produces, amongst many other things, the seemingly miraculous workings of literary coincidence that we nowadays call "inter-textuality."

The basic structure of a Wildean narrative is invariably a material miracle with a humane message. In *De Profundis* he was to write that Christ's miracles seemed to him "as exquisite as the coming of Spring, and quite as natural" (*Works*, 1029). Wilde's own miracles are natural in that sense. After all, the miracle of *Dorian Gray* is that in the long term human morality confirms human mortality and vice versa. The miracle of *The Importance* is that we are what we want to be, if we did but know it. And the miracle of *The Ballad* is that individual suffering need not be necessary for forgiveness, although that, admittedly, is a close-run thing.

But then it always is, which is the ultimate point. For it is precisely because Wilde's battle was with the very real tempta-tions of superstition and harsh doctrine that we should be credulous when reading him, and follow his cues. Wilde's gift of oracular speech infuses his writing, guiding us afresh through what we think we already know, or have forgotten, or have simply grown accustomed to. We should aspire to be entranced listeners rather than skeptical readers. His manner demands it of us, but we owe it to ourselves to let him transform the world back into its true materiality with his parables, his confidence tricks. "The English," he once told the playwright Maurice Maeterlinck, "have a miraculous power to change wine into water" (Ellmann, 351). Faced with the miraculous vision of Wilde, con-man, conjurer, and contortionist, we should remember that it is only the unimaginative who cannot see what is before their very eyes.

CHAPTER 2

Some gentle criticisms of British justice

For those at the center of the Wilde affair, the most pressing need after the sentencing on 25 May 1895 was to continue to protest at the verdict, and to provide justification of their own conduct without risking further incrimination. Both Wilde and Lord Alfred Douglas engaged in these activities, but their approaches were significantly different and by no means consistent.

Douglas opted for a self-regarding use of Wildean aesthetics: "All beauty is subjective and relative," he wrote in reply to his French critics, "I may be ugly as Hell: I am not aware of it and it does not trouble me. The only thing which matters here is that my friend found me beautiful. My beauty is the hypothesis of the discussion."[1] However deserving, Douglas's targets remained predictable: judges, politicians, journalists, the unofficial representatives of British philistinism. "What can they know of an artist's temperament, a poet's character, his love of the bizarre, his leaning for the fantastic, his search for the strange, his desire to tread all the paths of life?" he sneered of Wilde's jury. "How can you expect these twelve prosaic shopkeepers to understand all these things?"

Intended for an article in the *Mercure de France* in 1895,[2] this particular piece of rhetorical justification, which was to have been accompanied by quotations from Wilde's intimate letters, never saw the light of day because Wilde, although in jail, managed to forestall publication.

Crude counterattack was not Wilde's way: a love of paradox sustained him even now. "To be entirely free, and at the same time entirely dominated by the law, is the eternal paradox of human life" was to be the new note struck in *De Profundis* (*Works*,

997); though *The Ballad of Reading Gaol* does record a more
concrete sentiment: "I know not whether Laws be right, / Or
whether Laws be wrong; / All that we know who lie in gaol / Is
that the wall is strong" (*Works*, 896). For Wilde, too much
concern with the workings of civil law withheld realization of
those more elusive laws of human experience whose truths the
brutality of public justice had now ironically exposed.

Yet even Wilde had sometimes made his thoughts his prisons.
For all its show of humility *De Profundis* is an attempt at self-
assertion in which Douglas is treated as usurper. We will probably
never know exactly what part Wilde's comforters, Robert
Sherard, Robert Ross, and More Adey,[3] played in the raising of
this Mephisophelean devil, but certainly much of Wilde's ire was
brought on by Douglas's early campaign on his behalf in France,
which they must have reported back to Reading. As Wilde saw it,
Douglas's seditious activities were tantamount to an admission of
the legal charges; moreover, as Richard Ellmann observed,
Douglas "misjudged his man. Neither now nor afterwards had
Wilde any desire to plead publicly guilty to a charge of which he
had pleaded publicly not guilty. Confession, if it ever took place,
would be on his terms not another's."[4] In any case, Wilde had
already absolved himself, turning guilt into innocence with his
great defence of Uranian love at the Old Bailey – and had been
condemned none the less. His rage was most likely engendered by
Douglas's presumption, by his betrayal of Wilde's difficult,
though deepening, attempts at moral understanding.

In Wilde's beleaguered mind no one, least of all a man upon
whom so much time, love, and, as he increasingly remembered,
money, had been expended, could have substituted for the real
victim. A more politic man than Douglas would not have done
everything right. Given Douglas's volatility, his inability to
control a public face, everything was inevitably and hopelessly
wrong. Whatever he did, said, or wrote seemed to Wilde to be a
parody of the past, a distortion of the present, a detonation of the
future.

But Douglas's concerns were no longer those of his friend, if
indeed they had ever been. By the latter part of 1895 he had several
simultaneous projects in hand in addition to the exoneration and

possible release of Wilde. His justification was multiple: affirmation of homosexuality, promotion of his own art, humiliation of his father, elaboration of an aesthetic attitude. Douglas wanted justice, and at the same time he wanted revenge. Unlike Wilde, he did not see that these were no longer compatible aims. So Douglas remained simply and violently hostile to the law, even as Wilde was veering towards larger questions of moral nature. And if Wilde still sought confession without absolute disclosure, Douglas would always hold to the idea that if you proved the iniquity of those who dispensed the law you were bound also to reveal the heroism of those who had suffered from it.

In May 1895 Douglas moved to Rouen, where he took up residence in the Hôtel de la Poste, wrote letters, some of them to the press, and received visitors, among them French journalists and an Englishman who had traveled from Newcastle. Douglas repeated his sensational accusations to them all: Queensberry's solicitors had blackmailed and bribed witnesses; Rosebery, the Prime Minister, had been intimidated by the threat of personal exposure; Maurice Schwabe, nephew of Sir Frances Lockwood, the Solicitor General, had been shielded. In addition Douglas pronounced, as he always did, on the worth of his own poetry.

PLAYING FAIR

The English visitor was suitably impressed, and on his return to Newcastle incorporated Douglas's claims, together with a tribute to his poetry, in a pamphlet bearing the facetious title *Some Gentle Criticisms of British Justice*[5] and, perhaps inspired by Douglas, attributed the whole to a punning alias, "I. Playfair."[6]

"Playfair's" pamphlet is headed Part I (there is no apparent trace of Part II), and it is divided into ten short chapters. Chapter I introduces the Criminal Law Amendment Act of 1885; this is said to have failed, in that the number of prosecutions for the "vices indictable under this Clause" has increased enormously since it came into force. Then, barely signaling the shift, Playfair moves into satirical vein:

Now as these offences are not indictable at all in France and Italy, and only nominally so in some other countries, it behoves us more than ever to exhibit our righteous zeal in the face of all the sneers and detraction of foreigners.

Having alluded to the recent opinions of the bench (Sir John Bridge, the Bow Street magistrate before whom Wilde had first appeared, and Mr. Justice Wills, who heard the final trial and actually passed sentence), Playfair continues with his ironical suggestions. Drawing at first upon the opinions publicly expressed by W. T. Stead,[7] he proposes:

1st. – MR.STEAD had admitted that to carry out the clause consistently would involve an exodus from our public schools to our public prisons. Then by all means let us begin, unless we wish to be inconsistent. Any little inconvenience at first would soon right itself, as deaths would quickly occur.
2nd. – Let offenders of every rank be equally punished from Prince to peasant.
3rd. – Let hushed-up offences be brought now to light.
If anything less than the above be done, or if the public hesitates at all to carry out this lofty programme, then the whole of the late outcry from our noble and impartial Press, all the opinions of Magistrates and Judges, and all the denunciations of counsel, must be admitted to be hypocritical from beginning to end, which is, in fact, exactly what the Continental Press has had the insolence to say recently, with the most offensive unanimity and tenacity.

Playfair announces his scheme: we have "collected a few simple facts and disclosures," we shall "suppress names where we think the good people alluded to, would from motives of modesty rather be anonymous. Those whose names we cannot suppress will not dispute any of our facts, and we trust will take no offence where none is intended." Justification for the whole enterprise is provided by Alexander Pope: "Ask you what provocation I have had? / The strong antipathy of good to bad."

Chapter II announces that there are twenty or thirty black-mailers to be found in the Piccadilly area who regularly drink the health of "Good old Lab."[8] The police know of these people, yet do not act; Queensberry is said to have employed detectives who bribed some of them to testify against Wilde. Queensberry's solicitors, Russell and Day (one the son of the Lord Chief Justice of England, the other the son of yet another judge, Mr. Justice Day, as Playfair is anxious to point out), are accused of blackmail in turn. They are said to have placed a detective in an adjoining room and then threatened one of the young men (known here as "Hades")[9] with his own arrest unless he testified against Wilde.

This is Playfair's first major charge:

> Now supposing that Hades, under the influence of terror, had promised to say anything to secure his safety, what value could such evidence possibly have? Surely this was the mere sale and purchase of perjury?
>
> Do we put Judges on the bench to punish crime when they fail to teach their own sons the very rudiments of morality? Is it conceivable that these two Judges were quite unaware of what was going on in connection with a case so sensational as this one? Is it not possible that they were consulted by their dutiful children?

None the less, after "Hades" had told Russell "to go to a very dreadful place," he was allowed to depart, which leads to Playfair's next point:

> Was the detective there at all? If not, Russell lied. If he were, he equally lied, for the detective was not there for the purpose pretended, but only for the purpose of frightening the witness. Are the police expected by the rate-payers to act farces like this, to accommodate solicitors of this class? and what fee does an officer of justice usually charge for lending himself out as a private scarecrow?

The only conclusion, backed up with reference to Galileo's treatment by the Inquisition, must be that "extortion of evidence by terror has a suspicious family resemblance to blackmailing itself." Nevertheless, as Playfair concedes, Russell and Day did indeed find men (such as Alfred Taylor) who were willing to testify, and judges who were willing to listen. The conduct of judges is then held up for judgment itself.

> When next Mr. Justice DAY sends an old woman to penal servitude for SEVEN YEARS for stealing a rag, and who faints in the Court on hearing this considerate sentence from her humane Judge, let him think of the way in which the firm of RUSSELL and DAY earns its money, and put to himself Shakespeare's puzzling question "handy, dandy, which is the justice? which is the thief?" To complete the mockery Mr. Justice DAY

passes very heavy sentences of many years' penal servitude on weak-minded persons who write threatening letters.

Playfair now turns to "another beautiful and interesting character," a "gentleman named BURTON" who "keeps a seminary for blackmailing students, who we will call the 'Guild of the Wandering Nephews.'"[10] Burton's game is to train boys to entrap men in compromising situations, and then, posing as the boys' uncle, to demand money. "This also our good Treasury has long known, but the reasons why no case of REGINA v. BURTON will ever be heard of cannot be explained yet or in this Pamphlet."

An 1893 case is cited in which youths were encouraged to solicit men in order to bring about prosecution, their own morality being of no account whatsoever.

Is it not a curious reflection that thousands of honest decent lads are working hard for a small wage from early morn to night in pits and factories and shops and receive not an ounce of patronage from the Treasury – whereas "loathsome moral lepers blotched from footsole up to crown" are flattered and made heroes of Marquises and sons of her Majesty's learned Judges, and as we shall see later on, loaded with pecuniary rewards to an extent which would have shamed Gehazi.

Chapter III brings Playfair to the Wilde case and to a man he chooses to call "Macpelah," "Father of the Faithful," a blackmailing solicitor who also worked for Queensberry.[11] It was "Macpelah" who once proposed to "a famous and accomplished lady"[12] that he concoct a fraudulent will in her favor, and who had shown the same lady the notorious letter from Wilde to Douglas which she, in turn, had shown to a friend.[13] Wilde had warned her to have nothing to do with the man, but Queensberry came to hear of the letter and bought it. "Macpelah's" young blackmailers were then put to work, together with "two well-known actors, both of profligate lives."[14]

Playfair's strong condemnation of Queensberry is matched by his support for his son:

But to none of his children has this "loving father" shown so intense an animosity as to his son, LORD ALFRED DOUGLAS, whose persistent devotion to his broken-hearted mother, and whose chivalrous attempts to defend her from the utterly incredible persecutions of her cruel enemy, seem to act on this man's mind as a "poisonous mineral" on the digestive system.

In his fourth and fifth chapters Playfair turns to Edward Carson, Wilde's schoolfellow, who "used to walk about with him, with his arms round his neck, before he had discovered that gain could be made, by affecting to suspect wrong, in the most natural expressions of affectionate comradeship." Playfair questions the treatment, in and out of court, of the Crown witnesses Charles Parker and Edward Shelley, and makes references to other trials in which blackmailers have been involved. He goes on to query the protective intervention of the Solicitor General, Sir Frank Lockwood, whose nephew, Maurice Schwabe, had introduced Wilde to Taylor. Lockwood's reported remark to Clarke, Wilde's counsel, "You'll dine your man in Paris to-morrow,"[15] is cited as evidence that even the Solicitor General knew how dubious the testimonies against Wilde really were. At the same time, Lockwood's public charge that Wilde's supposed offenses made men "lower than the beasts" is set against a noble quotation from Wilde's own poem, "On the Sale by Auction of Keats' Love Letters."

Chapter VII is devoted to the letter to Douglas that begins "My Own Boy, Your sonnet is quite lovely," and to Playfair's own theories of how language can be misinterpreted:

The chief argument was that this language "would have had" a base meaning, "if it had" been addressed to a woman. Possibly so (though even then much would have depended on the relations of the persons to each other). But what an absurd test to apply! Why, every expression of affection in this or in any other language, depends entirely for its purity or impurity on the circumstances in which it is used. What does the word "Love" mean in the opening line of *In Memoriam*? And to what base use is the same word sometimes applied? Had Tennyson therefore a wrong meaning when he used it?

Playfair explicates the references in Douglas's poem:

Apollo was the inspirer of poetry, song, eloquence, music, painting, sculpture, – in fact, not to terrify our legal friends any longer with the black list – of false glamour generally.

Hyacinthus was his beloved pupil, whom he educated and to whom he taught the golden lyre. If they loved each other so enthusiastically and madly, it was through the sympathy of a common aspiration, – the bond between teacher and taught.

Then comes Playfair's ironical challenge:

Does the Crown aver, that if Apollo were still alive and were to visit this country, Scotland Yard would run him in?

The stupidity of Mr. Justice Wills and the "open foulness" of Queensberry are traduced, and Playfair subjects Wilde's letter to an alternative, positive reading in which the sonnets of Shakespeare and of Michelangelo are brought to bear and Whitman is mentioned. Spenser's list of great male friendships in *The Faerie Queene* Book III, Canto X, beginning with Hercules and Hylas, is quoted. These are all expressions of ideal and poetical attachment, since

it has long been held by those who have studied the laws of human emotion most closely, that it is precisely where an attachment is freest from a baser element, that it tends to become ideal, and the expression of it poetical and extravagant; – and would not this specially apply to friendships between those of one sex, where a coarse element is at least highly improbable, and is to most minds inconceivable?

Chapter X, the last, is given over to extravagant praise of Douglas's verse. The more mature writer, Wilde, is hailed as a mentor whose friendship enabled the young man to check the "bitterness" brought on by a father's hatred. No wonder then that Douglas's gratitude "should be so fervent and overflow into the music of song" and that he should want to make Wilde the dedicatee of his poems. With that rational plea Playfair's pamphlet, at least in the form that it survives, comes to an end.

In the event *Some Gentle Criticisms* was probably never published; even if it was, few can have read it. The legal situation after the spring of 1895 ensured that most protests against the punishment of homosexuals tended either to assume a euphemistic tone, as Wilde's own "justifications" were sometimes to do, or else became caught up in other debates and wider power struggles. Playfair's attempts to make the facts more widely known were to be inhibited at every turn. When evidence could not be made evident, then the conviction would remain convincing. As Wilde, and Wilde's friends knew, the problem with protest was that it only proved guilt.

JAMES H. WILSON

The real name of the author of *Some Gentle Criticisms*, Alfred Douglas's new ally, was James H. Wilson. Very little is known about him, even today. Yet (adapting the terms made familiar by Jonathan Dollimore in *Sexual Dissidence*) we can say that Wilson, though socially marginal, was symbolically central. He can stand not only for all those who were moved to tears and sometimes to action by Wilde's imprisonment, but for an even wider constituency of moral protesters who emerged in new formations in the late nineteenth century: the prison reformers, the members of the Humane Society and the anti-vivisection lobby. In that respect his very obscurity is a continuing mark of his significance.

We do know that Wilson lived in St. Ann Street, now demolished, close to the wharves; that he, or at any rate his family, were furriers; that he was a Quaker who had dealings with Robert Spence Watson and Elizabeth Spence Watson of the Newcastle Literary and Philosophical Society; and that he was a poet, whose volume *Zalmoxis and Other Poems*, dedicated to the Watsons, had appeared in 1892.[16]

Zalmoxis is, if only in its range, an impressive volume. It contains some forty-nine poems of which seven are classical monologues drawn from Herodotus and Homer, presented in Tennysonian mode. These include "Zalmoxis" (an Ionian slave who came to be worshiped as a god by the Thracians), "Ganymede," and "Calypso." There are also, as a concluding sequence, translations from the German of Heine and others, and of Moschus' epitaph on Bion and Bion's epitaph on Adonis. The last two are accompanied by notes which make learned comparison with Keats, Shelley, and Arnold.

Between these verses on classical themes Wilson offers poems in a variety of genres. There are several pieces complaining about injustice, such as "Suicide in Durham Gaol"; while in "L'Envoi" Wilson makes it clear that he sees himself in the role of outcast prophet:

Desert so wild and gray – bare rocks – and
wilderness places,

Here O friends! let me stray, though far from
the sight of your faces.

Whence were those bitter wails, those cries
which awoke us from slumber,

Tears from the darkness of jails, and sorrows
which no man can number?

These from the victims of hate, from the
outcast sons of oppression, –

Vengeance – the creed of the State! and Law –
the fierce Right of Possession!

Lawgivers hard as the stone! have ye joy of the
wrecks ye are making?

Flesh and blood are like your own, but hearts
that are broken and breaking!   (164–65)

There are landscape poems too, set in Northumbria, which
seem, with their mention of "our mysterious brotherhood," to
allude to a Whitmanesque sense of camaraderie. One of them,
entitled in fact "Comrades," opens with:

Spirit with your thirst unslakèd,
Earnest heart, laid bare and naked,
Comrade, from the first I knew you.
Take the kiss which I give to you.   (88)

It ends:

Therefore show me, unforbidden,
Secrets from the cold world hidden.
Be my friend, companion, brother;
Let us love and trust each other.
What I give is worth bestowing;
What I teach deserves your knowing;
Are there struggles, strivings, yearnings,
Loss of heart and hope, soul burnings? –
Comrade, by these signs I knew you.
Take the kiss which I give to you.   (90)

The Whitmanesque, or Carpenterian, atmosphere is palpable, yet *Zalmoxis* also has poems about a man who dreams that his dead wife has returned, and a sequence entitled *Clods of the Valley* commemorating a past love affair that certainly sounds as if it were a marriage.

Twenty years later, in 1912, Wilson was to publish, anonymously, a long dramatic poem in blank verse entitled *Iscariot's Bitter Love*, in which Judas' betrayal is shown to have been caused by his jealous, possessive love for Christ. The events of Christ's life take place offstage; onstage scenes include debates about the meaning of his teaching conducted by a Brahman, an atheist Roman, a pantheist Greek, and a Jewish scribe. Each gives a coherent explanation of Christ's meaning according to the tenets of his own beliefs, and Wilson provides source notes which range from the *Upanishads* to Walter Pater, from St. John of the Cross to the popular contemporary mystic Alice Meynell. The main character, Judas, declares as he leads the soldiers to the Captain of the Temple:

> The world itself is nothing but a sign.
> We wait; we have not found the meaning yet.[17]

But Judas is soon appalled by his own actions, and by a deepening realization that he has destroyed the prophet of infinite forgiveness. At the very end of the drama Judas maintains (with perhaps an echo of "Each man kills the thing he loves"):

> My love was poison, but it still was love.
> It did the deeds of Hate, but was not Hate.   (85)

All in all it is extremely difficult to determine much about Wilson's personal life from his poetry. That, of course, is part of its interest: it reflects a view of the world in which sexual alignments are intimately connected with, yet secondary to, expressions of love, grief, outrage. Nevertheless the poetry, the pamphlet, and the surrounding correspondence strongly suggest that Wilson was well read, pedantic, obsessive even, and he obviously sometimes felt sensitive about his provincial location. What is also very apparent is that his attitudes were a product of a synthetic but intense humanitarianism.

THE SUMMER OF 1895

Wilson's preparation and frequent revision of *Some Gentle Criticisms* was a lengthy business, his endeavors made more complicated by the problems he encountered in communicating with those friends of Wilde's, in particular More Adey, whose approval he considered to be essential if he were to avoid giving offense and betraying Douglas as the source of his information. He was obliged to make several journeys to London, where he stayed at the Friends Institute in Bishopsgate. Deferential yet determined, he bombarded Adey with letters, requesting meetings, seeking advice.[18]

By July, though, Wilson's plans were well underway, and he was hoping to publish chapters of his pamphlet as articles in *Reynolds' Newspaper*. On 24 July he told Adey that he had discussed the whole matter with a sub-editor who would try and persuade his chief to go ahead with publication. The purpose of both pamphlet and articles would be to expose the infamy of the law and to reveal the folly of relying upon blackmailers for evidence. A further article, he wrote, would deal with Wilde's letter to Douglas, which had been read out with such damaging consequences at the trial.

The absurdity of imputations is discussed in great detail. Shakespeare and Michelangelo are proved to be in exactly the same position. Then Spenser's *Faerie Queene* is quoted from very fully. Then the right view of a lofty friendship is explained.

However, on 2 August Wilson wrote to Adey that having heard nothing further from *Reynolds'*, he proposed to publish the first half of the pamphlet himself; if there was a reaction he would follow up with the second half. He still had hopes that *Reynolds'* would at least print extracts. By 22 August he was ready to publish, but was frustrated by his failure to arrange a meeting with Adey in spite of frequent visits to London and discussions with Dalhousie Young.[19] The sub-editor at *Reynolds'* now wanted to put a discussion of the Wilde case at the end of a series on police corruption. Wilson himself had had the idea that the newspaper might review his pamphlet and quote from it, but he was getting worried that the Editor might become "obdurate":

Then comes the most difficult of all questions. Shall I print it and distribute it by post, *now* or *later on* or destroy it? Or shall I so strip it of personal matter, that it will be publishable and saleable? It seems absolutely necessary for me to meet you and *go through it word for word!*. . . .A great deal depends upon extraneous circumstances that only you can explain; and a great deal upon the MS itself which you have never seen. Your opinion might be entirely altered when you see it. In view of possible publication I have got my own printer to print the Introduction, clearly understanding that it may come to nothing. In that case he will simply knock the type out again, charge a mere trifle for it, and the matter is ended. He sees nothing else, and has no idea of what is in the body of the pamphlet, and could not spread it about, and besides this I have confidence in his discretion. (25 August 1895)

By mid-September Wilson seems to have lowered his sights. The pamphlet might still provide *Reynolds'* with material for articles, the paper might review it (thereby reducing the risk of a libel action), but Wilson no longer intended to send copies to prominent MPs and magistrates. He had decided instead to confine distribution to "carefully selected friends, so as not to let it get broadcast – yet doing a little good in a quiet way by exposing the injustice and wickedness of the authorities even if only to a few people." As concerned as ever for Douglas's safety, he assured Adey that the pamphlet would not be properly published, and that Douglas "need not feel any annoyance" (Colby, 12 September 1895).

Come October and Wilson's mood had changed yet again. He had made another trip to London, had again failed to meet Adey, but he was now confident that *Reynolds'* would use his material. He was thinking of printing a thousand copies, with a thousand more to come. He was still anxious about Douglas though, and "Mr. H"[20] continued to warn that publicity might provoke the authorities into retaliation. Wilson claimed to be puzzled by this caution:

It seems to me outrageous that great men could stoop to such petty spite, as to revenge an attack on themselves in any sort of way like this.

I cannot but hope it is a mistake...But I anxiously await some definite information as to how it is is possible to make Mr. W[ilde] suffer by any public comment. (1 October 1895)

At this point Wilson added a "most telling passage" from Krafft-Ebing,[21] and he now noted:

I think this attack and correspondence in *Reynolds'* etc. might just open the door for a few good men to take up the question: if the medical men once boldly attacked these wicked and diabolical laws, they would soon be repealed, or at least employed less recklessly. The crimes of the authorities if exposed give the opportunity for this attack.

A few days later he writes:

I should very much like to have your opinion as to how far it would be wise to expose the iniquities of the authorities at the present time. If the individual has to suffer for what really concerns the public, it prevents me from making the exposure which I am convinced *ought* to be made. (10 October 1895)

References to the police are to be softened and a postscript added to the effect that "Mr. P[layfair] does not attack the law, but that it is badly administered, if we accept it as a good law. But great authorities in science attack the very law itself. Then Krafft-E[bing] is quoted."

Wilson was right to be cautious. Wilde's friends were in a quandary throughout his time in jail. It was widely held that it would be dangerous to the prisoner's interests (his dealings with his wife over money matters, in particular) to dwell upon his relationship with Douglas; and risky for several of Wilde's other friends too if the legitimacy of homosexuality were to be too loudly proclaimed. Unable to contact either Douglas, who had left for Italy, or Robert Ross, Adey rehearsed these arguments in an undated letter to Wilson.

With regard to the end of the pamphlet I hope that Mr. Playfair will understand the difficulties I have experienced in detailing the objections which I have felt to it before. I am equally the friend of Mr. Wilde and Lord Alfred Douglas, but this is not the case with many people who are most anxious to help Mr. Oscar Wilde. I think that allusions *at this time*, to the exceptional friendship existing between them are calculated to prejudice Mr. Wilde's cause in the eyes of those who are friends of his, and *not* of Lord Alfred. At present it is necessary to emphasize rather Mr. Wilde's excellent understanding with his wife, and not his romantic friendship with Lord Alfred Douglas, with which I sympathise so cordially and which Mr. Playfair so eloquently describes.

In another undated draft Adey wrote that as one of Wilde's friends it was essential that he take up a public attitude of "cold reserve and indifference." In his reply Wilson reiterated that he had not asked for the public support of Wilde's friends, and he would not do so now; Douglas would not be exposed. Moreover,

For many years I have observed the utter hypocrisy and diabolical cruelty (as it seems to me) of justice in this country, and have often been impatient to express some sort of protest. On seeing an opportunity now, I only relieve my *own* mind, and no one else is responsible for a word. (17 October 1895)

Here we can see very clearly not only the commitment that has sustained Wilson over the months, but a clash between the moral sense of the individual and the self-protective workings of authority, with consequent restrictions upon the opportunities for outright protest. The persecution of homosexuals was a public matter: Wilson knows of "three other most terrible cases, involving five cruelly wronged victims...cases more horrible than anything in Playfair's last Pamphlet," and yet, prompted perhaps by Douglas, he habitually refers to those who dispense the law as if they were simply private persons. He says he needs to ascertain whether the authorities will act with what he calls "the repentance which becomes them" or with "a mean revenge."

When he decides that a thousand copies will be published, Wilson is necessarily vague about distribution: "fifty copies to men like Bernard Shaw." On the advice of his contact at *Reynolds'*, the praise for Douglas's poetry will be retained in only a small private edition – "not that the estimate of Lord Alfred Douglas's poems is exaggerated, but the public may think it is."

What seems to have been Wilson's last letter to Adey (who was by this point himself engaged in preparation of a petition on Wilde's behalf to the Home Secretary) is dated 16 November. With it Wilson enclosed a cutting from *Reynolds'* which mentioned Playfair in the context of an exposure of police methods and their habit of blackmailing male prostitutes in order to entrap homo-sexuals. There was some consolation in this, but Wilson was tired, and had by now given up all hopes of distributing his pamphlet.

Personally when I contemplate the injustice and wrong, it becomes almost more than I can endure...I feel that left without assistance I could do nothing, though if I had access to the press I am certain a very great deal could be done.

WHY "REYNOLDS'"?

James Wilson had tried his utmost to gain access to the press and had very nearly succeeded. The reasons for his ultimate failure were several, and they tell us a great deal about the material world of late nineteenth-century England: about the interaction between sexual conduct and class attitudes most obviously, but also about the slow, inadequate, and often compromised pro-cesses of negotiation between individuals, the communities to which they belonged, and the public organs that claimed to represent them.

By deciding to enlist the help of *Reynolds' Newspaper* Wilson was following a long tradition as well as responding to recent events. Although founded in 1850 in the wake of Chartism, *Reynolds'* had remained the natural home for outspoken attacks on class and legal corruption.[22] In January 1895 the Editor, W. H. Thompson, an Irishman with a history of radical involvement, was still able to claim that his was "the only avowedly Republican paper – the only journal that demands 'Government of the People by the People for the People.'" Famous for its attacks on royalty and the upper classes, the paper had a clear sense of its readership, boasting: "We write for the working man, and publish nothing that we think pitched in a key too high for the average. We are for facts and sentiments appropriate to our aims and do not appeal to all classes." [23]

By July 1895, which is when Wilson first engaged with the *Reynolds'* sub-editor, the paper had begun to wind down a coverage of the Wilde scandal that had always been extensive and initially extremely virulent in its attacks upon all concerned, including Wilde himself. Yet on Sunday 30 June the paper was prepared to publish a poem by Percy T. Ingram called "The Democratic World," which ended:

> And still today the damning record runs
> Ungrateful England blights her rising star
> And thrusts her brilliant poet where felons are.

Back in early March, when Wilde had charged Queensberry with libel and the story had first broken, the paper's approach had been very different. It had seized a heaven-sent opportunity for a full-scale attack on aristocratic mores, and had gone on to provide some of the most detailed reports of the subsequent trials, with stories spread over two or three columns, sketches of the protagonists, careful character studies, and as much local color as it could muster. Although the bitter feuding within the Queensberry family provided the delicious spectacle of the ruling class divided against itself, this was hardly to Wilde's advantage, since everyone knew that he moved in those social circles too. *Reynolds'* traditional support for the Irish and for the victims of legal injustice was challenged by Wilde's own manner, and certainly by that of many of his acquaintances who were indelibly associated with the corrupt world of High Society. Everything about Wilde's personal life suggested that however satirical his plays, he was himself contaminated with an upper-class "decadence," empty and self-indulgent, that cruelly exploited others in the pursuit of its own pointless pleasures. Wilde was, quite literally, what "decadence" looked like and *Reynolds'* had gone for the kill.

Accordingly, in April, when Wilde was actually in the dock, it had embarked upon a series of judgmental editorials in which an epic range of prejudice was energetically displayed. For recent scholars these articles have become famous for their comprehensive homophobia, misogyny, and overall philistinism.[24] Here, for example, almost in its entirety, is what was offered on the front page on Sunday 14 April:

THE NOTORIOUS MR. WILDE

The records of romance, and even of reality, furnish few, if any, instances where the tables have been turned with such pronounced definiteness as in the notorious case of Oscar Wilde against the Marquis of Queensberry. Hitherto the scandalous revelations of courts of law were mainly concerned with the gross indecencies, and the domestic horrors of people in high life whose animalism, nurtured by a lazy, luxurious mode of living, dominated all the ordinary rules and conventions by which men and women are supposed to regard and treat one another. But, as the times, the fashion in scandal changes, and in the era of the "new women", it is not astonishing to discover that the sex-problem is putting on a new face and marking out a fresh course for itelf. It would be trite to recall the fact that ancient Rome, in the days of its idle and wealthy classes, furnishes a parallel and a precedent for the immoral revolution upon which we have just entered in this divine century.

Consider the combatants, who have attracted within the last few days the interest, the curiosity, the unwholesome attention of tens of thousands of English men and women. On the one side we have the Marquis of Queensberry – a man of considerable natural gifts, when compared with the majority of the hereditary automatons who happen to be of his own rank. Whatever may be his little weakness in the direction of the turf, and however eccentric his unmuscular patronage of the prize-ring, it stands to his credit that he has had in his public life the courage of his opinions – he is not a mere man–doll. Avowedly because he is an Agnostic, he was intrigued out of his Seat in the House of Lords, where he, an elected representative peer for Scotland – the land which is a pleasanter place from the point of view of its natural, rather than its theological mists. And Mr. Oscar Wilde, his accuser, what of him? A poet, a writer, a dramatist of the most brilliant achievement, equally distinguished throughout an honourable college career, and a more or less struggling existence as a man of letters; a personage to whom, a month ago, every reviler of the worst side of his life – which has the disadvantage, from which many worse men are saved, of being found out – would have fawned, cringed and "lionized". Here indeed is the material of no ordinary exposure, and from it we shall learn more than enough of the corruption of modern life.

The morbid interest which the persons on the street have taken in the case throughout suggests certainly that there is a lack of moral stiffening – a decadence – in the community. Women, boys, girls, eagerly peruse the latest intelligence and excitedly canvas it...

There is no defence for the vice of which Oscar Wilde is accused. Yet it is by no means new or unfamiliar. Similar practices are carried on daily, in an intensely grosser form, under the eyes almost of English tourists in Oriental countries. It is not a noble sign of the national character of such nations that the vice is almost commonplace; but the fact remains. In our own country, and especially in London, such practices have grown apace, unchecked by police authority or Vigilian

Society. The reason doubtless is that the sinners and law-breakers have, in the past, been such as could afford the costly orgies of the Cleveland Street Bacchanalia.

We shall say not a word to prejudice the case of the unhappy man whose conduct is now undergoing investigation in a criminal court. But we may be allowed to point out that in a recent case Mr. Justice Wills sentenced a youth to seven years' penal servitude for threatening a well-known City merchant for exposure for having, as he alleged, committed with him an infamous crime. The Judge said that the conduct of the prosecutor was suspicious and that he would impose upon the prisoner the mitigated sentence mentioned above – having given penal servitude for life in similar instances previously. A series of cases in England have shown that bestiality is rife in our Society. When such a crime is proved, the seducer ought not to be less lightly dealt with than the seduced. Moreover, the public will regard it as very extraordinary if, in the hearing of Wilde's case, there be any concealment of the names of any "exalted" or other personages. Were it a case of a poor man, no names would be hidden under any mysterious formula, such as "Mr B." as we have seen in the Queensberry–Wilde trial. It is peculiar to notice how frequent are such suppressions when the allusion concerns persons probably of social status. The reputation of the Home Secretary and the Public Prosecutor are concerned in this matter, and the public expect they will do their duty.

The real lesson taught by the recent appalling revelations should not be lost sight of by the public. That there is a danger of this cannot be doubted, for with one accord the public prints have carefully avoided any specific reference to the source of the abominations which contaminate the minds of thousands of English lads yearly. That source is to be found, we grieve to state, in the great public schools of England. It is a fact, atrocious to all acquainted with the subject, that at certain educational establishments of the highest class the morality of the students is past praying for; innocent lads, with the purity and refinement of home life in their hearts, become tainted with the traditional vices of these schools and colleges before they have been many months within their walls. Who is responsible for this terrible condition of things? Perhaps the real burden of blame should be laid on the shoulders of wealthy parents, who encourage the extravagant propensities of their children, giving mere lads three or four hundred a year for pocket money, and indulging them in directions which must inevitably lead to the contraction of vicious and depraved habits. Then again, the scholastic authorities were too prone to wink at the irregularities of the sons of men of wealth and position, deeming them privileged, so to speak: and being mindful, too, of the patronage and

influence which the future might place at the disposal of their aristocratic pupils. The result of this method of training is written in vivid
characters in the social records of the country, where we now see in the
scandals and infamies and follies of Society the outcome of vices planted
by the great public schools of England. The latest contribution to these
records should rouse the conscience of the public to demand that drastic
measures of reform be taken to purge these schools from the peculiar
forms of iniquity which poison the social life of England at its very
fountain-head.

Reynolds' followed this the following Sunday with a leader on
"Sex-Mania," where the emphasis was once again on the
depravity of the aristocracy, as it always was, even when an
additional phenomenon such as the "New Woman" was brought
into play.

Yet it is also possible to detect in the columns of *Reynolds'*, as
the year continued, a counter or at any rate an alternative
current of opinion. On 12 May there appeared two letters notable
not just for their frankness, but for their subversive potential. One
was signed "A Schoolboy":

In the study hall, in the classroom – nay at very prayers – I have known
masturbation carried on. Such was the daily *régime*, and yet the powers
that be never made an attempt to check the mischief. Of its existence
they could not have been unaware, for soiled bed clothes and torn
trousers' pockets, apart from the pimpled foreheads and emaciated
appearance of the boys, told their sad tale.

Another letter, signed T. G. Roy, headed "Oscar Wilde and
the Democracy," protested against the recent leaders, referring at
some length to *The Soul of Man Under Socialism*: "Trusting in your
sense of justice to at least modify your sweeping denunciation of
Mr. Wilde's writings, and only regretting that the enclosed
extracts give so meagre an idea of a brilliant and splendid essay."

Reynolds' treatment of Wilde was now about to move into a new
phase, and it was this, surely, that James Wilson was responding
to. Between 12 May and 2 June, when the correspondence was
officially brought to a close, the paper ran a series of letters and
commentary on immorality in the public schools and the ancient
universities. The feature belongs with those half-contrived, half-
spontaneous controversies, beginning with "Marriage or

Celibacy?" in *The Daily Telegraph* in 1868 and continuing through
to "Is Marriage a Failure?" in the same paper twenty years later,
which were such a feature of the late Victorian popular press.[25]
The notable aspect of the *Reynolds'* brouhaha, however, is that it is
about homosexuality, specifically about pederasty. It includes a
comparatively wide range of opinion ranging from rabid hostility
to tolerance (or at least charity), to something that is initially hard
to categorize.

"EXPERTO CREDE"

Alan Sinfield has recently argued that it was not just that
homosexual activities thrived in the public schools (a fact about
which the Victorians were absolutely in agreement), but that
"public schools were crucial in the development of homosexual
identity":

Despite the official taboo they contributed, in many instances, an
unofficial but powerful cultural framework within which same-sex
passion might be positively valued...The school ethos was seized for just
those purposes it was supposed to be repudiating.[26]

Read in this way some of the letters to *Reynolds'* take on the air
not simply of exhibitionist confession but of something very close
to affirmation. There are even letters that, for all the moral
bluster, go beyond the public schools altogether to enter a world
of general rational discourse.

On Sunday 19 May the first of a series of letters from "Experto
Crede" appeared:

I have been interested and somewhat amused at the contributions of
some of your correspondents on these sexual questions now cropping
up. One writer says there are "*hundreds*" of M.P.s, lawyers, authors,
artists etc who indulge in what are called unnatural practices. Well, this
is true, I dare say, as it goes. But, to tell the whole truth, it should be
added and there are "*thousands*" of tinkers and tailors, soldiers and
sailors, costers and loafers who do the same. The fact is, the propensity
is common to all men at all times and in all countries.

"Severe and cruel laws" are therefore quite inefficacious:

The practices of big schoolboys on smaller ones is merely a "make-believe"; it is the ordinary male passion for the female, prevented by circumstances from taking its normal course. When the impediments are removed, the young fellows rush after the real thing, and the sham is rejected. But is is undoubted that there is in all Societies a certain minority of men (relatively small, but actually very large) who never know any inclination for the female, whose attraction is constantly and exclusively for the male – the younger for the adult male, the adult for the younger. This is a problem that has been ignored and shirked by us, but which will force its way to the front.

This prompted a reply the following week from "ETHICUS":

The able letter of "Experto Crede" in your last issue introduces an important problem which to quote from the writer "has been ignored and shirked by us, but which will force its way to the front". The problem is that of pederasty. The fierceness of denunciation which men of all classes mete out to this failing rivals the legendary zeal of the Spanish Inquisition and suggest an enquiry as to wherein lies its heinousness. You sir, are the first, as far as I am aware, sufficiently above suspicion, to allow the question to be opened in your columns. May I invite one of those who are so implacable in their condemnation to set forth the plain facts of its enormity as being the best deterrent from its practice?

I have asked a doctor what the physical injury is and he replied he knew of none; I have asked a lawyer what the injury to the state is, and he told me it would mean a decrease of population; I have asked a clergyman, and he answered that it was unnatural, disgusting, degrading.

Surely it would be no good for the State, even if it were possible, that every single spermatozoon should fertilise every single ovum!

What is meant by unnatural? in a sense it is unnatural to shave or eat an egg. "Experto Crede" says "the propensity is common to all men and all classes of men and at all times and in all countries." All who have good opportunities of knowing what goes on at present, or who have access to something more explicit than the schoolboy history, will agree with him. It is to be observed also in animals. In what sense, then, is it unnatural?

What about disgusting? It evidently does not disgust those who practise it. On what is the principle founded that what is disgusting to some is illegal to all? Moreover, it is never done openly. And then it is degrading! Some of the ablest men have been charged with it. Where are the statistics to prove that it induced physical weakness? It is not so debilitating as masturbation or sexual excess, nor so degrading as prostitution and adultery.

I am not defending the habit, but asking for solid reasons against it, and, to clear the ground, have discounted some of the usual replies.

A week after that there appeared a letter signed "C.S.M.": Christopher Sclater Millard, who was later, under the name of "Stuart Mason", to become Wilde's first bibliographer:

Mr. Oscar Wilde has been sentenced to two years' imprisonment with hard labour. What for? For being immoral? No. A man may commit adultery with another man's wife or fornication with a painted harlot who plys her filthy trade in the public streets unmolested with impunity. It is because this man has dared to choose another form of satisfying his natural passions the law steps in. Yet he has not injured the State or anybody else against their will.

Why does not the Crown prosecute every boy at a public or private school or half the men in the universities? In the latter places "poedirism" is as common as fornication, and everybody knows it.

May I say a word about the conduct of the Press in this case? *The Daily Chronicle* and yourselves are the only papers which have ever given the poor wretch now in prison a fair hearing. Other papers, which a few weeks ago devoted columns to reviews of his splendid plays or books now scorn him as poison. Because a fellow-creature has fallen, why should they cast stones at him? Are the writers of such articles themselves immaculate in their passions?

Prosecuting a man on such a charge as this does not tend to diminish this form of immorality; it rather increases it tenfold.

Even when the correspondence finally ceased, the topic continued to be referred to. Concurrently *Reynolds'* own references to Wilde became more generous, sometimes even defensive, describing him, for example, as "the greatest playwright since Sheridan" and comparing him to Marlowe.

Once Wilde was in jail, and could be seen as society's victim rather than its jester, the paper was clearly prepared to present a more understanding attitude. He could now be seen (though admittedly in a limited way) as representative of a sexual group that, whatever the moral and legal aspects, had been harshly treated. When James Wilson decided in July to co-opt the resources of *Reynolds'* for his personal stand he had reasonable grounds for hoping that his moral precepts would now automatically win some support.

And even though his articles were never printed as he intended, Wilson's faith in *Reynolds'* was in the long run borne out to a significant extent. Throughout Wilde's two years of imprisonment the paper provided snippets of information, sympathetic in tone, about his condition, and devoted a positive-sounding column to his release in May 1897. It was to *Reynolds'* that Wilde himself thought of sending *The Ballad of Reading Gaol* later in the year. "It has, for some odd reason, always been nice to me, and used to publish my poems when I was in prison, and write nicely about me. Also it circulates widely amongst the criminal classes, to which I now belong, so I shall be read by my peers – a new experience for me" (*Letters*, 663). When Wilde died in 1900 it was to *Reynolds'* that George Ives instinctively sent his memorial poem.

In more recent years radical historians, including Raymond Williams, have tended to castigate *Reynolds'* for its sensationalism, its outmoded reading of class politics. Williams held that the radical attitudes which had fired *Reynolds'* in the 1850s suffered irreparable damage in the course of the nineteenth century as the "market" took possession of a journalism that had once represented "a community or a movement." The supposedly "popular" appetite for temporary diversion, for sensation and for scandal, made demands that were often incompatible with the long-term aims of radical politics. As a result, papers such as *Reynolds'* underwent a "critical transformation," losing much of their potential as forces for change.[27] Such complaints can obviously be used in support of the criticism that *Reynolds'* continued to endorse an "old analysis," based on simple class antagonism, long after the working-class had found its political coherence.

In many ways the story of James Wilson confirms that view, yet scandal can have its constructive side too, and the upper classes are, after all, still with us. It is better perhaps to think of communities within communities: the community of a shared sexuality that by crossing class seeks to defy class, or simply the community of humanitarian outrage that takes on mindless Authority – the one community to which both Oscar Wilde and James Wilson unquestionably belonged.

LOST SHEEP

In his despair at the crimes of Authority James Wilson has "I. Playfair" several times turn to *King Lear*, quoting in a slightly abridged form the lines beginning "Thou rascal beadle, hold thy bloody hand." The Wilde that Wilson recognized was likewise more sinned against than sinning, the enemy of official hypocrisies, a humanitarian Wilde most clearly visible in *The Soul of Man Under Socialism*, with its contempt for the patronizing superiority that motivates organized charity. This is the Wilde who realized himself most completely in those models of moral protest, his first writings on his release: the two letters to the *Daily Chronicle* about conditions in prison. With their impassioned insistence that humane feelings and common sense are essentially the same, their anger at the chaplains ("well-meaning, but foolish, indeed silly men"), their respect for doctors as "the most humane profession in the community" (and consequent anger that the profession should be falling down on its prison duties by giving priority to private practice), these letters speak out with a fierce moral clarity. Here, more than *The Ballad*, with its gestures towards universal guilt, or *De Profundis*, with its susceptibility to martyrdom, are direct appeals to the community of the truly humane.

We have so many images of Wilde: as a romantic boy poet in Byronic cloak and hat; as a *bon viveur* parading the stalls; as the bloated and rouged Roman emperor that Toulouse-Lautrec painted, Westminster mist behind him; as one of the "zanies of sorrow" in convict stripes. I want to add another, to my mind at least as heroic as any of these. It is of Wilde in the chapel at Reading, one among many horribly bored "lost sheep," as he sat "in a listless attitude with his elbow resting on the back of his chair, his legs crossed, and gazed dreamily around him and above him."[28] This picture has been left us by Warder Martin, whose "simple humanity" (*Letters*, p.571) in turn so impressed and moved Wilde himself. "There were times," says Martin, when Wilde was "so oblivious of his surroundings, so lost in reverie, that it required a friendly 'nudge'...to remind him that a hymn had been given out, and that he must rise and sing, or at least appear to sing his praises to God" (390–91).

Martin follows that with a wonderful sentence which builds with impatience as his memories take hold:

When the Chaplain was addressing his shorn and grey-garbed flock, telling them how wicked they all were, and how thankful they should all be that they lived in a Christian country where a paternal Government was as anxious for the welfare of their souls as for the safe-keeping of their miserable bodies; that society did not wish to punish them, although they had erred and sinned against society; that they were undergoing a process of purification; that their prison was their purgatory, from which they could emerge as pure and spotless as though they had never sinned at all; that if they did so society would meet and welcome them with open arms; that they were the prodigal sons of the community, and that the community, against which they had previously sinned, was fattening calves to feast them, if they would but undertake to return to the fold and become good citizens, – the Poet would smile. (391)

Out of such smiling *ennui* humane feelings are re-born.

"I long to rise in my place, and cry out," said he, "and tell the poor disinherited wretches around me that it is not so; to tell them that they are society's victims, and that society has nothing to offer them but starvation in the streets, or starvation and cruelty in prison!" (391–92)

CHAPTER 3

Wilde at bay: the diary of George Ives

Poet and penologist, humanitarian recluse, self-styled "evolutionary anarchist," George Ives will attract more attention now and in the future than he ever risked in his lifetime. As a friend of Oscar Wilde it is no more than he expected. The sheer bulk of his legacy – innumerable scrapbooks, endless manuscripts, and a gargantuan diary (122 volumes, over three million words), asserts an unshakable confidence that sooner or later his day would come.[1] Ives's unpublished papers are his buried monument to his times as well as to himself and he fully intended that at some later stage they be excavated.

For all its size, Ives's diary constitutes a text of a peculiarly recalcitrant kind. An interlocutor is often presumed, an anonymous presence who sometimes seems to be actual, perhaps one of the sequence of boys with whom Ives lived; sometimes to be imagined, a later reader who, as a member of the public, is berated for his insensitivity or ignorance, whilst at the same time exhorted to admire Ives's moral commitment. Leading characters are occasionally apostrophized: both Wilde and Lord Alfred Douglas come in for this treatment.

In the end Ives's paranoia, historically understandable as it is, exhausts the defensive opportunities of his genre. By controlling their distribution and reception, most diarists try to protect the secrets they disclose. Ostensibly repositories of truth, diaries are also intended to serve as protectors of self. But if we simply recognize this fact and read Ives with a measure of the infinite patience he expects from us, then it begins to be possible to appreciate the sustaining power that the image of Oscar Wilde (the "superman," as Ives once called him), had for an obsessively private but sometimes courageous man.

George Ives was a humanitarian who not only looked forward to a future when homosexuals would be free to live as they wished but, more than that, believed that they would be able to instruct the rest of society by their tolerance and moral concern. The range of moods in the diary reflects the extremely idealistic nature of his project, and some degree of sympathy with Ives's vision is taken for granted throughout.

Moreover although, in the sexual battles of the 1890s, Ives and Wilde were unlikely allies by virtue of temperament alone, the inherently antithetical nature of their friendship does offer a key not only to the diary, but to shared aspirations. When Wilde wrote *The Importance of Being Earnest* in the summer of 1894, he thought of Ives's homosexual ménage at E4 Albany, Piccadilly, and originally had Ernest Worthing occupy those chambers, thereby converting a den of simmering conspiracy into the beleaguered home of a heterosexual dandy. The joke was at everybody's expense, including the author's, since Ives embodied a movement and a mood which Wilde had sometimes allowed himself to take with unusual seriousness.

The illegitimate son of aristocratic parents, George Cecil Ives, born in 1867, was brought up in England and on the Continent, educated at Cambridge and London Universities, and lived most of his adult life in London until his death in 1950.[2] At Cambridge he mixed with a rich sporting set: he gambled and rode to hounds, though he also found time to take part in debates at the Union.[3]

As a young man he took his expected place in High Society. The diary records a typical dinner in 1888:

Dined with W. Rothschild[4] at his house in 148 Piccadilly in the evening – it was very splendid, the dinner and the decorations being superb – on the table were four huge silver candelabra blazing with light and beautifully carved. The plates were silver and the dessert knives very fine, the whole of the forks and spoons being gold on silver gilt. I met a lot of old friends there...(21 June 1888)

Ives holidayed at his grandmother's house on the French Riviera, where he attended fancy-dress balls, and also spent time at the family home: Bentworth Hall, Alton, Hampshire. It is clear, nevertheless, that he was already much concerned with the sufferings of others. An entry written in Nice in January 1890 is mainly taken up with a description of London slums:

> In many parts of London the only open spaces that exist are old burial grounds or back yards, every other inch being covered by miserable houses, except where huge warehouses raise their heads, shutting out only too effectively both light and air. The Italian community – in these houses are numbers of these poor foreigners – men, women, children and their monkeys all herding together in the same room. They have no beds, and so they sleep on the floor, never taking off their clothes...but many years work among the poor has impressed me with a deep sense of their wrongs, and of their inability to help themselves...no amount of remedial measures could be of any avail if our Metropolis is to be flooded by strangers from the Continent. (29 January 1890)

Although this reads like sincere concern, it also betrays strong hints of a Malthusian interest in population control. "It may be morality to many, to bring into the world a lot of helpless creatures uncared for and destitute, but it is the morality of sin," he had written earlier (22 July 1889). The interest was, if anything, to increase over the years,[5] for Ives always acknowledged links between his own sexual preferences and social principles. In the diary, awareness of his own sexuality sometimes combines with an inquiring habit of mind to produce a confessional mode in which philosophical speculation is mixed in with erotic fantasy. So, for example, a recurrent theme: the transience of youth, on this occasion prompted by gazing at sailors at work:

> I am always fond when looking at some coarse ugly creature or even at aged good looks of mentally rejuvenating it; and what a difference it makes even done roughly and incompletely in the imagination. How much more therefore must it have been in the reality. The unwonted and unwanted sharpening of the outlines which age, even middle age, unfortunately produces, how it transforms the soft graceful outlines of youth – the question is really interesting – for what is it that lies so long dormant in the human countenance which ultimately comes out to disfigure? (4 January 1891)

At the same time Ives was drawn to the kind of utopian

androgyny that can sound misogynistic. He once wrote to Edward Carpenter about the development of women:

Of the average girl I feel inclined to say what the cat spoke unto the dog in Alice, "you wag your tail when you're pleased and growl when you're angry; I growl when I'm pleased and wag my tail when I'm angry; one of us must be mad" – I quote from memory. The old style female is eminently uncompanionable, but this will be changed till there will be but slight difference between girls and boys. In the next world, I trust even this will be removed and each will require what the other lacks. Some indeed say, and it is a beautiful thought, that in the far future matter will be subjected to the will; this indeed is stated in Milton's conception of the angel. (13 September 1894)

Elsewhere he expressed a preference for post-menopausal women, past "the uterine stage," because then they become "reasonable and intellectual" (5 August 1899).

Ives had a taste for self-dramatization that he built into his more practical commitment to homosexual rights as well as into his diary. At some early point in his life, probably in 1893, he founded a secret homosexual society, giving it the name "The Order of Chaeronea" in memory of the band of young Thebans destroyed by the Macedonians at the Battle of Chaeronea in 338 BC. His papers contain innumerable veiled references to meetings, ritual, insignia, codes, and so on, all of them along vaguely Masonic lines, though the mixture of portentousness and evasion makes it extremely difficult to determine just how this Order operated and who belonged to it.[6] Perhaps in time some scholar of gay history will fathom the mysteries: meanwhile, for any literary historian, Ives's main claim for attention must remain his friendship with Wilde.

This began in 1892. On 30 June, having spent much of the day at Lord's watching cricket, Ives proceeded to the Authors' Club, where a formal literary dinner was being held:

By one of those rum coincidences which seem my fate, I got talking with Oscar Wilde, with whom I have friends in common, and went with him to the Lyric Club. He was most amenable and has asked me to lunch at the Berkeley – of course the leader of the aesthetic movement is very interesting to meet, for it is, so far as I know, a great change for Art in the age and one with which I have always been in full sympathy. Our meeting was quite droll and romantic, and would be pronounced far-fetched in a play but such meetings are not new to me or to W.

A note, probably added years later, comments:

P.S. First meeting with Oscar. I spoke to him as he sat in the passage waiting (for he arrived very late). He looked at me with his sleepy eyes and said: "What are you doing here?" I replied I was attending the literary dinner. "But," he answered, though I forget the words he used, it's so long ago, "Why are you here among the bald and the bearded?"

This double acccount makes it fairly clear that what drew the two men together in the first place was a sexual interest, though Ives seems to have known little about Wilde beforehand. It was not until September, for example, that he got round to reading *The Picture of Dorian Gray*, and when he did so he immediately sensed an unbridgeable gulf between its author and himself:

It seems very brilliant as far as I have gone – Lord Henry in particular is a second Chester [presumably Lord Chesterfield], but though admiring the acting and the cold cutting cynicism I am not of it. Under control, patient, immovable, crushing down good and evil under the ice mantle of suppression – with the few exceptions, neither loving nor loved – yet I have a Cause: I feel an instrument and in that above the weakness of my nature – ah, the world is a terrible school.

The deliberation is characteristic: Ives frequently makes a point of contrasting temperaments as a preliminary to reaffirming the common cause. Although he took great delight in compiling lists of famous men whom he knew or believed to be homosexual, and was fascinated to hear from Wilde that, for example, Whitman's homosexuality was beyond question[7] and that Byron and Shelley had been lovers, Ives, throughout his life, found it a challenge to reconcile the variety of homosexual personalities with his own somber ideals and retiring nature. Thus, on 14 August 1892:

Had letters from two celebrities today, O. Wilde and E. Carpenter, the authors respectively of *Lady Windermere's Fan* and *Towards Democracy*.[8] The latter E. C. criticises my book, i.e. *The Lifting of the Veil*,[9] saying, "I think among the mystic symbols and aspirations of the book there are signs of poetic ore…" He seems to complain of the regularity of my metre. Of course Ed. Carpenter, who writes in the strange metre – or rather, style of Walt Whitman, and that too is a vein full of life and I must say beautiful idealism, strongly interwoven with practical life, or, to be more exact, idealised earth-life – can hardly like a book at once mystic gloomy and sombre.

Well, the cause must be served and followed by all sorts of men, each to work in their particular sphere; the issue and the hope is great enough to bind even the most heterogeneous society and, if only organised, which we have never been before, we shall go on to victory.

When Carpenter told him that "the working classes are often by far the nicest of the population," Ives commented that "no doubt he had some ground for so saying," but concluded nonetheless that "we must teach them the Faith" (27 August 1894).

The responses of his heroes were less gratifying than Ives was prepared to admit. Carpenter never joined his secret society, and there is no evidence that Wilde did either. A note added later to an entry for October 1892 recording Wilde's advice that he set up a pagan monastery on some rocky Mediterranean island suggests an early impatience with Ives's clandestine schemes. Nevertheless Ives was soon in close contact with John Francis Bloxam, Charles Kains Jackson, John Gambril Nicholson, H. S. Salt, Theodore Wratislaw, all of them caught up in the sexual politics of the moment. When, in the spring of the following year, would-be blackmailers threatened Wilde with exposure of certain compromising letters to Douglas, he went out of his way to consult Ives and even suggested that he meet with Robert Clibborn, one of their number.

It was not until October 1893 that Douglas personally came on to the scene, when Ives was introduced to him by Wratislaw at a luncheon on the 14th. Ives "had an idea that we shall influence one another greatly." It was an eventful day in another respect. Apparently at Wilde's request, though he also required the permission of his grandmother, Ives shaved off his moustache. "Moving very rapidly now at last but I am prepared, it is well," begins the entry. The following night Ives and Wilde dined at the Savoy with two other guests whom Ives had invited, probably André Raffalovich[10] and Sir Egbert Sebright.[11] They sat from eight to eleven, and Ives was bedazzled:

A teacher [i.e. Wilde], he either cannot or will not give the key to his philosophy, and till I get it I can't understand him. He seems to have no purpose, I am all purpose. Apparently of an elegant refined nature and talented as few men are, brilliant as a shining jewel, yet he teaches many things which cannot be held and which are so false as not even to be dangerous.

Well, I shall find out in time, no one can conceal their real nature for ever, meanwhile we have one thing in common which covers a whole multitude of differences.

I feel it is a terrible task to fight the battle of Our Truth, weighed down by weakness and all manner of littleness, yet when I look at the goal, at the wonderful future which will come to man, then I remain loyal.

This is, as usual, a rather garbled explanation of what should have been a memorable occasion. Ridden with self-consciousness Ives, even at this early point in their friendship, could not understand how Wilde could be so flamboyant, so careless of himself. That night he could not sleep, blaming his restlessness on Douglas, "about whom I am spinning a friendly web." Bosie ("X" in the following extract) had perhaps joined the previous evening's gathering or at had least been discussed:

I want X to pause, to reflect on himself, to conquer himself and obtain freedom. I want him to change his life, for his own good, but especially for the Cause, which is sacred to us both: shall I do all this? I don't know frankly. It is a difficult character, swayed by passion, shaken by impulse; but people of strong emotion have often strong will, though it may be dormant. All will depend upon this. But of course the Cause must not be injured by an individual, however charming. (16 October 1893)

On the 19th Wilde was again Ives's guest, together with Douglas, who was "decidedly ruffled" and "so lost some of his fascination." "I felt bound to take a certain line but now I've done my best and must leave matters to take their chance," was Ives's cryptic comment at the time, though he added later: "I believed I warned Lord A. more than once, that he was indulging in homosexuality to a reckless and highly dangerous degree." A week afterwards he again met with Wilde to consider Douglas's future. On 25 October, back at Bentworth Hall, he told his diary that he "would like to go for one long midnight walk, or ride, with Bosie through the black, deep woods. He would learn the

Kingdom of the Night, and the beautiful wild soul would understand" (25 October 1893).

Much of 1893 was given over to systematic study. Ives read Charles Pearson's account of evolution in *National Life and Character: A Forecast*,[12] but found Pearson's fear of an increase of "coloured races" to be unwarranted, since "if the coloured races ever become strong enough to menace us they must also become highly civilised" (7 November 1893). He turned to the critique of Pearson's ideas mounted by the Positivist Frederick Harrison,[13] to Herbert Spencer on "The Inadequacy of Natural Selection,"[14] and to Thomas Huxley's celebrated Romanes lecture on "Evolution and Ethics" (30 March 1893). In addition he read Moll on homosexuality, Schopenhauer, Charcot, Lombroso, and some historians.

Ives found reinforcement of his ideas in all of these, though intellectual convictions were of little help in curbing Douglas, whose extravagance and promiscuity were on the increase. Wilde's difficult summer had ended with Douglas being dispatched by his family to spend the winter in Egypt, and Ives does not mention any further consultations with Wilde until a dinner at the Albemarle Club on 13 December, when he sported a buttonhole of lilies of the valley which, if not of green carnations, still won approval. The following day the two men lunched at a restaurant, encountering some of the staff of the *Pall Mall Gazette*. On the 15th Ives wrote that the previous day had been "all creativity, laying plans and plots for the great movement of the future." When he left to spend Christmas in France, Wilde came to the New Travellers' Club to see him off and kissed him goodbye, "passionately" (23 December 1893). The sadness of this parting was, it seems, alleviated by Ives's chance meeting with a sympathetic soul on the boat train: "When the lights of the sleeping cabin were put out, he kissed my hand in the darkness. This time, instead of an Etonian, it was a middle-aged Frenchman" (27 December 1893).

Back in London in January 1894 there was a major crisis, probably involving one of Ives's boyfriends, with whom he had been living in Albany since mid-July. Ives felt insecure because he could not communicate with "some of Us," though he was in touch with Wilde and Douglas throughout 1894 and frequently entertained them in his rooms along with other homosexual guests. Ives had reservations: "Their ideals of life are so different from mine and, though I appreciate their brilliancy and charm, we can never I fear work together for public ends" (5 July 1894). The entry for 27 July records a gathering at which Douglas was "very cross" and Wilde "ruffled." On 24 August Douglas spent the night, and the diary again offers a double perspective – immediate, incoherent guilt: "The voice of the faith came to me and said, 'Thou shalt not play with Souls for they are priceless. . . shame shall come upon thee who has broken the bond of friend-ship'"; and later, rationalization supported by hindsight: "That miserable traitor. . .I knew he had faults and more or less insanity all along, but I thought him rather the victim than the villain he proved to be."

When set against this background of continuing private turmoil, of failure in human relationships, and faith in humane ideals, Ives's most public action of 1894 takes on greater import. In March Grant Allen, novelist, journalist, and Spencerian philosopher, had published a provocative article in the *Fortnightly Review* entitled "The New Hedonism." Taking as his motto the Greek precept that "self-development is greater than self-sacrifice," Allen had argued that "self-development" included the free expression of sexuality, but only within the family. This limitation so incensed Ives that he wrote a reply, which appeared in the *Humanitarian* in October.[15]

Invoking Plato, John Addington Symonds, and Walter Pater in support of the proposition that, in Pater's words, the figure of the Greek hero shows "the material and the spiritual fused together," Ives maintained that the true Greek ideals had been wholly obscured by modern prejudice. Genuine "Hedonism" must embrace all love and all pleasure, including, the implication was unmistakable, homosexuality. Ives's article caused some stir,[16] and played a part among the polemics of what was, for the homosexual vanguard, a remarkably active year.[17]

The combative mood was soon further intensified by tragedy. The suicide of Lord Drumlanrigg, Douglas's brother, which, it was strongly suspected on all sides, had homosexual implications, prompted a letter from Wilde describing his lover's grief and congratulating Ives on having been criticized for his "New Hedonism" article: "When the prurient and impotent attack you, be sure you are right" (*Letters*, 375). Later that year Ives was sufficiently reconciled to Douglas to praise him, "if he has made Oxford what it is" (15 November 1894), and to join in with plans for the fateful Uranian magazine that, at Ives's suggestion, was to bear the title *The Chameleon*. When Ives expressed reservations about the political wisdom of publishing overtly homosexual material Wilde, who had initially voiced similar doubts about Ives's reply to Grant Allen, was now able to riposte: "You have thrown a bomb and you object to a cracker...It will do a great deal of harm – that is good" (12 February 1914). Ironically, the greatest harm done by *The Chameleon* was, of course, to Wilde himself, for his association with the magazine was to be used against him to great effect at his trials.

The diary insists that all through his life, but particularly in the nineties, Ives brooded on little else but what he identified as "the Cause." This may be misleading, since Ives had several other longstanding passions, including sport. He was a keen cricketer, turning out for a team that included J. M. Barrie, Jerome K. Jerome, and Arthur Conan Doyle (28 May 1893) and a keen swimmer who frequented the baths at the Regent Street Polytechnic.[18]

Certainly his faith in the homosexual ideal led him in directions which might at first glance seem incongruous. A convinced Darwinist, he studied the many pseudo-biological treatises which attempted to diagnose contemporary problems, and became especially fascinated with the "non-functional" or "extra-organic" habits of animals: actions which seem not to correspond with inherited physical structure, such as the friendships that develop between cats and dogs, apparently homosexual ties between mammals and birds, and the capacity of fish to make love without physical contact, to retain their eggs in their mouth or to swim upside down. He claimed to find in such phenomena clues to an evolutionary process based on the interchange between structure and function. The fact that the elephant uses its nose as a hand, or that the snail walks on its stomach, seemed to him of immense significance in demonstrating the variety and complexity of the physical world.

This interest in biological oddities probably began as a "rational" attempt to find parallels for the essential naturalness of that other "anomaly," the human homosexual, who followed his instincts irrespective of procreative "purpose." It clearly became compulsive. Yet Ives's motivation was always to assimilate the unusual rather than simply to accumulate a collection of freaks. His extraordinary scrapbooks (they run to forty-five volumes) contain clippings on Jack the Ripper, the Loch Ness Monster, Aleister Crowley, outbreaks of Siamese Twins, Wolf-Children, strange mutant births, the stock-in-trade of popular newspapers. Certain themes do emerge: injustice and abuse (to children in particular), the death penalty, transvestism, drug addiction, religious extremism, and racial persecution.

Early in the 1930s Ives was worried about the rising tide of fascism. By juxtaposing a cholera plague with stories of witchcraft, putting a lynching in South Africa alongside praise for Mussolini, it is as if he were trying to document the whole world according to the single taxonomical principle of the dominance of suffering. While cultural taboos are shown to outlaw what is present in nature, unusual natural phenomena mirror what is grotesque in social behavior. This is a world without clear boundaries other than those that human morality chooses to impose; and human morality, founded upon religious superstition, is usually cruel.

History had a way of confirming Ives's beliefs. He objected strongly to warfare, writing to *The Freethinker* in 1917: "Truly, all wise men contend against the same enemies. And they have no worse foe than Christianity, which corrupts the minds of the living through the fears of the dead."[19]

It was the same campaigning spirit, as well as his acute awareness of the particular injustice meted out to homosexuals, that drew Ives to progressive criminology, and he developed a lifelong compassion for the wrongly treated that he backed up with wide reading. Continuous but unmethodical research enabled him to produce a series of short but encyclopedic books: *A History of Penal Methods* (1914), *The Continued Extension of the Criminal Law* (1922), *Obstacles to Human Progress* (1939). These deal chiefly with attitudes to offenses which legal opinion had long ago learnt to consider as obviously anachronistic (witchcraft, for example), or as medically or biologically endemic. Although Ives maintained a conventional distinction between "crimes of impulse" and "crimes of circumstance," he restricted the first to behavior which he found it easy to claim as harmless to others such as homosexuality and suicide, while he treated the second, theft, murder, and so on, as the products of an entirely undifferentiated "environment." In short, his humanitarian aspirations tended to lead him to underestimate the question of jurisdiction over offenses in which he was not personally interested.

In addition, Ives considered himself a poet, and he produced several books of verse. *The Lifting of the Veil*, which contains verses on his habitual themes, prison and suicide, was reviewed (probably by Kains-Jackson) in *The Artist* in 1894.[20] This was followed by *Book of Chains* (1897) and *Eros' Throne* (1900), both of which contain evangelical poems on Wilde.

In his preface to *Book of Chains* dated August 1896, Ives defends his own decision to publish the volume anonymously and distances himself from the effeminate image of the poet strongly associated with Wilde in the 1880s:

To be made to read or recite my own verses, or to have to explain my inmost thoughts – which, however badly expressed and critically faulty, are at least sincere – gives me much the same intolerable sensation as it would to go about quite naked before strangers. I hope also to escape the epithet poet (and any qualifying adjective), and thus avoid being associated in people's minds with weak, spoony eyes, and long and unkempt hair.

But I do not wish to come forward as a worm and apologise for wriggling; the following verses were written, I trust and believe (but how often do we deceive ourselves), apart from fear, or hope, or palliation. If they give courage to any fellow sufferer, if they should move any heart, old or young, to fight the cause of our unhappy prisoners or any other victims of the crimes of State, I shall be glad indeed.[21]

The imagery of chains present in the title contains the same double reference as it does in the insignia Ives designed for his secret society: chains are a symbol of imprisonment, in the tradition of Rousseau and Socrates, but also of unity. One of the poems, "A Message," wishes an unnamed prisoner the alternative comforts of sleep or death. Later references to "chains" often invoke Wilde's sufferings in Reading Gaol as well as the bonds that continued to unite the two men. Carpenter, for one, responded positively: "There is a delicate aroma of freedom and love about all you write, which yet is almost too subtle and indefinite. You have caught the scent of morning in your hair...I am in good spirits, for the threads of a great movement are coming to hand from all sides" (13 December 1896).

Apart from a handful of poems attacking Empire, *Eros' Throne* is a more conventional volume, firmly in the tradition of the Uranian poetry of the 1890s. In his diary, writing of *Eros' Throne*, Ives defines the theme of the title-poem as "the sweet separation, the Boy-Love, the beauty incarnate of the world. Eros the winged Spirit of Love enthroned in the height of heaven, in unutterable glory!" (12 February 1900). It is, in fact, a long philosophical piece that brings together most of Ives's favorite concerns: the differences between the sexes ("Even should you be companions, Yet the fatal rift is there"), the unknowability of the cosmos, and the consequent power of Love and Pity.

Ives was always unshakable in his beliefs, always, in his melancholy way, concerned for others. Even in the optimistic early nineties he had sometimes found it hard to derive much comfort from the growing solidarity among his homosexual friends in London. His forebodings were soon to be brutally confirmed. On 1 January 1895, revealing a tendency to self-fulfilling prophecy which was to enmesh Wilde himself, he confided to his diary: "After going among that set it is hard to mix in ordinary society, for they have a charm which is rare and wonderful. I wish they were less extravagant and more real; so gifted and so nice yet...I see the storm of battle coming." In mid-March J. F. Nisbet's *The Insanity of Genius* helped him understand something of his own condition, though not perhaps that of Wilde. The book seemed to confirm what he "had so often thought":

That the intensely delicate if not morbid condition of the nervous system is often the key to celebrity, hence also the explanation of why solitude has been termed the cradle of genius. Some people may term the abnormal nerve state "degeneracy", but I don't know where the world would now be without it. (16 March 1895)

Ives's immediate comments on the Wilde trials are fairly scanty. This may be attributed either to caution or to his exclusion from the support groups because of some recent quarrel, the nature of which he does not disclose.[22]   On 5 April the case against Queensberry was withdrawn, and later that day a warrant was issued for Wilde's arrest. On 6 April, not for the first time, Ives considered suicide, peering down the barrel of his revolver at the "little messenger" it contained:

What art thou, such a little thing, but it is thine to save me from the force of all the State, it is thine perhaps to convince many, and to open the gates of justice. Who shall understand, who reads this passage, what matter, for I understand and think on the words of Seneca of Rome. Thanks little minister, remain patiently until I call for thee, it may be soon or not for many years, God knows...meanwhile I must go forth into the hatch of life, even for the good of many...

April passed. Ives suffered in sympathy and meditated on the meaning of events:

There is nothing to be done yet, though it may do good in the future – I have been so grieved about it, but the greatest movement will go on, though individuals fall; if it were a true case of the Faith we should stand side by side but this would be impolite and useless now. (25 April 1895)

The second trial ended with the jury unable to agree, and Ives's relief was matched by his hope that in the next hearing the witnesses would finally be revealed as blackmailers and Wilde would be saved. Come 5 May and Wilde's great speech on "the love that dare not speak its name," which Ives transcribed from the *Daily Telegraph*, he was hailing Wilde as "a man who sticks to his colours" and one of "the great of the earth" (5 May 1895). Wilde was put on bail, retried, convicted; and for Ives, the transfiguration from master to martyr was well underway. Wilde was one of those who "though they may have erred, at least created no actual victims or sorrow" (26 May 1895); his enemies "do not know how brutal they have been, and if we could show

them the truth I believe they would be both sorry and ashamed"
(2 July 1895). Ives considered visiting Wilde in jail but in the end
decided that it was enough that Robert Sherard should have
made the effort, for "the whole affair would have been painful
and more or less imprudent for me and no use for the victim"
(27 August 1895).

Throughout 1896 he reassured himself that Wilde was not,
would never be, forgotten. Sometimes he despaired:

I do not love now; I am dead once more, O[scar] and B[osie] awakened
me out of my sleep, the one of charm, the other of pity and beauty, now
it is over; but the Ideal of Faith still leads me. If it please the Great
Power to try me, then It will give me strength. I think the body can be
cured and overcome – as a means of freedom for others not as an end of
an ideal. (26 March 1896)

A deepening trust in the "ideal" was accompanied by heady
fantasies: he would acquire a yacht with "a grand Greek crew"
and sail away "from man and tyranny" (17 March 1896); if he had
been with Wilde in the spring of 1895 he would have died –
whether with or for Wilde is unclear; he would have challenged
Queensberry to a duel (18 April 1896). There were practical
gestures too: he sent an article to the *Echo* on prison conditions
(14 May 1896),[23] and he supplied Frank Harris with evidence
from parliamentary papers to help with the petition to the Home
Secretary then being planned (26 August 1896). As a private
protest he refused to go the opera while Wilde was in jail
(26 November 1896) and renounced alcohol for life.

At last he was rewarded with a poignant message from the
prisoner himself, sent via Sherard:

Please remember me very kindly to George Ives. I was terribly touched
at hearing of his desire to come and see me. In this terrible solitude and
silence in which one lives a message or a memory means a great deal. I
hope he is hard at work writing books. I am very glad you know him.
He is such a good fellow and so clever. (*Letters*, 407)

This tribute consoled its subject in entirely characteristic ways:
it freed him from a lurking sense of betrayal and it made him feel
part of history. Reinvigorated, he dreamed of infinite prospects
for his "Cause": " 'We' are disciplined, careful, fanatical, a power

that one day must be known; but for the victims, ah the poor victims" (11 December 1896).

When May 1897, the time of Wilde's release, finally came round, Ives offered his home, sent a message via Harris that he would meet Wilde anywhere, but for the time being stayed where he was, in Cambridge, reading Max Nordau, whom he was surprised to find prophesying homosexual marriages (18 May 1897).

The essence of Ives's devotion is best revealed in a later episode which is recorded with unusual care. Early in October 1897 he set out for Berneval, the village near Dieppe where Wilde had spent the summer. He traveled second class, slept in his boots and high collar, and arrived in Dieppe at 4 A.M. After a cup of hot milk he strode through the rainy gas-lit streets, a thornstick in his hand, a loaded revolver in his pocket. He climbed the hill of Le Pollet and left the town:

Ferns were growing out of the thatch and the lanes were wooded and muddy; it was like a little home hamlet all over, and the people so nice, many of the urchins saluting me just as they would at home, and of course, I raised my hat in reply – then over a cliff and down a steep path, so steep, and then I saw a little village nestling in a cove in the cliffs and the great rosechalk headlands, meadow-covered right up to their jagged uncompromising edges, and without any guard rail or protection whatever. The road down to the sea was through a deep cutting, and the beach seemed just a sort of opening in the line of interminable cliffs, a little homely sheltered spot. (3 October 1897)

When on arrival in Berneval he discovers that Wilde has left, Ives registers no disappointment. It was enough to have made the effort:

But he whom I sought had been gone three weeks; and all my long journey was vain; how good and kind he was, the woman said: he is. Well, I went up to the "shrine" and saw the room he had and his chair – see how a great man carries honour through all that man can lay upon him; and after a run to the shore, I started back by a different road, through Braquemont and Puy and such lovely lanes, such dear little shell-cemented cottages; all seemed so fair and restful in the beautiful early morning. I felt so glad he had been there; to drink in the deep tranquillity and receive the scene into his soul, and be strengthened by Old Mother Earth, who cares for us all. (3 October 1897)

That the word "shrine" should be singled out does not necessarily imply a total self-awareness in Ives's narrative. Nevertheless, it was at this point that Wilde, about whom Ives had repeatedly expressed grave moral doubts, achieved typological apotheosis. The visit to Berneval was even more gratifying once it became a pilgrimage to a deserted scene. Eager for witnesses, Ives began corresponding with Warder Martin, who had been sympathetic to Wilde in Reading Gaol (19 November 1897).

It was not until the spring of the following year that he saw Wilde again. The place was Paris, and the apparent naivety of the diary is strikingly revealed when offset against Wilde's own account. After receiving Ives's anonymous volume of poems, *Book of Chains*, late in 1897, Wilde had written to Ross: "George Ives has sent me his books of poems – of course without an inscription. His caution is amusing. He means well, which is the worst of it" (*Letters*, 673).

In Paris in March 1898 Ives reported a rather different opinion: "Thursday and I am still here but the place this time is full of interest. I have seen him the poet and he likes my book. Yes and I have told him so much, it is well, at last, that we met after that terrible block of time and are unchanged" (9 March 1898). Wilde told Ives about the dreadful privations of his prison experiences and sent him a letter with the celebrated prophecy:

Yes: I have no doubt we shall win, but the road is long, and red with monstrous martyrdoms. Nothing but the repeal of the Criminal Law Amendment Act would do any good. That is the essential. It is not so much public opinion as public officials that need educating. (*Letters*, 721)

Away from Wilde, Ives reverts to his old doubts. "Not exactly intimate friends," he admits (25 September 1899), but "much as we disagree in the philosophy of life,"

there is nothing in the wide world would give me greater joy than would thy happiness. Thou hast been wounded beyond all healing. For the sake of many hast thou been offered up; the fairest and most brilliant soul I ever knew, lovable beyond words, princely, generous, most noble. I'd rather stand by thee than have the favour of the unworthy hounds that bayed at thee...Greeting dear heart, thou hast made one firm friend that knew thy mind and loved it well. (30 November–3 December 1899)

They met again in Paris in 1900. One evening early in February they talked past midnight. Ives drank his customary hot milk, Wilde took whisky. The Boer War was underway and Wilde "was full of patriotism which seemed to me strange, considering how the country had treated him" (8 August 1902).[24] They talked about witchcraft, Wilde told parables:

But he would not let me go home to his door, nor could he see me there today; some café, he said! And that means a crowd where all must be said in public (all the more as he is growing a little deaf!). In the end, I declined, and am going home tonight so it is uncertain if we meet again. (6 February)

In fact Ives must have attempted a further meeting, for on 12 February 1900 Wilde complained that he had called twice at the Hôtel d'Alsace without leaving his address. It was an angry, impatient letter, the kind of rebuke that Wilde frequently issued during the awful last days, but surely faithful to the maddening effect Ives now had upon him:

Don't have with me the silly mania for secrecy that makes you miss the value of things: to you it is of more importance to conceal your address from a friend than to see your friend...Also, when you send a petit bleu to ask me to make an appointment with you, please put your address: otherwise I can't reply...On the whole, George, you are a great baby. One can't help being angry with you. (*Letters*, 815–16)

Back in London Ives told his diary that he found Wilde's handwriting "most difficult to make out" (13 February 1900). In September a letter arrived asking for a loan of ten pounds; Ives sent five (8 September 1900). Then on 30 November 1900 Wilde died. Ives announced the event several times over, contributed a hallowing poem to *Reynolds' Newspaper*:

> He lives in the soil of France
>   Whose heart England has broken;
> He sleeps from that nightmare-trance
>   Where no more words are spoken
>
> And a weight of guilty shame
>   Spreads thorough the cold foggy air
> Yet it rests not on his name
>   But on some who honours bear!

Far better in grave to lie
  Than be one who had betrayed,
And joined in that coward cry
  Of those who were much afraid.

Some day on History's page
  Shall his mournful fate be told,
Young eyes in a better age
  Shall weep at this tale of old.

In the pages of his diary he lamented at length:

1 December 1900. Oscar Wilde, victim and martyr, died yesterday in Paris.

2 December 1900. The greatest tragedy of the whole nineteenth century makes me pause and think. But there is no justice in the world I have seen, that the land is full of tears I know: we must leave to time and evolution and then our day will come.

Like almost everyone else, Ives had the partial revelations of Wilde's prison letter still to confront, though when excerpts appeared under the title *De Profundis* in 1905 they seemed "like a fifth gospel" and did little but confirm his dedication to the sacred memory:

The papers are full of Oscar Wilde's great book *De Profundis*, it appears most wonderful, for the first time the world will behold him as I saw him, as the great glorious soul, noble beautiful generous being, who never injured anyone intentionally, but whose philosophy never revealed him at his best and whose acts were light and careless in their consequence; and harmful most of all to him.

I am not blaming his manner of loving: only one person had cause against him in the light of justice and she began no action. His economic life, and even his influence upon young men, was very bad, I may even say poisonous and pernicious. But not from his love or his inversion, but from the artistic sense overbalancing him – and others. He looked so deeply at the Light of Beauty that he saw only that; it dazzled him all round, or blinded him. . .

But he *had* a soul; the sweetest and most lovely that I ever met; not strong, not heroic, not grand, but oh how splendid, how glorious, how consecrated. Yes, for he looked on Beauty till he grew so like it. He perceived, he understood another soul; God in Heaven! one dwelt *nearer* him than single flesh and blood permit; our souls were nigh in pure intellect. Oscar *meant* well, to all.

He had not the gift of responsibility, he could not estimate consequence, he was all Art, and all Emotion, and I looked up to him as to a superman (and do still, while utterly disagreeing with his written philosophy, and even with his life, on many sides). (23 February 1905)

De Profundis helped Ives to justify his own feelings about Douglas whom he had apostrophized in 1898 from his own position as "a socialist," writing "You are a gentleman and an Artist and very beautiful. But you have no more principle or heart than a courtesan: that will not do for the Faith" (19 May). When in May 1899 they had met up again after a passage of time Ives thought he "seemed fairly well but looked rather worn and I do not wonder" (9 May 1899). In 1905, after the appearance of *De Profundis*, Douglas went back to being a "courtesan" and a "cockatrice" (4 March).

For all the emotional pull of *De Profundis* Ives always insists on establishing a basic distinction between Wilde and himself.

"His view of life – with all its morbid sense of 'sin' and Roman Catholic substitution of mere ritual for reason – was poles apart from my Whitmanic paganism," he writes (23 February 1905), registering a sense of betrayal in the fact that they could have had so much in common and yet differed so greatly when it came to conduct. One thing they had certainly agreed upon was the finite nature of human life, as later memories record:

Oscar Wilde once said to me, The world was created when you were born; it will come to an end at the time you die – so this world will, for me and for each one living. I forget Oscar's exact words, but they were something like those above. (18 August 1921)

I was talking to Oscar Wilde, and saying to him, that as one got older, the lines of the colours seemed less vivid and the keen edge of life was taken off. And he said (to the effect) that at the end of the day, life looked grey and we died. (18 February 1922)

Perhaps the disagreement was more about style than fundamentals. Certainly when Bernard Shaw told Ives that he thought that Wilde had been wrong to "make passion into a religion," Ives strongly disagreed:

I think not so. It is a religion and the most inspired of all religions, as Socrates, Plato and the Sufis well know. Nay, Oscar was quite right there. On many points I cannot defend him. He was superstitious, a respector of the so-called great, and, about money, as hopelesss as ever an Irishman can be. But that is the worst I can say of him. I do not know enough of his domestic relations (though I knew Mrs. Wilde) to say what he may have been as a husband, but I should fancy a neglectful one. But who shall dwell on mere weaknesses in the face of such wrong as he incurred in the world? Not I. (6 January 1924)

Inevitably it was the points of agreement with Wilde that Ives chose to perpetuate in his diary. He did so by the simple expedient of adding or repeating anecdotes. The secret life remained a secret, partly because the law demanded it, partly because Ives was ultimately less interested in a precise reflection of the bright surface of daily exchange than in perusing his own subterranean self-involvements. His portrait of Wilde undoubtedly suffers as a result. Time and again, he half-remembers some Wildean epigram, fumbles to repeat it, fails, resorts to cliché, and then passes the moment off with an unapologetic "words to that effect." In 1899 he attempts to cite *The Ballad of Reading Gaol* and blunders into banality: "Is that terrible sentence true, 'we can always be kind to those we don't love'?" (2 March 1899).

"Morbid" was what Wilde called him on one occasion (27 December 1893), meaning that he took undue pleasure in concealment. In contrast, when Ives used the same word about Wilde, he was referring to his final conversion to Catholicism (23 February 1905). Just as telling was Wilde's surprised comment on looking into a volume of the diary: "How systematic!" (6 April 1896). The fact is that despite their moment of programmatic allegiance Ives had soon become everything that Wilde could not accept, while Ives's own commitments had taken him further and further away from Wilde's public panache.

"St. George" to Robert Ross in 1893 (29 July 1893), but a "great baby" to Wilde in 1900, Ives never managed to achieve an ironical perspective on his own fate. In the tragic context of sexual oppression he could find little place for Wilde's public manner.[25] Their lasting point of agreement: a firm conviction that, in Edward Carpenter's words, "the Outcast of one age is the Hero of another."

Monumental bore, gauche intruder among the devious and the complex, class casualty: all these Ives could certainly be, but he still commands sympathy and admiration for commitment and perseverance, gratefully appropriating each new intellectual discovery, whether Bertrand Russell, Shaw, Havelock Ellis, Freud, D. H. Lawrence, or A. S. Neill, for "the Cause."

Throughout his life he would record the deaths of those he had known or felt to be of significance, sometimes repeating previous information, sometimes adding new. "When homosexual people die (and never before) I like to furnish such evidence as I can in the interest of truth" (21 May 1929). Consequently the death of J. F. Bloxam prompted the observation that "he became mediaeval, and was practically a Catholic," though "his life might have been more peaceful but for his religion, which put him in conflict with his whole nature" (21 April 1928). When the painter Henry S. Tuke died aged seventy in 1929, Ives identifed him as "one of the eminent band of Inverts (homosexuals) which included Lord Ronald Sutherland Gower, and others still living" (14 March 1929), adding that Tuke was always afraid that knowledge of his homosexuality would stop people from buying his pictures (3 August 1932). Charles Kains-Jackson, who died in 1933, was claimed as a member of the Order of Chaeronea who "did good service for the movement when he was editor of the *Artist*" (4 December 1933). And when Lord Rosebery died in May 1929 Ives took up yet another opportunity to fill in some important background:

I saw him once at Lord Rothschild's. He was very small but good looking. He was said by almost everybody to have been a homosexual. I was told by a deputy coroner, that one of the chiefs of the C.I.D., Dr. McNaughton, told him that the Hyde Park Police had orders never to arrest Lord R. On the principle that too big a fish often breaks the line. What I complain of is that the small fish are hooked, and nobody troubles. I was also told that he (Lord Rosebery) wanted to obtain the release of Oscar Wilde (whom he, and Arthur Balfour knew) but that the Home Secretary, Asquith, told him that if he did, he would lose the election. And that was enough for a politician. Still, it is to Lord R's credit if he tried. I believe that he and A.J.B. sent Oscar money at one time. (21 May 1929)

Ives was convinced of the homosexuality of Balfour as well and repeated the point when he died the following year (entry for 20 March 1930). The death of Edward Carpenter in 1929, however, was obviously an event of much greater personal significance:

An Eastern saint: he gave one the sense of calm. Like a mountain he seemed to rest over the wide earth and to be founded on the archaic rocks. He was never a Member of our Order though he was the greatest mover in our work. But he refused to be bound or (as he thought) limited by a system. Never the less, we held the same Faith; along with Socrates and the Sufi poets. (29 January 1929)

Other old acquaintances have briefer mentions: Lord Russell (5 March 1931) and Frank Harris (27 August 1931). Increasingly, the diary reveals how closely and how percipiently Ives was watching the growth of fascism. On 23 May 1935:

Called at the Sexological Society. They have just received a mourning card from Nice announcing the sudden death of Dr. Magnus Hirschfeld. A good and kindly old man, who was driven from Germany on the advent of the Nazi terrorists. Fortunately he had had time to cross the frontier, and received no personal ill usage.

He was a great pioneer of sex reform and his work is known throughout the criminal world – and will go on, and will ultimately bring justice.

I am so sorry that he died in a very dark period of persecution, suppression, and ignorance. Yet perhaps he saw ahead and into the dawn of better times. I hope so. For I feel confident that this and nationalism and fascism will not endure. The truth and the solid party now established, have nothing to fear from investigation, and only taboo can justify the long ill treatment of the homosexual minorities. (23 May 1935)

Then, some three years later:

The papers say that the Nazis are ill-treating Sigmund Freud, another of the great Jews, whose work is influencing thought throughout the civilised world. I foresaw the possibility of that happening, weeks ago.

Dr. Hirschfeld would have been served the same, probably, only he escaped in time and died in France, some say by suicide. (22 March 1938)

Sadly the confirmation Ives found in the opinions of others was of dubious assistance when it came to the daily tribulations of his own life. Throughout the diary he gloomily notes the stages of his own mortality, a habit that dates from the very start of the project. "I begin these notes with a declining year, like all of us sinking fast to its end," he had written when he was nineteen, "soon to be counted with the things that were; forgotten by mankind as most of us will be" (20 December 1886).

Yet for all his despondency about the future, Ives was to go to extraordinary lengths to ensure that he would never be forgotten. The great diary was intended to secure immortality; nothing less would do. At some profound level of conviction Ives knew that time was ultimately on his side. We should take pleasure then, now that their mutual day may at last have come, in commemorating the somber determination of George Ives alongside the impatient wit of Oscar Wilde.

CHAPTER 4

Romantic reincarnations

There are always consolations, or so Wilde tried to persuade himself. In Reading Gaol the consolation, as well as the curse, was time: to think, to read, to write. The result was *De Profundis* in which, quoting *The Borderers*, he was to pronounce:

Better than Wordsworth himself I know what Wordsworth meant when he said:

> "Suffering is permanent, obscure, and dark
> And has the nature of Infinity."   (*Works*, 1018)

Wilde went on to declare that should he ever write again, it would be on "Christ, as the precursor of the Romantic Movement." This had long been a favorite theme, but it was now darkly stained with the realization of where identification with Romantic attitudes might lead.

In this chapter I set out to define the distinctiveness of the Wildean reconstruction of the Romantic hero by drawing comparisons with the very different perspective on Romanticism achieved by Wilde's near contemporary Arthur Symons. In 1909 Symons was to complete *The Romantic Movement in English Poetry*,[1] a lengthy book made up of previously published essays on the great poets – Byron, Wordsworth, Coleridge, Shelley, Keats, and Blake – together with pieces on many minor writers: eighty-eight sections in all.[2] Read in the light of Wilde's quite different aesthetic (and of the critical predecessors both men shared: Swinburne, Arnold, Pater) *The Romantic Movement* can be seen as a revealing symptom of a bias towards metaphysical abstraction that was to last long into the twentieth century.[3]

For Symons, writing at the turn of the century, Romanticism

presented itself, in retrospect, as the source of a continuing split between artistic visions and historical phases. That same division is reflected in the contrast between the title and the preface of his book. For while the title proclaims this to be a study of a "movement," from which we might expect to find some distinct and shared purpose among the writers who compose it, the preface denies any such collectivity. Almost predictably, the epitaph to the book is Blake's "Ages are all equal; but genius is always above the age": a favourite aphorism of Symons as it had been of Pater,[4] used here as an endorsement of Symons's own ideology which was increasingly individualist, vitalist, Nietzschean.

If the individualism of Romantic writers came from their awareness that they were living through a revolutionary epoch, it followed that the Romantic tradition should produce a criticism that searched for individual identity at the same time as it surveyed the *zeitgeist*. By coupling the highest estimation of the artist with an appreciation of his moment the Romantic inheritance was felt to be prolonged, whilst devotion to the principle of creative energy, in whatever guise it appeared, could even act as a rebuff to despair at what Romanticism had failed to achieve. In this sense all late nineteenth-century critics, including Symons, continue to write under the shadow of aborted or incomplete revolution, the psychological burden that M. H. Abrams famously discovered among the Romantics themselves and called the "High Romantic argument":

In the ruling two-term frame of Romantic thought, the mind of man confronts the old heaven and earth and possesses within itself the power, if it will but recognise and avail itself of the power, to transform into a new heaven and earth, by means of a total revolution of consciousness...The great Romantic works were not written at the height of revolutionary hope but out of the experience of partial or total disenchantment with the revolutionary promise.[5]

Certainly Symons was not alone in seeing in the aspirations of the Romantic writers evidence of the remoteness of their revolutionary moment, as well as proof of the unhistorical nature of "genius." Already, in a cultural pessimist such as Matthew

Arnold, the very thought of Romantic poetry had provided the consolation of nostalgia; even Pater had on occasion found himself identifying with the inevitable failure of grand Romantic projects. In other respects, though, Symons's survey marks a characteristic shift away from both Arnoldian moral absolutes and Paterian materialist convictions towards the realm of the spiritual. Oscar Wilde, in marked contrast, was to record the historical distance from Romanticism by turning his personal response to individual poets into the stuff of high drama.

What did remain constant was critical procedure. The typically mid-Victorian approach to the Romantic inheritance had been through a comparative method. Here, for example, is the very well-known concluding passage from the preface to Arnold's volume of selections, *Poetry of Byron* (1881), which attempts to capture Byron's unique qualities:

Wordsworth has an insight into permanent sources of joy and consola-tion for mankind which Byron has not; his poetry gives us more which we may rest upon than Byron's – more which we can rest upon now, and which men may rest upon always. I place Wordsworth's poetry, therefore, above Byron's on the whole, although in some points he was greatly Byron's inferior, and although Byron's poetry will always, probably, find more readers than Wordsworth's and will give pleasure more easily. But these two, Wordsworth and Byron, stand, it seems to me, first and pre-eminent in actual performance, a glorious pair, among the English poets of this century. Keats has probably, indeed, a more consummate poetic gift than either of them; but he died having produced too little and being as yet too immature to rival them. I for my part can never even think of equalling with them any other of their contemporaries; – either Coleridge, poet and philosopher wrecked in a mist of opium; or Shelley, beautiful and ineffectual angel, beating in the void his luminous wings in vain. Wordsworth and Byron stand out by themselves. When the year 1900 is turned, and our nation comes to recount her poetic glories in the century which has just ended, the first names with her will be these.[6]

Wordsworth *or* Byron; Wordsworth *against* Byron rather than *against* Keats or Coleridge or Shelley; finally Wordsworth *and* Byron: these shifting permutations are set against certain values, some of which, though not all, are specifically Arnoldian. They include "joy and consolation," "pleasure," "actual performance," "poetic gift," the "immature," and famously, the "beautiful and ineffectual." A final sentence invokes the historical principle which prompts adjudication: the approaching end of the century will require a roll-call of national achievement. Although the method which has resulted in the isolation of Byron and Wordsworth from their contemporaries has been prolonged and often equivocal, decisions have nevertheless been reached and an overall critical responsibility fulfilled, an endeavor that both Symons and Wilde were to repeat in their own treatments of Romanticism. So, for instance, Wilde has Gilbert mimic the Arnoldian method in "The Critic as Artist" when he pronounces:

Wordsworth saw in *Endymion* merely a pretty piece of Paganism, and Shelley, with his dislike of activity, was deaf to Wordsworth's message, being repelled by its form, and Byron, that great passionate human incomplete creature, could appreciate neither the poet of the cloud nor the poet of the lake, and the wonder of Keats was hidden from him (*Works*, 1150).

Symons's tribute to the Arnoldian method was to be considerably longer and far less whimsical than Wilde's brief parody: the compilation of his own *Romantic Movement*.

BYRON

To appreciate more fully what was involved in late Victorian feelings about Romanticism some recapitulation is needed, starting with Arnold on Byron, an engagement that goes back at least to "Memorial Verses" (1850) where Arnold had proclaimed:

> When Byron's eyes were shut in death,
> We bowed our head and held our breath.
> He taught us little, but our soul
> Had *felt* him like the thunder's roll.[7]

By the time Arnold came to make the 1881 selection, Byron's English reputation had sunk with many traces. This unfashionableness did nothing but help Arnold's cause, which was to rehabilitate the poet's reputation against the narrow-mindedness of Arnold's own partly self-created enemy, the philistine middleclass. Thus the penultimate paragraph:

As the inevitable break-up of the old order comes, as the English middle-class slowly awakens from its intellectual sleep of two centuries, as our actual present world, to which this sleep has condemned us, shows itself more clearly, – our world of an aristocracy materialised and null, a middle-class purblind and hideous, a lower class crude and brutal, – we shall turn our eyes again, and to more purpose, upon this passionate and dauntless soldier of a forlorn hope, who, ignorant of the future and unconsoled by its promises, nevertheless waged against the conservation of the old impossible world so fiery battle; waged it till he fell, – waged it with such splendid and imperishable excellence of sincerity and strength.[8]

Sympathy with Byron depended upon recognition of his prophetic powers coupled with a sense of Victorian society as imprisoned in class relations. Arnold's own essay turned upon an acknowledged borrowing from an essay by Swinburne first published in 1866 (revised version 1875), in which he had written admiringly of "the splendid and imperishable excellence which covers all his offences and outweighs all his defects: the excellence of sincerity with strength."[9] For Swinburne, Byron had been the magnificent poet of unmediated nature, a figure of irrepressible courage to whom nature was essential reality, to be felt and pursued like some physical, or more precisely, erotic challenge. Swinburne compared the style of *Don Juan* with the fluctuations of the sea, an Aeschylan image for the source of all experience, brilliantly extemporizing the same marine analogy over more than a dozen sentences. The poem embodies the mutability of nature, which is sometimes hospitable, sometimes hostile, seductive, and malicious; to read it is to become immersed in an elemental world. Borrowed by Arnold, "sincerity and strength" came to signify something quite different: the resigned hope for a Romantic revival that had been endlessly delayed, or so he believed, by mid-century materialism.

Prompted by this misrepresentation and by his own changed aesthetic Swinburne replied to Arnold in 1884 with a long rambling essay, "Wordsworth and Byron,"[10] in which he partially reneged on his own earlier position. Announcing that the supreme tests for poetry are imagination and harmony, Swinburne now determined that Arnold had mistaken personality for

art. Much of Byron was technically incompetent, his lyricism
abused and strained. This was consistent with Swinburne's earlier
approach to Byron in that it continued to keep aesthetic values
separate from simple moral messages, but subtly treacherous in
the light of his later requirement that poetry be brought to order,
his deepening conviction that poetry is in essence the untransla-
table record of profound meanings. Byron's exuberance could not
easily satisfy this revised rubric.

The exchange between Swinburne and Arnold on the subject
of Byron was but one skirmish between two very deceptive critics.
Both were attracted by Byron's lack of interest in metaphysics, yet
both found his weakness to lie in worldliness. Although they have
come down to us as polar opposites – one the Aesthetic wildman,
haunted prophet of Decadence, connoisseur of the sexual *frisson*,
the other the austere Victorian moralist, school inspector, public
man, apostle of "culture" – in their later careers the similarities
sometimes seem to be as great as the differences.

This tendency towards cultural pessimism is greatly extended
by Symons in *The Romantic Movement*, where the essay on Byron
(first published in 1900) gives a portrait which at least alludes to
the appeal of Byron as a pathological failure. In some ways
conventional (he retains the comparative method that Swinburne
and Arnold had used, and stresses "sincerity" above all things),
Symons is in other ways more typically *fin-de-siècle*. In this reading
Byron's imaginative *ennui* competes with his revolutionary energy:

His mind was never to him a kingdom, but always part of the tossing
democracy of humankind. And so, having no inner peace, no interior
vision, he was never for long together the master of the obedient vassal
of his imagination; and he has left us tumultuous fragments in which
beauty comes and goes fitfully, under pained disguises, or like a bird
with impatient wings, tethered at short range to the ground (248).

And compared with the mid-Victorians Symons is, as always,
far more responsive to the tragic potential of evasive moments:
"Byron gives us, in a overwhelming way, the desire of life, the
enjoyment of life, and the sense of life's deceit, as it vanishes from
between our hands, and slips from under our feet, and is a voice
and no more" (262).

It is exactly this sense of frustrated vision that Wilde prides himself on having reached beyond. In *The Soul of Man Under Socialism* he complains that Byron's personality "was terribly wasted in its battles with the stupidity and hypocrisy and Philistinism of the English" (*Works*, 1179), while in *De Profundis* he echoes Victorian cliché: "Byron was a symbolic figure, but his relations were to the passion of his age and its weariness of passion," only to add his own subversive boast: "Mine were to something more noble, more permanent, of more vital issue, of larger scope" (*Works*, 1017).

WORDSWORTH

When mid-Victorian critics argue strongly about Romantic poetry the subject is most likely to be Wordsworth.[11] Swinburne, who in 1866 had said that Wordsworth used nature "as a vegetable fit to be shred into his pot and pared down like the outer leaves of a lettuce for didactic and culinary purposes,"[12] was by 1886 paying tribute to Arnold's recognition of "Wordsworth's healing power, his gift of direct or indirect refreshment, the comfort and support of his perfect and pure sincerity in all his dealings with nature."[13] It is true that Arnold's poem "In Memory of the author of 'Obermann'" (1849) had included, along with a tribute to "Wordsworth's sweet calm," the qualifying remark, "Wordsworth's eyes avert their ken / From half of human fate," but in "Memorial Verses" (1850) he had attempted to ease the dichotomy. This he achieved by collapsing three phases into one: the lost world of orphic poetry, the Romantic era of heroic regeneration, a personal revelation of the power of pristine nature:

> He found us when the age had bound
> Our souls in its benumbing round;
> He spoke, and loosed our heart in tears.
> He laid us as we lay at birth,
> On the cool flowery lap of earth.[14]

That passage brings together not only widely separate moments, but three distinct ways of conceiving of experience:

mythic, historical, and individual. Yet each view makes a similar point about the failure of the nineteenth century to sustain poetic inspiration. Interplay of contexts enables Arnold to present Wordsworth's poetry as an escape back into innocence rather than as a corporate retrieval of historical potential. Arnold found this "healing power" particularly soothing, but Wordsworth came to the rescue of many other Victorians beset by their various crises of faith, among them John Stuart Mill, Leslie Stephen, John Morley, William James, and, most problematically, Ruskin. There were exceptions though, including the critic who had the greatest, if most complex, influence upon the late nineteenth century.

Walter Pater's essay on Wordsworth, first published in 1874, displays a self-awareness about the Wordsworthian mood that contrasts strongly with the gloomy regression derived by Arnold and even with the reassurance of "tranquil contemplation" gained by Mill:

It would come sometimes, like the sign of the *macrocosm* to Faust in his cell: the network of man and nature was seen to be pervaded by a common, universal life: a new, bold thought lifted him above the furrow, above the green turf of the Westmoreland church-yard, to a world altogether different in its vagueness and vastness, and the narrow glen was full of the brooding power of one universal spirit.[15]

As the allusion to Faust implies, these are dangerous feelings. For Pater the modern increase in knowledge (especially scientific knowledge) had radically altered concepts of truth and the perceived reality of the present, although he remained insistent that theory not be allowed to do service for discovery. For Arnold, despite his appeals to the open mind, ultimate truths persisted, even when they had been obscured by presumptive modern knowledge to the point when the world had become so intolerably confused ("Multitudinous") that it was best viewed as a kind of nightmarish illusion. Paterian appreciations were rarely acquiescent, Arnoldian ideals invariably conservative.

The contradiction of Wordsworth's influence in the nineteenth century was that he had gained reverence at the expense of power. Some of the reasons for this waning are obvious, such as the poet's own failing gifts and public ignorance of *The Prelude* until 1850. More crucial was the need to find in his poetry traces of a corporate basis for felt experience that would survive the disruptions of industrialization, a quest sometimes associated with a sentimentalized version of the pastoral community. We can trace the different directions taken in this search by noting the meanings given to the word "common": from Wordsworth's "common air"[16] in "Michael," where the air is literally "held in common," to Mill's inspirational "common feelings and common destiny of human beings,"[17] to Pater's association of Wordsworth's "passionate sincerity" with "incidents and situations from common life,"[18] to innumerable manipulations of the phrase "the common people."

Because Arnold's judgments reflect a cyclic approach to history coupled with a static concept of nature, his defining phrases are bids to entrap each poet in his own essence by relating him to ultimate values. Developing an alternative to Arnold involved a fidelity to the principles preached by the younger Swinburne, and to the more authentically Romantic characteristic of insatiable striving: the struggle with an idea of nature as that which has the capacity to inspire change yet, if accorded too much sober reverence, might actually curb man's potential. In Arnold's early poetry such as "Empedocles on Etna" the Romantic battles against incorporation were forlornly reenacted, but in his maturity Arnold instinctively reached towards the preordained conclusion that nature contains a hidden positive which the mirroring mind of the poet must strive to reflect, and that modern civilization is merely fantasia, a false or corrupt nature whose bewilderments only the greatest poets will resist. The power of the external world of nature was maintained, yet in Arnold's later aesthetic the Romantic ideal survived in a greatly reduced form as simply the reward for contemplating the lapidary moral import (the "ideas") that lie within natural phenomena.

It is from this delusive discovery of ultimate truth that Pater deliberately distances himself, concluding that Wordsworth's over-interest in the workings of memory could lead to something close to madness:

Sometimes as he dwelt upon those moments of profound, imaginative power, in which the outward object appears to take colour and expression, a new nature almost, from the prompting of the observant mind the actual world would, as it were, dissolve and detach itself, flake by flake, and he himself seemed to be the creator, and when he would the destroyer, of the world in which he lived – that old isolating thought of many a brain-sick mystic of ancient and modern times (55).

To the Romantic fear of the "despotism of the eye" (Coleridge's phrase about Wordsworth, and Wordsworth's phrase about himself) we may oppose Pater's fondness for such phrases as "the eye of the mind" and "the capacity of the eye," signs of his materialist commitment to the self-sufficient powers of perception. It was precisely because Wilde shared this same commitment to human potential that he could, at times, be scathing about Wordsworthian natural wisdom, most famously when he had Vivian sneer in *The Decay of Lying* that Wordsworth "found in stones the sermons he has already hidden there" (*Works*, 1078).

In his rather more opaque commentary on Wordsworth, included in *The Romantic Movement*, Symons, a professed admirer of Pater who never hesitated to invoke Arnold, quoted Wordsworth with the euphoric comment:

What a responsiveness of the soul to the eye, "the most truly despotic of our senses", the sense of sight, as he calls it, truly!...The eye is realised by him as the chief influence for good in the world, an actual moral impulse, in its creation and radiation of delight. Sight, to him, is feeling (95).

Since his involvement with Yeats in the mid-1890s, Symons had been more and more drawn to mystical notions, and an increasingly acute sensitivity to the glories and treacheries of visual perception accompanied his drive to rediscover the infinite. This culminated in a tribute to Wordsworth as someone for whom "external things existed so visibly, just because they had no existence apart from the one external and infinite being; it was for the principle of infinity in them that he loved them, and it was this principle of infinity which he seemed to recognise by a simple act of memory" (97).

Symons here is doing nothing less than embracing "that old isolating thought of many a brain-sick mystic" which Pater had so scrupulously avoided, and which Wilde tried to eliminate with epigram. When he came to review Pater's *Appreciations* (the 1889 volume of collected essays in which the Wordsworth essay subsequently reappeared), Wilde quoted with considerable approval some thirty uninterrupted lines from the master, ending with a tribute to the Romantic poet's sense of human life:

He sees nature full of sentiment and excitement; he sees men and women as parts of nature, passionate and excited, in strange grouping and connection with the grandeur and beauty of the natural world: – images of his own words, "of men suffering, amid awful forms and powers".[19]

The choice of passage was entirely apt, the length of the quotation a deliberate act of critical bonding, designed to replace the guardian of eternal values and the universal spirit with the observer of human life: the Wordsworth that Pater and Wilde had "in common."

COLERIDGE

The special distinction of Pater's approach to Wordsworth, and, correspondingly, the full extent of Symons's *fin-de-siècle* appropriation, as of Wilde's playful revisionism, becomes even more apparent if we go back twelve years to Pater's essay on Coleridge, Arnold's "poet and philosopher wrecked in a mist of opium." For it is in Pater's early study that we can best perceive his admiration for active achievement over and above the metaphysical abstractions that may have prompted it, the priority that Symons was later to question.

The essay opens with a theory of natural, that is to say "organic" growth:

Nature, which by one law of development evolves ideas, moralities, modes of inward life, and represses them in turn, has in this way provided that the earlier growth should propel its fibres into the latter, and so transmit the whole of its forces in an unbroken continuity of life.[20]

This should not be mistaken for the organicism that Coleridge had made use of. Pater's organicism explains change as the product of biological antagonism: the pressures between inner and outer, between old and new, which take place in all cellular life. Ironically, one word for that process might be "continuity." Indeed, Pater's recognition of the necessary and creative function of antagonism in organic processes is what finally enables him to celebrate the poet within an act of rejection. Over and again his essay relies upon sentences whose circular structure disrupts the apparent direction of their meaning almost to the point of negation. For example:

And whatever fame, or charm, or life-inspiring gift he has had is the vibration of the interest he excited then, the propulsion into years that clouded his early promise of that first buoyant, irresistible self-assertion: so great is even the indirect power of a sincere effort toward the ideal life, of even a temporary escape of the spirit from routine (8).

The rhetoric is at one with the double motion which gives Romanticism in general, and Coleridge in particular, its historical placing: the "charm" of a past writer increases as his pastness comes into view. As it was to be with Wordsworth, so it had been with Coleridge: the correct, the only, mode of appreciation of such writers is a lingering backwards look.

That is particularly true of Coleridge's concept of "genius," and of his attempt to link great imaginative achievement with more commonplace thought processes through their shared obedience to natural law. Pater tracks the origins of that idea back through German Romanticism to Greek philosophy, noting a division between the deistic version which views nature as the product of divine design, and a pantheistic alternative which sees nature as vaster in scope than the human mind, though made up of essentially the same kind of intelligence. "Genius," according to Coleridge, occurs when "ideas become effective: the intelligence of nature, all its elements connected and justified, is clearly reflected; and the interpretation of its latent purposes is fixed in works of art" (14).

Pater questions this definition on the grounds that it belongs with the lost cause that his essay ironically mourns: the search for an "absolute," or all-encompassing meaning in life. The modern "relative" spirit which supersedes that quest is typified by precise observation leading to new classifications based on what were previously taken to be discrete opposites. Modern "analysis" produces fresh subtleties and complexities, hidden interplay between categories, a scientific procedure that is reproduced by Pater's analytic style.

Yet Pater's essay on Coleridge was to undergo significant revisions by its author. When it reappeared in *Appreciations* in 1889, the attacks upon Christianity and upon religion in general, together with the extended discussions of theories of epistemology, had been greatly reduced. "A transcendentalism that makes what is abstract more excellent than what is concrete has nothing akin to the leading philosophies of the world" (2–3): provocative sentences such as that had disappeared.

Symons, for one, had approved of these changes even as Pater was considering them, writing to a friend in 1888: "I find he is working into his later essay on Coleridge some bits of the earlier one – which, however he rightly disowns as it stands."[21] And in his obituary essay of 1896 Symons was to observe that Pater's "first published essay was an essay on Coleridge, in which Coleridge the metaphysician, and not Coleridge the poet, was the interesting person to him."[22] These direct responses are merely the most overt signs of Symons's ambivalence towards his supposed critical mentor. Similar sentiments are present, by implication, in Symons's own essay on Coleridge, with its tolerance for Coleridge's lifelong search for "the absolute, an absolute not only in thought, but in all human relations, in love, friendship, faith in man, faith in God, faith in beauty"; and with its welcoming of Coleridge's double interest in both poetry and philosophy: "One sees truth for its beauty; the other finds beauty an abstract, intellectual beauty, in the innermost home of truth. Poetry and metaphysics are alike a disengaging, for different ends, of the absolute element in things" (130).

For his part Wilde was quite happy, despite the revisions, to continue to praise in his review of *Appreciations* Pater's "very blameless work" for its "insistence on the necessity of the cultivation of the relative, as opposed to the absolute spirit in philosophy and its ethics,"[23] making an implicit link with the Hegelian (and theatrical) enthusiasms that had once led him to pronounce that "the truths of metaphysics are the truths of masks" (*Works*, 1173).

SHELLEY

Pater on Coleridge was a difficult precedent for the *fin de siècle* to deal with, more difficult, for example, than the cult of Shelley.

"Beautiful and ineffectual angel, beating in the void, his luminous wings in vain": Arnold's image casts Shelley's idealism in a pallid hue, rendering it helpless. For others, the apparent gap between the diaphanous poetry and the coarser, if still obscure, record of Shelley's life indicated a more rewarding puzzle. So dedicated was the nucleus of Shelley's admirers that they founded The Shelley Society in 1886 and set about staging *The Cenci*, a production that Wilde attended and much admired.

The major Shelley debates at the turn of the century, and there were several, involved established rhetorical ploys. Yeats attacked the appropriation of the poet by those "scientific minds" that he abhorred (for Yeats, of course, "science" meant not only Darwin, Spencer, and Huxley but also George Eliot), and he added the bitter complaint that confronted with the collapse of traditional beliefs, these writers merely made out of their own abstractions a substitute religion. In an extended treatment of Shelley, an essay of 1900 entitled "The Philosophy of Shelley's Poetry," Yeats saw Shelley's triumph to lie in the revelation of symbols – tower, cave, moon, and shell – whose multiplicity signifies something rather different from the liberation of the individual from tyranny. These symbols stand for eternal aspirations, or "desire," which are, of their essence, unappeasable. Nevertheless the essay ends with gnomic allusion to missed potential: "But he was born in a day when the old wisdom had vanished and was content merely to write verses, and often with little thought of more than verses."[24]

This is not far from the mood of Symons's chapter in *The Romantic Movement* which quietly rebukes Shelley for the times when "he thought that his mission was a prophet's rather than a poet's." "A dreamer, never a visionary" (369–70): Symons's Shelley is a sentimentalist who "desired impossible things, and his whole theory of a reorganisation of the world, in which anarchy was to be spiritual deliverer, was a dream of the golden age which all mythologies put in the past." Consequently, "when Shelley thought he was planning the reform of the world, he was making literature." "He teaches us nothing, leads us nowhere, but cries and flies round us like a sea-bird" (280–81).

Where Shelley was concerned there was among skeptical critics something of a consensus that the insubstantiality of the poet's vision was confirmed by the impracticality of his demands. More lively disagreement was left to the disciples.

"A great poet," wrote Wilde in *The Soul of Man*, identifying Shelley as someone who, unlike Byron, had managed to escape, at least to a degree, the "stupidity and hypocrisy and Philistinism of the English." Had the English realized Shelley's greatness "they would have fallen on him with tooth and nail" (*Works*, 1179). By the time of *De Profundis* Wilde's identification was inevitably more complete. Shelley and Sophocles, he now wrote, belonged "in Christ's company"; by which he meant, of course, that Christ belonged in theirs, and in his own (*Works*, 1028).

KEATS

If, in the 1890s, Shelley was a demanding model, Keats was a tempting example: Shelley the poet of misty essence and the heroic rebel against political orthodoxy; Keats the poet of sensuous imagery and victim of the literary establishment. Keats provides the line or picture, Shelley bequeathes the symbol; Shelley is the deceptive beacon and Keats the warning echo. Moreover, Keats was often seen as both the precursor of *l'art pour l'art* and the evidence of its failure, so that the differences between the image of Keats and the image of Shelley can be said to be much like those between Decadent and Symbolist poetry. Wilde saw both poets as offering ways in which life, or the perception of life, could profitably imitate art, for "we can see the dawn through Shelley's eyes, and when we wander with Endymion the Moon grows amorous of our youth" (*Works*, 1138). In Arnold's poetry the Keatsian mood had served as a syphon for emotions that were unacceptable yet irrepressible. In the eyes of the aesthetes and decadents who came later this was no longer the case. Keats offered a seductive paradigm of artistic endeavor.[25]

According to Wilde in 1877 when he was twenty-three, it was "a noble privilege to count oneself of the same race as Keats or Shakespeare" (*Letters*, 40). A sonnet, "The Grave of Keats," written during the Continental tour with Mahaffy in the same year, puts Keats alongside St. Sebastian as a martyr to feeling. "As I stood beside the mean grave of this divine boy, I thought of him as of a Priest of Beauty slain before his time; and the vision of Guido's St. Sebastian came before my eyes as I saw him at Genoa," wrote Wilde about this sacred moment. It was a vision of "a lovely brown boy, with crisp, clustering hair and red lips, bound by his evil enemies to a tree, and though pierced by arrows, raising his eyes with divine, impassioned gaze towards the Eternal Beauty of the opening heavens."[26]

Five years later Keats was still "that god-like boy, the real Adonis of our age" (*Letters*, 108). In his lecture on "The English Renaissance of Art," delivered in America, Wilde went further, offering Keats as the type of all poets, a Christ-figure with a "thorn-crown."[27] A further sonnet, "On the Sale by Auction of Keats's Love Letters," written in 1885, was to be bitterly recalled some ten years later when the contents of his own Tite Street home were put up for sale (*Works*, 1007).

Symons's essay on Keats also perceives a great sensualist, though costumed, prototypically, as *un poète maudit*: "Keats was more than a decadent, but he was a decadent, and such a line as 'One faint eternal eventide of gems,' might have been written, in jewelled French by Mallarmé" (305). As an example of the pathological hero, Keats could hardly compete with Verlaine or Baudelaire, whose *nervosité* persisted with fascinating results into strenuous middle age. There is a dichotomy, however, between Symons's admiration for the precursor of *l'art pour l'art* and regret at his limitations: "He had none of that abstract quality of mind which can take refuge from realities, when they become too pressing and painful, in an idea. Ideas with him, were always the servants, never the masters, of sensation" (302). Keats "is the type not of the poet, but of the artist. He was not a great personality; his work comes to us as a greater thing than his personality"

(306). In this formulation absence of personality is the artist's self-transformation in his work, and must be differentiated from the Wildean idea of a "personality" that finds expressive completion in art.

Although Symons ends with a prefiguration of T. S. Eliot's modernist "unified sensibility" ("To Keats, the thing itself and the emotion were indistinguishable; he never saw without feeling, and he never felt without passion" [315]), the pronouncement floats in the air. Keats's place in *fin-de-siècle* poetics was problematic: no longer was he the inspiration he had once been for the Pre-Raphaelites, and was always to remain for Wilde. Symons's phrase, "unhealthy nerves and something feminine and twisted in the mind" (305), a far cry from Wilde's "god-like boy," suggests just how much the cultural climate had changed as a result of the social purity campaigns of the 1880s, the decadence and doom of 1895.

BLAKE

The one Romantic poet to whom Matthew Arnold seems to have paid no attention whatsoever was William Blake. The reason for this may simply have been one of accessibility, though it is hard to imagine what the fastidious Schools Inspector would have made of "the road of excess." Pater certainly read Blake, but the discovery and championship of the poet was first and foremost a Pre-Raphaelite achievement, and his legend remained exclusive to that circle in a way that Keats's did not, at least not until the 1890s when more concentrated study began to get underway.

Immured in Reading Gaol Wilde was to remember Blake's great line, "Where others see but the Dawn coming over the hill, I see the sons of God shouting for joy," finding in it support for the consoling philosophical principle that "a thing *is*, according to the mode in which one sees it" (*Works*, 1059). In general, though, Wilde shows little sustained interest in Blake, despite their shared interest in the liberating power of paradox.

But Symons was particularly devoted to Blake and wrote a whole book on him in 1907,[28] as well as the essay that appeared in *The Romantic Movement*. Increasingly, throughout the nineteenth

century, Blake had become one of the great test cases of the
conundrum: "madman or genius?"[29] He could be seen as a
uniquely free spirit whose innocent spontaneity, whether understood according to a Swinburnean dialectic or not, rendered all
matters of direct moral instruction quite irrelevant; alternatively
he could be hailed as a mystically inspired prophet whose vision
was accessible only to those who were similarly equipped with
arcane knowledge. In a powerful association of sensibility with
evolutionary progress Blake could even become a significant
"special case," to be studied scientifically as a way of estimating
the place held by any anomalous individual in relation to cultural
process.

"Scientific" the issue had certainly become: through the spread
of Spencerian sociology, the rediscovery of the work of Francis
Galton, and the publication of books such as Cesare Lombroso's
The Man of Genius, with its discussion of Baudelaire and Verlaine
(English translation 1891), Max Nordau's controversial *Degeneration*
(English translation 1895), J. F. Nisbet's long and comprehensive
The Insanity of Genius (1891), William Hirsch's *Genius and Degeneration*
(English translation 1897), and, more locally, the work of Have-
lock Ellis. These were all writers who strove to produce a
pathogenic definition of the artistic temperament that would lay
to rest its claim to visionary power; and they were all well known
to the writers and critics of the 1890s.

At the turn of the century, there was, in addition, a powerful
new influence at work which seriously affected Symons's readings
of Blake. Nietzsche's works had just become available in England,
and for a time both Yeats and Symons were strongly attracted by
the German philosopher's antipathy to conventional ideas of
reason and by his stirring conceptions of heroism.

"It is true that Blake was abnormal; but what was abnormal in
him was his sanity," wrote Symons in *The Romantic Movement* (50).
The synthesis of Nietzsche with Blake offered Symons a way of
reconciling eccentricity with the future, of explaining the coming,
though endlessly deferred, revelation, along with an aesthetic
commitment to the here and now; finally, of preserving, with or
without the aid of science, the traditional conjunction of madness
and genius. In Symons's extensive writings upon Blake, Nietzsche

exerts an interpretative influence, more deeply paradoxical, but quite as pervasive as Carlyle's upon earlier writers on the subject. "Like Nietzsche," said Symons about Blake, "but with a deeper innocence, he finds himself 'beyond good and evil,' in a region where the soul is naked and its own master" (46).

ROLE MODELS

"Ages are all equal, but genius is always above the age": it does now become apparent why Blake's aphorism and the Romantic cult of genius should have held so much fascination for the individualistic writers of the *fin de siècle*. As M. H. Abrams explains it, the "High Romantic argument" allows the hope that whereas the establishment of social harmony through political revolution has failed (and will fail again), the unity glimpsed through a regenerated poetry can still survive. Both Wilde and Symons would have agreed with him about that, though Wilde would probably have insisted that the flame could be kept alive only by rejecting those false revelations that proffered social progress without structural change. Even so, Wilde would willingly have conceded that historical process can sometimes be understood as the transvaluation of the status quo by individual agents who point the way to a more general liberation.

His own "individualism" was always of this kind: Romantic, revolutionary, theatrical. He started off by acting out the Romantic ideology as modern comedy. "I have nothing to declare but my genius," as he supposedly said to the New York customs in 1882 (*Ellmann*, 152). When, in 1897, he confessed, "I became the spendthrift of my own genius" (*Works*, 1018), Wilde was in tragic mood, though the idea of "genius" as a capital resource would always remain useful to someone who conceived of his life not only as an aesthetic mission but as a rather expensive spectacle.

For those such as Arthur Symons who, unlike Wilde, continued writing into the twentieth century, a more spiritually based doctrine of "individualism" would eventually prepare the way for a more dangerous Nietzscheanism. This too is explicable. "The mind will occupy itself less and less with works of genius," Charles

Pearson had prophesied in his *National Life and Character* (1894) "and more and more with trivial results and ephemeral discussions" (355). "Ours is certainly the dullest and most prosaic century possible," says Vivian in *The Decay of Lying* (*Works*, 1089). In its closing decades a general apprehension had spread out among intellectuals: a fear of those encroaching systems, of those popular syntheses of science, of politics, and of metaphysics, which would reassuringly reduce experience to the preordained and the easily understood, co-opting even the expansive vision of poets. Conversely Romanticism had become identified with those impulses that refused incorporation on the grounds that all orthodoxies suppress, through assimilation, the mind's potential for advance. It was hardly surprising, then, that opposition would sometimes lead towards strange gods and exotic creeds which went beyond conventional science, to spaces where some alien spirit might be conjured up, or that there should be attempts to broaden scientific inquiry to include the kind of supernatural explorations in which Wilde, for one, was so interested.

The late Romantic *animus* against scientifically based theory was not that it destroyed self-consciousness entirely (the Hegelian, and certainly the Paterian, influence strongly suggested otherwise), but that in practice science was limiting consciousness to the quotidian, replacing belief (the Romantic "joy" or "hope") with lame verification (what was left when doubt had done its work). Poetry was by definition without definition, and the poet the figure the system excluded: the "genius," his gift still the traditionally mysterious "inspiration."

And antithetically the reinforcement of these Romantic convictions explains why the textbooks on madness and genius held such a perverse attraction for artists, who seized upon would-be scientific notions of the pathological and turned them upside down, re-converting the social outcast back into a Romantic hero.

"Pathology," wrote Wilde, "is rapidly becoming the basis of sensational literature, and in art, as in politics, there is a great future for monsters."[30] Not that Wilde ever considered himself to be a monster, leaving that particular insult to the Marquess of Queensberry. Wilde had always had a higher destiny in mind.

When he wrote in *De Profundis*: "I see in Christ not merely the essentials of the supreme romantic type, but all the accidents, the wilfulnesses even, of the romantic temperament also" (*Works*, 1034–5), he was keeping faith with a vision originating some twenty-five years earlier when, prompted by Keats, he had promised that "the thorn-crown of the poet will blossom into roses for our pleasure."[31]

CHAPTER 5

Beardsley / Jarry: the art of deformation

No more masterpieces

Antonin Artaud[1]

The grammar of art exists only to be violated

Robert Ross[2]

It is said that one night in the early 1890s Oscar Wilde dined at the Paris home of the legendary courtesan Liane de Pougy together with Aubrey Beardsley, Jean Lorrain, two professional wrestlers, and a French journalist, and that after the meal the wrestlers staged an orgy.[3] Sadly, this story is almost certainly an invention, though, like other myths in the Wilde connection it does point to certain truths. If Wilde and Beardsley were ever to meet in Paris (and there is no evidence that they did, though they may at one point have planned to do so)[4] then it surely should have been at the home of a courtesan and dancer, and there should have been wrestlers present too, practitioners of a skill rather like their own: a spectacular prowess, where few can say where improvisation begins or ends, and the result is a mixture of the graceful and the grotesque with more than a hint of the erotic.

This chapter looks for the workings of that aesthetic in the parallel developments and intimate exchanges of two of Wilde's creative contemporaries: Aubrey Beardsley and Alfred Jarry. Both were young in the 1890s; both were notable for their multiple interests among the visual, literary, and theatrical arts; and both were harbingers of what was to be called "l'esprit nouveau."

As far as the theatre is concerned the new spirit was born with the collapse of naturalism and of historical archeology, brought on by the undermining of the positivistic principles of detail and accuracy upon which both styles had been based. A wave of revolution swept through the European theater at the turn of the century and it was out to change the role of the theater by changing the way it looked. Scenic design was the cutting edge. It is hard to imagine that Aubrey Beardsley would not have contributed to this modern movement, had he lived. He might well have been employed by his contemporary at Brighton Grammar school, the impresario C. B. Cochran. He had, after all, altered the history of the theatrical poster at a stroke with his design for *A Comedy of Sighs* at the Avenue Theatre in 1894. On matters of scenic design, as on so many other things, Beardsley has spoken through his posthumous influence – which, of course, is everywhere: most immediately in the work of Charles Ricketts, most colorfully in Bakst's designs for the Ballets Russes,[5] most exuberantly in Aleksander Blok's *The Puppet Show* (1906), but also contributing to the modernistic salons of the twenties, and even more directly to Noel Coward's *Bitter Sweet* (1929), John Gielgud's "black-and-white" production of *The Importance of Being Earnest* (1930), and Cecil Beaton's two-tone Ascot scene for *My Fair Lady* (1956).

That is not all: Beardsley's drawings were studied by the great modern pioneer Edward Gordon Craig, and Craig may well have picked up some hints for his über-marionette theory from Beardsley too, along with the writings of Maeterlinck, of Wilde, and of Arthur Symons, in whose *Studies in the Seven Arts* of 1906 Craig read about Alfred Jarry's essay "L'inutilité du théâtre au théâtre."[6] Modern theatrical style in general can be said to have drawn upon the example of Beardsley and the example of Jarry in about equal parts. Yet although they inhabited the same historical moment, it is as if the two men stood at a tangent to one another, viewing the future from different angles. From Beardsley comes what Peter Brook, thinking not only of the elegance of Gielgud but of Jouvet, of Bérard, and of Massine as well, calls "romantic theatre";[7] from Jarry comes not only Brook's theatre of mockery and abuse, "rough theatre" (77), but his "holy theatre" too, in the form of Artaud, who founded his own "Théâtre Alfred Jarry." The Collège de Pataphysique has included both the absurdist playwright Eugène Ionesco and the novelist and jazz-man Boris Vian among its members.

The forcing ground for this spirited modernity was Paris rather than London, amid a growing entanglement between hieratic Symbolists and popular entertainers, which left as its most visible sign the multitude of acrobats, cabaret artists, and assorted *saltimbanques* who appear in Impressionist and Post-Impressionist painting as well as in the theatrical practice pioneered by Jarry. Both Wilde and Beardsley met with Jarry in Paris, but independently. Wilde and Jarry were brought together in May 1898 by Henry Davray, translator of both Wilde and H. G. Wells. Jarry sent Wilde some of his writings. Wilde thought that these had "sometimes the obscenity of Rabelais, sometimes the wit of Molière, and always something curious of his own," but that in person Jarry was "most attractive...like a very nice renter" (*Letters*, 746–47).

Jarry may well have been among the "long-haired monsters of the quarter" who accompanied the novelist Rachilde when Beardsley lunched with her at Lapérouse in April 1897. "They all presented me with their books," he wrote to his sister Mabel, adding in parenthesis, "which are quite unreadable."[8] But critical distaste did not prevent him from making a portrait of Jarry (now long lost). Jarry was equally generous when he inserted the complex prose-poem, "Du pays de dentelles," dedicated to Beardsley, into his *Gestes et opinions du docteur Faustroll* of 1898. To the wider implications of that verbal tribute we shall eventually return. First, the picture.

Were it to turn up now Beardsley's portrait of Jarry would provide one of the great souvenir images of the *fin de siècle* – assuming that we would be able to recognize it. Would it be Beardsley at his most attenuating, a Jarry stretched and twisted into elegance? Or would the sitter have obliged the artist to find some squat outline commensurate with his monstrous ideas? A boyish ephebe ("a very nice renter") like the young page in Beardsley's illustration to Wilde's *Salome*? Both Beardsley and Jarry had seen the play at the Théâtre de l'Œuvre in February 1896 when Lugné-Poe staged its first performance there in its author's tragic absence. Or would Beardsley have portrayed Jarry

as a "long-haired monster," a troll, the part that Jarry played in
Peer Gynt at the same theater in November?

To pose the question in such a way acts as a reminder that
Lugné-Poe's Théâtre de l'Œuvre could draw upon several scenic
styles at once. Its designers, Bonnard, Vuillard, and Lautrec
among them, covered all the varieties of the garish, the ethereal,
and the merely exotic, even matching up to Jarry's own *Ubu Roi*
when it was performed in 1896 to an audience that included,
famously, Arthur Symons and W. B. Yeats. Their responses –
"symbolist farce" and "Savage God" – were those of foreigners
looking for, and finding, portents. All the actor who played Ubu
would say later was that "it never occurred to us to find out the
meaning of the words that we delivered. What we liked was the
fact that we didn't understand them."[9] And Jarry himself could
be equally relaxed about meaning. Ubu, he said, could be
considered as merely "the deformation by a schoolkid of one of
his teachers who represented for him everything grotesque in the
world."[10]

Beardsley made fewer statements about his art than Jarry (he
had, it is true, even less time), but his most famous remark,
made in an interview, suggests that he shared something of
Jarry's aesthetic starting-point: "If I am not grotesque I am
nothing."[11] For Jarry the grotesque is achieved through "deformation," as in his tribute to the Symbolist painter Filiger, who is
"a deformer, if that's the right word for a painter who paints
what really is...and not just what is conventional" (*I*, 1024). The
formula parallels Wilde's tribute in *The Critic as Artist* to "the
Archaicistes" of Paris who, "rejecting the tedious realism of those
who merely paint what they see, try to see something worth
seeing" (*Works*, 1148).

"Deformation" was the means by which an underlying reality
could be revealed by violating the conventional forms of representation; a mode of illusion, not of realism, that relied upon the
contingency of images, not of things.[12] This, in turn, was to
become a conventional justification of modern painting of many
kinds, but the immediate significance is considerable: Jarry
would apply the principle of "deformation" to theatrical representation as well as to the purely pictorial arts; and among the

pantheon of "deformers" he would happily include Aubrey
Beardsley himself.

Given the breadth of the gap between their national cultures
the initial similarities between Beardsley and Jarry are impressive.
Both were precocious and though instinctive scholars, classicists
even, both enjoyed caricaturing their teachers and playing with
toy theaters and puppets, providing their own family entertainments. Their mutual interest in marionettes – an enthusiasm that
was shared by Wilde, as least for a while (*Letters*, 310–13) – lasted
them into their brief maturities. Beardsley would surely have
appreciated the punning opening of Jarry's "Guignol," published
in April 1893, with its reminder that comic *lazzi* can easily turn
into another favourite motif of the *fin de siècle*, the dance of death:

As the ghostly curtain swept up into the flies – a great red wing that
made the noise of a fan – so it revealed a dark pit that yawned in front
of us like a hellish mouth. Like glow-worms, resin candles dripped from
their elegant eyes to the nails of their stately hands, like the spiral at the
end of a horn, and that made us suddenly shudder with the thought that
the marionettes were going to mock our gloomy faces with *lazzi*, that
these wooden actors would demand to be applauded with the clap of
jaw-bones (*I*, 180).

For Jarry in particular the preference for puppets was a
"deformation" of a "deformation," a protest against the unnatural expressiveness of "great acting," and the way some classical
texts substituted a gallery of roles for the interchange of life.
Racine, for example, was a mere vehicle for star performers (*I*,
413). In any case, Jarry complained, the audiences at the Comédie
Française habitually listened to plays without understanding them
(*I*, 405), just as they did at the Châtelet, the Gaité, the Ambigu,
and the Opéra Comique (*I*, 412).

Beardsley, on the other hand, enjoyed many kinds of theater,
including the theater of the Paris boulevards. Yet, although a
large number of his pictures have theatrical subjects, these are
rarely portraits of performers or records of performances; more
often they are improvisations upon play-texts or, most myster-
iously, purely theatrical inventions: the three *Comedy-Ballets of
Marionettes*, for example, which relate to no known work or
troupe. Beardsley's brand of "deformation" began early on. His

sketch for *Ghosts* (1890), though crudely drawn, is notable for the handsome angular profiles he gives both to Oswald (upon whom the first onslaughts of syphilis should surely be making their mark) and to his mother. *Hamlet Patris Manem Sequitur*, much more in the style of Burne-Jones, has its tragic hero pushing blindly through misty woods, which may make a symbolic or Freudian point, but has no obvious counterpoint in any contemporary production, let alone, of course, any specific reference to the play-text. A very crude sketch of Sarah Bernhardt (*c.* 1890) has the odd effect of flattening those famous features, again into masculinity. But then Bernhardt was always good material for caricature. Jarry once praised a circus clown for looking like her (*II*, 334).

Wagner was a major obsession of Beardsley's from the very start (*Götterdämmerung* in particular, several drawings of *Das Rheingold*, one or two of them exceptionally obscene), but his most typical theatrical imagery is drawn from the traditional *commedia dell'arte* troupe of Pierrot, Doctor, and Columbine.[13] These may be seen singly or in groups, but are rarely pictured acting out *scenarii*. The frontispiece to John Davidson's *Plays*, for example: the full title, *The Comedy-Ballets of Marionettes as performed by the Theatre Impossible*, would suggest something much more contemporary, but what? Similarly *The Scarlet Pastorale* is neither scarlet nor obviously pastoral. *Commedia* theater had many attractions for Beardsley, irrespective of any dramatic narrative based upon it. It is improvised theater, phallic and ritualistic in origin, non-verbal, gestural (so much depends upon the pointing finger and the indicative body), and it makes explicit acknowledgment of its spectators. As Brigid Brophy says about *The Death of Pierrot*, which shows a troupe of masked *commedia dell'arte* personages tiptoeing in a line towards Pierrot's deathbed, their fingers to their lips: "You can tell they are on a stage because they are looking not towards their destination but towards an audience."[14]

When Beardsley does draw individual figures the results can be just as defiant: *La Dame aux camélias* is neither Bernhardt nor Duse. Réjane is obviously Réjane, but it is not always clear which role she is playing.[15] Mrs. Patrick Campbell, an actress renowned for her gaunt physicality, is reduced even further, to a wasp-waisted silhouette. Later projects are illustrations of plays, such as

Lysistrata and *Volpone*, that Beardsley could not have seen in performance. Interestingly, some of his contemporaries were not in the least worried that Beardsley could no more be said to directly "illustrate" theater than he did any other kind of subject matter. The obituarist in *The Studio*, for example, wrote of Beardsley's Wagner drawings: "Certainly, they owe nothing to the stage effects the composer himself arranged etc."[16] But presumably he saw what Arthur Symons also saw in Beardsley: "an art of the day and hour" competing "not merely with the appeal and the popularity of the theatrical spectacle, but directly with theatrical methods, the methods of stage illusion."[17]

Beardsley's theatricality has little to do with plot or psychology; it is much more concerned with mimicry and disguise, tastes revealed in the artist's own remarks about Ben Jonson's *Volpone*, with his "passion for the theatre":

Disguise, costume, and the (theatrical) attitude have an irresistible attraction for him, the blood of the mime is in his veins. To be effective, to be imposing, to play a part magnificently, are as much a joy to him as the consciousness of the most real qualities and powers; and how perfectly Volpone acts, how marvellously he improvises! He takes up a role with as much gusto and sureness as a finished comedian for whom the stage has not yet lost its glamour, and each new part gives him the huge pleasure of developing and accentuating some characteristic of his inexhaustibly rich nature, and exercising his immensely fertile brain.[18]

Sometimes Beardsley exercised his own "immensely fertile brain" by being as disrespectful as he reasonably could be about what passed for theatricality in London at the time. The results can be seen in the series of drawings that he produced when employed by the *Pall Mall Budget* early in 1893. This was admitted to be an unfortunate engagement even by the man who hired him,[19] and one can see why: the pictures show Beardsley to have been unable to resist adding satirical comment to a convention that normally respected the boundaries of genial caricature.

On 2 February he made a contribution to a feature review of Henry Arthur Jones's *The Bauble Shop*. The review, unsigned, is accompanied on the same page by a composite sketch, not by Beardsley, which shows in the usual manner of the period a number of moments from the production. *The Bauble Shop* is a

morally inspiring play about a politician who is waylaid by a
street gang and takes refuge in a toy bazaar where he discovers,
and immediately sets about importuning, the proprietor's
daughter. Repentance eventually follows. It was fitting, then, for
the professional illustrator to reproduce a significant episode
which had the politician amusing himself by playing with a
mechanical doll. Beardsley's drawing is on a separate page. It is a
solid black outline showing the playwright Jones pulling the
strings of some diabolical toy jester who, shaped like Big Ben,
waves a baton with the outline of a crucifix. The real "Bauble" is
Jones's mechanically mischievous play.

On 9 February the performance was Tennyson's *Becket* at the
Lyceum with Irving and Terry. Beardsley contributes a whole
page frontispiece: a Gothic, Faustian Irving, largely black,
merging into the background, and a number of smaller figure
sketches. These are drawn in accordance with sentiments expressed in the review: "Mr. Irving's talents heretofore are triumphs of
melodrama," where "the acting was of more importance than the
play acted." Irving's Becket is superior to his Lear ("which was
marred, by an aggravation of action that approached the grotesque"), but only because of the inferiority of Tennyson's play.
Even so, "not all the energy of Lyceum acting...not all the
archaeology of Lyceum costumes...can make the piece seem real,
or human, or attractive." Its characters are "as wooden as
marionettes without the animation." Beardsley reciprocates with
a static silhouette of Terry in what was to become the style of
Craig's famous "black figures."[20] It is left to another artist,
E. Sullivan, to illustrate an actual scene.

An apparent impatience with the job in hand marks the four
sketches for the review of the Bancrofts' revival of *Diplomacy*
published on 23 February. All are totally undistinguished, average
likenesses rapidly achieved, barely an improvement upon the
portrait of Squire Bancroft by the actor William Kendall on the
same page. The most that can be said for them is that they go
some way toward establishing the Bancrofts' ambiguous status as
superannuated personalities who had drifted somewhat from the
public memory.

On 16 March the subject is Gluck's *Orpheus*, performed by

students of the Royal College of Music with Clara Butt in the title part. Beardsley contributes one small sketch of Irving ("a visitor to the rehearsal"), and three of the opera. These are unmistakable: experiments in the full-blown style of 1893 in which gracefulness expresses dramatic tension, with a subversive hint of something willed or premature in the effort. The reviewer could not help but remark on a chorus who showed "every sentiment of earnestness and deep resolution to be serious," and "a frowning effort after gracefulness which is extremely laudable." Beardsley shows careful posing, obvious sexual ambiguity in the case of Clara Butt, and in a single instance, "one of the spirits," a Medusa-haired fury straight out of *Salome*, which he was illustrating at about the same time. This study clearly belongs with those other menacing and difficult configurations: "The Kiss of Judas" and "Of a Neophyte." When confronted by some of the pretensions of the late nineteenth-century stage, Beardsley could not keep a straight face.

Nor could Jarry, who believed that the true theatrical tradition had been lost, buried under rhetoric and bourgeois respectability. Like Beardsley he was fascinated by the *commedia*. In the several manifestoes he issued at the time of *Ubu* he demanded a Rabelaisian, which is to say Shakespearean, which is to say Ubuesque theater. "What are the conditions that are indispensable to the theatre?" he asked himself.

I do not think it is still necessary to know if there are three unities or the single unity of action because the unity of action is observed if everything important is to do with a single character. If we are supposed to respect the pudeur of the public then we cannot argue from Aristophanes either, since many editions have notes on every page saying, "The whole of this passage is full of obscene allusions". Nor can one cite Shakespeare for one only has to re-read certain words of Ophelia's, or the famous scene (frequently cut) in which a queen takes French lessons. The least we could do would be to follow Messieurs Augier, Dumas, Labiche, etc., whom we have had the misfortune to read and with deep boredom (*I*, 415).

As far as *Ubu* was concerned the means for reaching the ideal conditions were at hand. First and foremost the actors should be marionettes, or at least, if human they should look and act like marionettes (*I*, 399–400). Costumes would preferably be modern, "since satire is modern, and sordid, too, so that the play appears even more shabby and appalling." They should be "as far as possible from local colour or period" (*I*, 1043). Décor in general is a hybrid, neither natural nor artificial: "if it resembled nature it would be a pointless duplication...It is not artificial, in the sense that it isn't, for the playwright, the realisation of the outside world as he has seen and recreated it" (*I*, 70). The aim should be that "every spectator sees a play in a décor which does not contradict his own view of it. For the general public, on the other hand, it doesn't matter how artistic the décor is, because the mass doesn't understand anything of its own accord, only what authority tells it" (*I*, 406). Only by repudiating bourgeois specification will the imagination be released, and with it the universal. *Ubu*, then, was as determinedly ahistorical as it was outrageously theatrical.

Jarry believed archeology to be as tedious in painting as it was in the theater: "Classical plays were acted in the costume of their time; let us do the same as those old painters who wanted to make the most ancient scenes look contemporary. All the historical stuff is a bore, that's to say, useless" (*I*, 414). His 1901 lecture, "Le Temps dans l'art," probably with reference to Gustave Moreau, does acknowledge the seductive charm of historical reconstruction: "Painters are charmed by an unusual colour or by a strange woman covered with jewels, just as writers find the language of past ages to be more sonorous and expressive than the language of their own time, even when they don't understand the words" (*II*, 638). But Jarry goes on to argue that sweeping away "historical reconstruction" will reveal a bedrock of eternal feelings, above all, sexual feelings.

Like many of their contemporaries Beardsley and Jarry were greatly taken by the semi-mythic figure of Messalina, wife of the Emperor Claudius, who was said to have worked as a prostitute in order to slake her own apparently endless desires. Although most familiar as the "heroine" of Juvenal's sixth satire, Messalina makes many other appearances in the literature of the late Roman empire. Her case was one that seemed to have a particular significance for the *fin de siècle* because of its double reference: on the one hand, to the claims for sexual freedom currently being made by the New Woman, on the other to what was widely seen as a veritable plague of prostitution right across Europe. These meanings could be further played off against each other to suggest either the complicated causes of sexual exploitation, or to provide ancient evidence of rapacious female desire.

There was an opera, *Messalina*, pictured by Lautrec,[21] and Wilde has Lord Henry Wotton joke that Dorian Gray would still be interesting even if he were to marry Messalina (*Works*, 64). Later Wilde complained that the English upheld Messalina (standing for heterosexual debauchery) over Sporus (Nero's lover standing for the homosexual kind), and that the aim of life should be to overcome "the hunger of the body and the appetite of the flesh which desecrate always and often destroy" (*Letters*, 594, 604, 621–22). But this was after his spell in jail when he was not the man he once had been.

Messalina was a demanding mistress, which is why it has often been said that she appeals to the misogynist artist. In Jarry's version of her story, *Messaline*, first published in 1900, her desire becomes the driving force of the State itself (Roma as a palindrome of Amor) through a complex pattern of associations involving Rome and the image of the she-wolf, Lupa. Not that this makes it any easier to decode Beardsley's Messalina pictures. Jarry tells us how the Empress's features are customarily represented:

A face of exaggerated fullness, round like a breast, or with something forcibly swallowed. The mouth is tiny but nevertheless occupies the entire face, for the jaw-muscles are powerful and would serve an animal; the nostrils wide like Cleopatra's, inherited from Mark Antony her great-grandfather...Not beautiful in fact.[22]

Some, but not all, of these characteristics are conveyed in Beardsley's pictures: a Messalina with stern masculine brow, set mouth and brutal jaw. As in Jarry's version this may well look like female desire as a compulsion, as viewed by Nietzsche or Schopenhauer, though it has also been seen as an image of a strong, independent woman determined to pursue her own sexuality come what may.[23]

Jarry's *Messaline* goes in a different direction, suggesting that

MESSALINA.

2. Aubrey Beardsley, *Messalina Returning from the Bath*

desire is driven by phallic rule. About such matters he is entirely explicit: above the brothel hangs what is described as an image of the "divine generator," "the emblem of universal life" (12). Messalina is a figure from the Roman past with worldwide significance. It would not be difficult to read Beardsley's own archeological carelessness in a similar fashion. However, there is one scene in Jarry's text that does offer a clearly alternative view of the Empress. It involves the acrobat Mnester who, adorned with moon-shaped jewelry, adopts, at the climax of his dance, a completely spherical posture. Messalina is left imploring for this symbol of androgynous wholeness – "I want THE MOON" (75). It could almost be a "deformation" of Wilde's *Salome*, where the heroine's desires are more often associated with the moon as an image of sterile, vengeful, sexual division.

Sometimes pornography brings fundamental differences into the open. Compare, for example, Jarry's *Le Surmâle* (*II*, 187–271) with Beardsley's *Under the Hill*, published in an expurgated form in the *Savoy* in 1896. Both opt for excess, but where Beardsley is endlessly inventive, Jarry is infinitely repetitive.[24] Yet both were New Men of the nineties who responded positively to the New Woman, perhaps enjoying the thrilling possibility that she might reveal more of herself than ever before: that progression and transgression might intertwine. In *Le Surmâle* the dream of endless orgasm, "pornutopia," is almost made possible by the scientific invention, "la machine-à-inspirer-l'amour," a rather specialized view of technology, as well as of sexuality.

Beardsley had no qualms whatsoever about technology in the form of modern printing techniques, nor about mass distribution, nor about modern marketing. He welcomed the new art of the poster, he said, because "London will soon be resplendent with advertisements, and against a leaden sky skysigns will trace their formal arabesque. Beauty has laid siege to the City, and the telegraph wires are no longer the sole joy of our aesthetic perceptions."[25]

Jarry's sense of technology was much more theoretical, almost on a Wellsian level. He was interested in time machines, and in the aesthetic implications of new discoveries about the nature of matter. Beardsley could see that technology affected production, but does not seem to have been aware as to how it might affect conceptualization. Yet the wide variation in their perception of that modern world, or of how science might influence those perceptions, did nothing to inhibit Jarry's final appreciation of Beardsley's art, in which he saw signs of a modernity that no one else, not even Beardsley, would have known how to express.

The novelty of that appreciation can be grasped more completely if it is compared with what French contemporaries were saying at the same time. In France, Beardsley had come quickly and widely to the fore.[26] Pictures by the artist were included in Samuel Bing's "Art Nouveau" display at 22 rue de Provence in 1895, and at the 1900 Paris exhibition the British contribution to the "Décennale" in the Grand Palais included "Venus and Tannhauser." Lautrec asked for a book of Beardsley drawings,[27] and Robert de Montesquiou (Huysmans's Des Esseintes and Proust's Baron de Charlus), a major publicist for Art Nouveau, wrote a prose elegy for him in 1898. He did so under the lubricious title "The Perverse," listing Beardsley's typical props as if they were the contents of a cupboard hidden away in a brothel. Not surprisingly he was particularly taken with Beardsley's drawing of another French citizen famous for dressing-up, Mademoiselle de Maupin, confiding:

If I had to write the funeral oration and provide an epitaph for Beardsley, I would say: he loved, with a guilty love, peacock's feathers; candles; flames, with their obscene drips like miniature stalactites; actresses' make-up tables; pompoms full of rice powder; wigs in the style of Louis XIV; voluminous sleeves; untied shoes; velvet face-masks; and vine leaves that are the masks for what lies lower down.[28]

There are, of course, similarities in vocabulary between Montesquiou and Jarry: "deformation" is mentioned and, from Gautier, "transposition," but Montesquiou is still pursuing a combination of Wagnerian swoon and sexual naughtiness rather than the more radical possibilities of Beardsley's line:

Geometric lines, curves traced with a compass, which indicate at a single stroke an arm or a piece of drapery, and yet with grace, and in that evolving spirit of ornamentation, without which one cannot change a style, overcome a difficulty or astonish the world (95).

For Montesquiou, Beardsley's art still hovers between ornamentation and insinuation. For Jarry it already outlines an alternative world. Not for Jarry a cataloging of effects, but the reconstruction of an imaginative whole. In his tribute to Beardsley he improvises a new kind of art criticism for a new kind of art. Compare this with Montesquiou's salacious items:

The king of Lace drew out the light as a rope-maker plaits his retrograde line, and the threads trembled slightly in the dim light, like cobwebs. They wove themselves into forests, like the leaves which hoarfrost engraves on windowpanes; then they fashioned themselves into a Madonna and her Child in the Christmas snow; and then into jewels, peacocks, and gowns, intermingling like the swimming dance of the Rhine maidens. The Beaux and the Belles strutted and preened in imitation of fans, until their patient gathering broke up with a cry. Just as the white junoians, roosting in a park, complain raucously when the lying intrusion of a lamp apes prematurely the dawn's reflection of their ocelli, so an artless shape burgeoned in the forest of raked-over pine pitch; and as Pierrot serenades the confusion of the moon's entwined ball, the paradox of day burrowing underground arose from Ali Baba screaming in the pitiless oil and the jar's darkness (*I*, 677–78).[29]

The sources for that paragraph are many but they are brilliantly selected: the "Madonna" of 1893; assorted monkeys, Rhine-maidens, and Pierrots with mirrors and candles; "Les Beaux et les Belles" from *The Rape of the Lock* with their fans; peacocks from *Salome*; the mysterious Ali Baba. These details, however enchanting, are in themselves of less importance than the fact that the sequence is generated by the same principle of association that operates throughout the *Gestes et opinions du docteur Faustroll.*

Faustroll is perhaps Jarry's most astonishing production. In part an imaginary voyage ("From Paris to Paris by sea"), with Dr. Faustroll as a cross between Gulliver and Alice, in part a series of tributes to friends and heroes, largely expressed through affectionate parody, it is also a comic-book version of recent scientific thought. Indeed the first sentence of the Beardsley passage hails the artist as one who created out of waves of pure light, following Lord Kelvin's pronouncement in his *Popular Lectures and Addresses*, a work much studied and admired by Jarry, that "One thing we are sure of, and that is the reality and substantiality of the luminiferous ether."[30]

The tribute is both precise and heartfelt. Beardsley, like all great creative spirits, works with elemental resources. *Faustroll* is also, notoriously, the repository of one of Jarry's deceptively concise definitions of his own new science, "pataphysics": "The science of imaginary solutions, which symbolically attributes the

properties of objects, described by their virtuality, to their linea-
ments" (193). This is a logical accompaniment to the principles of
representation outlined in such essays as "L'Inutilité du théâtre."
The effect is to co-opt Beardsley as a fellow conspirator among
those who would free representation from the constraints of
verisimilitude by using art, paradoxically, as a polysemic means of
rediscovering both quiddity and subjectivity – as in *Faustroll*, with
a verbal evocation of the pictorial which flattens narrative into a
spatial game. Liberation through "deformation."

How much of that was in Beardsley's imagination, and how
much in Jarry's mind, we are left to guess. As spectators with
hindsight we can still only speculate as to the true modernity of
Beardsley's art. But when literary or "narrative" readings tend to
break down, other approaches do suggest themselves. And it is
Jarry's pataphysics, after all, that insists that the possible always
becomes the necessary.

Pataphysics is both the absurdist fancy of an out-and-out
subversive and the entirely serious proposition of a man well
versed in contemporary scientific thought: a mischievous alternative to the Symbolist theory that, as J. E. Chamberlin has
explained, was itself closely paralleled by much scientific discourse.[31] Pataphysics allows for what Wells, in an 1891 article that
was greatly admired by Wilde,[32] called "The Rediscovery of the
Unique." The great revelation of modern times according to
Wells is that *"All being is unique,"* or "nothing is strictly like
anything else."[33] In the brave recognition of the uniqueness of
particulars and the hypothetical nature of universals (including
number, language, and morality) lies the way to a terrifying
liberation: from now on it will be up to the spectator to make the
connections. Released from realism by a new subjectivity, modernity would be free – to sink or to soar.

CHAPTER 6
Dieppe: 1895 and after

My dear friend...your Dieppe is a reduced Florence, every type of character for a novelist seems to gather there...that enchanting Olga learnt more at Dieppe than my *Maisie* knew.

Henry James to Jacques-Emile Blanche[1]

Yes, dear Aubrey is always too Parisian, he cannot forget he has been to Dieppe once!

Oscar Wilde to Charles Ricketts[2]

Like culture, respectability, and the suburbs, the summer holiday has turned out to be among the more lasting of Victorian inventions. They belong together: by-products of capitalism, attempts to appease the reality of industrial labor. Even holidays can have, at most, only that "relative autonomy" from the work process which modern sociologists sometimes allow. Produced, even as negation, by the conditions of modern life, holidays are occasions for consumption rather than for carnival in the Bakhtinian sense, nor does Bakhtin's liberating "grotesque" have much of a place on holiday.[3] There is little stepping outside of roles and little role-reversal. Holidays preserve most of the structures of social life, and respect to a large extent the usual rules of what is and what is not permitted. At the same time they add a few rules of their own, such as "enjoyment." Proposing themselves as an escape from time's tyranny, they are still our regulated hours.

In the course of the nineteenth century the Normandy coastal town of Dieppe established itself as a particularly suitable site for the idylls of the English.[4] The Rouen–Paris railway opened in 1848, speeding communications between London and the French

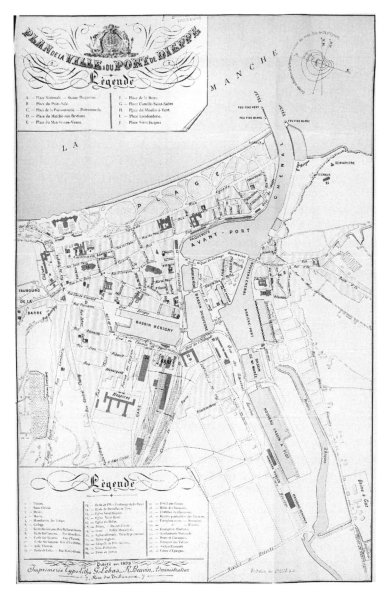

3. Map of Dieppe in 1898

capital with Dieppe as a convenient stopping-point, and eventually the port's function as a cross-channel terminal came to overshadow its usefulness as an international harbor (an official status that went to Le Havre). Dieppe countered by developing its ship-building and fishing trades.[5]

In 1889 dredging operations were completed which allowed a new ferry service: boats could now cross from Newhaven in three hours, and according to a regular timetable. Later in the century, better ferries steadily improved the London connection. By a familiar law of modern tourism, these speeded-up communications promoted a mood of nostalgia in the visitor, turning Dieppe, with its encircled harbor, its eighteenth-century arcades, cliff-top castle, and minaretted Casino, into the ideal location for a rendezvous with the past as well as for cultural encounter.

The elite had long appreciated Dieppe's natural advantages: visits by Marie-Caroline, Duchesse de Berri, in the 1820s had made it fashionable among the French, and annual holidays taken there by Lord Salisbury and his family from the 1860s onwards made it respectable for the English. As the painters had always known, Dieppe's coastal views and architectural variety have a unique charm: artists both French (Delacroix, Corot, Daubigny, Renoir, Degas, Helleu, Monet) and English (Haydon, Cotman, Turner) had sought out its opalescent beauty.[6]

By the 1890s the attractions of Dieppe were on offer to an ever widening clientele so that, for the summer months at any rate, a microcosm of English society could be found there, displaced by sixty miles of sea. To Dieppe, to join the long-established horse races, the English brought sports: golf, tennis, football, cricket even. Dieppe was and was not French, was and was not English, a border town, a liminal place.

For some of its admirers, the aesthetes and decadents of the *fin de siècle*, it was that uncertainty which made Dieppe so attractive, such a challenge to observation. English or French? Port or resort? Designed for leisure or made for adventure? Anxious to distinguish themselves from the other holiday-makers, the aesthetes came to Dieppe believing that they could combat respectability with refinement, could substitute for mere consumption an active mode of "appreciation."

1895

In the summer of 1894, when the *The Crown* pub had shut, Aubrey Beardsley and Ernest Dowson would sometimes walk the London streets waiting for the early boat-train that would let them escape across the Channel. But it was in the following year, in the aftermath of the Wilde trials, when temporary exile had become particularly desirable, that Dieppe saw its greatest concentration of artists and writers from London. The group (if such it can be called) consisted of Beardsley, Arthur Symons, Charles Conder, William Rothenstein, the publisher Leonard Smithers, and, for a while, Ernest Dowson. Symons drafted the "Editorial Note" to the *Savoy*, a new periodical to replace the ailing *Yellow Book*, while sitting outside the Café des Tribuneaux, Dieppe's social center. He composed poems and produced journalism while soaking up the town's atmosphere and in the end decided to pay tribute to local inspiration in a work of impressionist prose.

"Dieppe: 1895"[7] is typical of its author and of much aesthetic writing because it affects a surface casualness that belies a tense structure. It is, as its title suggests, a product of the time and place it describes. For example, sexuality is stressed by Symons not just because he had his own special problems in that area (in the summer of 1895 he was recovering from a tortured love affair), but because Dieppe had its own peculiar sexual ambiance. And money is important in Symons's essay not just because Symons was looking for a backer (and finding one in Smithers), but because Dieppe was at one and the same time expensive (the grand hotels, the Casino) and relatively economical (the cheaper hotels near the port).[8]

Dieppe was much represented by the English, most of whom came to it by boat, the *quai* being both *point de départ* and *point d'arrivée*: the margin of a marginal town. A railroad to Paris ran alongside; beyond that there was a narrow elevated platform, put there to ease the lifting of goods from storage sheds into freight cars. Beyond that people clustered, hotel touts offered rooms, friends reached out to greet visitors, others simply gazed, including those who made a point of regulating their daily walks according to the movements of the ferries. Stepping off the

Newhaven boat on to the Dieppe *quai* became a repeated motif in the literature of the time.

In 1883 Walter Sickert traveled via Dieppe in the company of Whistler's *Portrait of His Mother*, which was intended for exhibition at the Paris Salon. It was a decisive moment in Sickert's life, and for years afterwards he would recollect "the vision of the little deal case swinging from a crane against the star-lit night and the sleeping houses of the Pollet de Dieppe."[9] Because he was to have in Paris his first meeting with Degas, a profound influence upon his own work, so in his mind the Dieppe *quai* came to mark a symbolic threshold between English and French art.

Even the blundering surburban hero of Reggie Turner's *Imperial Brown of Brixton* (1908) undergoes mixed feelings of dislocation and possession on arrival at Dieppe:

> He tripped as he stepped off the woooden structure on to the cement, but, remembering an old legend, he took it as a good omen, and with a good-humoured snigger, not altogether devoid of self-consciousness he echoed the louder laughter of the gazers who pressed behind the rope which held them back from the voyagers. Thus he took possession of France, the land of his dreams and waking visions. England was now separated from him by a wide strip of water. Brown was abroad.[10]

And Dieppe is equally strange to the middle-class heroes and heroines of the novels of "John Winter," pseudonym of the prolific writer Mrs. Arthur Stannard. "Winter" set two of her novels, *A Sea-side Flirt* (1897) and *A Summer Jaunt* (1899) in the area, and in 1897 struck up a brief Dieppe friendship with Oscar Wilde, allowing him to pay her most popular (and mawkish) book the grownup compliment of being *une œuvre symboliste* in which "it is really only the style and the subject that are wrong" (*Letters*, 586). Invariably for "Winter's" heroines the trip to Dieppe is a first venture abroad. In *A Summer Jaunt* the narrator recalls this moment:

> My first impresssion, as we passed in between the Calvaries set at either side of the entrance to the harbour, between the tall white cliffs on the left and the tall white houses on the right, was that we had got to a foreign-looking town at last. Indeed, it seemed, when we left the sea behind us, as if we had passed into a quiet corner of another world.[11]

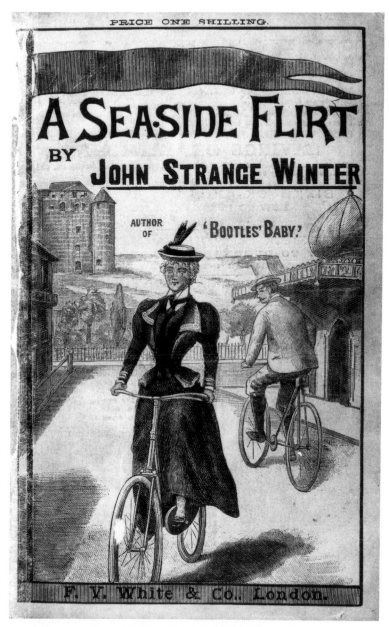

4. Cover of *A Sea-side Flirt* by "John Winter" (1897)

For most people the main question was where to stay. The choice was large and varied. For the affluent and respectable there were the grand hotels on the promenade, like the Hôtel Royal. Sickert, the town's "Canaletto" (as he was to be described by the Anglophile painter Jacques-Emile Blanche), said that it was the Hôtel Royal that made him a "rectangular" artist,[12] though in most of his paintings its rectangle is surrounded by disruptive detail and human accessories. One version (now lost, but reproduced in the *Yellow Book* in 1895) shows imaginary crinolined figures from an earlier age circling the foreground, softening the view with nostalgia. Elsewhere Sickert developed a highly influential approach to color entirely appropriate to the sentiments he wanted to express: a mixed strategy in which predictable grays, greens, and blues are countered by unexpected emotional effects.

The grand hotels were massive, impersonal, and institutional, a far cry from the place where Max Beerbohm, Reggie Turner, and William Nicholson stayed from the nineties through into the Edwardian period. First discovered by Whistler, the Hôtel Chez Lefèvre in the Rue de la Halle au Blé, opposite the old summer palace of Napoleon III, was small, domestic, and shabby. Staying at the Lefèvre became a genial habit, like so many of the incidentals of a Dieppe holiday. Visitors went there "not caring that it is perhaps not quite crème-de-la-crème, quite pleased with it and themselves, and only wanting it to remain unchanged."[13]

Wherever they chose to stay the English would soon settle into a similar ritual, usually based on the Casino, "where you met everybody in the morning at the bathing quay, and in the afternoon at the children's dance, and in the evening at the concert, and all day at the gaming tables where you put your money on the 'little horses.'"[14] That's according to Evelyn Sharp, a friend of Henry Harland, founder of the *Yellow Book*, but the daily round sounds much the same in "John Winter's" *A Sea-side Flirt*:

One goes down on to the terrace in the morning, watching the bathers and listening to the band, meeting all one's friends, looking at each other's dresses, and talking scandal...There are dozens of things with which to fill up the rest of the morning before déjeuner time – a turn down the Grande Rue, a hunt among the curiosity shops, a little spin on one's bicycle, a glance into the reading-room; or one can cycle up to the Hotel at Puys to breakfast, to Martin Eglise, or the Château d'Arques, or past the golf links to Pourville. Then, in the afternoon, there are a hundred and one excursions to be made, the concert at the Casino, the little horses...After that there is afternoon with one's friends at one resort or another, or what is now the smartest thing of all, to spend the afternoon and have tea on the Golf Green...We dine with somebody different every night, and spend the evening in the Casino or at the theatre.[15]

And should, of an afternoon, tedium set in, as in *A Summer Jaunt*, then Dieppe provided other alternatives – it was "just the kind of place where a girl would get entangled in a love affair..." In the evening there was "a little dancing or music, and lemon squash, an ice, a walk on the terrace – and for you men, the excitement of the little horses, and the baccarat room."[16] For men like Turner and Beerbohm the custom was to read the *Daily Telegraph* at the Café des Tribuneaux in the afternoon before strolling down to the Casino later.[17]

For the more privileged holiday-makers the routine was leavened with visits to one or another of the famous Dieppe *salons*. These were to be found at the painter Fritz Thaulow's Villa des Orchides in the Faubourg de la Barre and, at the far end of the beach, beneath the castle, at two houses among the row of buildings known as the Bas Fort Blanc. The mother of the painter and socialite Jacques-Emile Blanche had a villa here in which he was brought up – later it provided him with a studio.[18] Close by was the Villa Olga, home of Olga Alberta, the daughter of the duchess Cariociolo, herself the half-Portuguese, half-American mistress of a Polish equerry of Napoleon III.

To the Villa des Orchides came, in addition to Wilde, Beardsley and Conder who, at Thaulow's invitation, painted murals.[19] To the Blanches' Bas Fort Blanc came Sickert, George Moore, Symons (in the summer of 1895 Blanche painted Symons's portrait there) and, again, Beardsley. To the Villa Olga came on occasion and in secret the Prince of Wales. The sets, artistic and aristocratic, rivaled each other, overlapped and to some extent, intermingled. That there was a strong element of conscious play-acting in all of this is admitted by the portraits they produced of each other. Blanche made Beardsley quite Hogarthian, with black patches on his cheeks; William Rothenstein gave Conder a satyr-like swagger.

For the middle-class English family, in contrast, it was above all the famous promenade that counted, as *A Summer Jaunt* testifies:

> ...this great stretch of grass, those sheltered seats, the pebbled beach beyond, where Nanna can sit for hours in the sun if she likes. No great distance to get anywhere, no steep cliffs to climb that would tire the old woman to death. We could not have chosen a place more absolutely good for us all.[20]

No mention there, naturally, of the town's native population, the Dieppois, whose basic geography was rather different. For them a dividing line stretched between the holiday town with its Casino, hotels, and shops, all to the south and the east of the harbor, and the poor fishermen's quarter of Le Pollet, to the north. Yet within these broad swathes there were subsidiary areas, each with its own possibilities. Dieppe was still, even in the nineties, an unresolved place.

Symons's "Dieppe: 1895" begins with him flaunting his independence in the most elementary way, insisting upon his freedom to linger, to ignore regulated time. "I went to Dieppe this summer with the intention of staying from Saturday to Monday," he announces. "Two months afterwards I began to wonder, with a very mild kind of surprise, why I had not yet returned to London" (227). Not for Symons and his set (there have been, he says, "relays of friends") the treadmill of leisure, but rather a kind of midsummer madness. "There is a fantastical quality in Dieppe air which somehow turns us all, at our moments, into amiable and enthusiastic lunatics" (227). Prose evokes pose with a characteristically "decadent" use of surplus language, of redundant modifiers, a style in which the individual parts, single sentences and paragraphs, overreach in detail, underplay in tone, the conventions of the travel essay. Symons's key words – "charm," "fascination," "delicious," "enchanting," "pretty," "adorable," "attractive" – may be mild, but they are brazenly repeated. With such devices he sets about turning the map of Dieppe into a

personal menu, rearranging its spatial delights in his own sequen-
tial order, introducing a Dieppe whose social zones have been
marked by his individual patrol. Motifs are kept in suspension,
stretched across whole sections before issuing into silence. At the
same time, almost subliminally, Symons confesses his private
response to Dieppe, admits the true nature of his appreciation,
implies a more subtle side to the town, a sweet frustration
underlying the tourist's jaunt that only he (or his kind) can feel.

The fascination of Dieppe, he insists, is rarefied, appealing to
"the not quite conventional Englishman," the "sensitive and
appreciative Englishman," who sees in the town "nothing and
everything," "something of that 1830 air which exhales for us a
picture of Bonington" (227).[21] On the other side of the channel,
Symons reminds us, is London; at the other end of the railroad,
Paris, where one's "duties" and one's "realisable pleasures" are
respectively to be found. Yet all round Dieppe there is "the
moment's vague immense, I say again, inexplicable, satisfaction,
which broods and dawdles" (228). To the truly "sensitive and
appreciative," who resist blatant consumerism, Dieppe's momen-
tary satisfactions offer themselves as the perfect answer.

Eight sections follow, of roughly equal length, each ending with
an informal comment reasserting Symons's own quizzical position
as a satisfied observer. Section I begins conventionally enough,
with a vista:

At Dieppe the sea is liberal, and affords you a long sweep from the cliffs
on the left to the pier on the right. A few villas nestle under the cliffs;
then comes the Casino, which takes its slice of the *plage* with excellent
judgement. (228)

The approach is that of a landscape painter, who guides the
eye of a spectator across the surface of his picture with a sequence
of particulars that eventually, in a broad perspective, completes
the field. This view is then replaced with another: the sights to be
seen from the terrace of the Casino. Half seascape, half landscape,
it is filled with appropriate figures: "beautiful, well-dressed
women, princes, painters, poets, Cléo de Mérode" (228).[22] At
such luminous moments solid figures appear to dissolve into signs
of organic nature: "...a flow of soft dresses, mostly in sharp, clear

colours, vivid yellows and blues and whites, the most wonderful blues, more dazzling than the sea...delicious hats, floating over the hair like clouds: great floating sleeves, adding wings to the butterfly" (228–29); "bright dresses glitter in the sunlight, like a flower garden" (230), leaving only the merest impression of color and movement. By the sea, it seems, the signifier is free to play.

This induction via pleasure and vivid visual stimuli is deceptive.[23] The act of male gazing that recent critics have rightly stressed in Symons's account[24] was actually built into the bathing experience. And the conventions that held sway on the beach had a great deal to do with the conventions that operated away from it. According to the *Pall Mall Gazette* in 1893, the bathers at Dieppe offered a sight that had no equivalent at any English resort:

The majority of the visitors assemble either on the beach or in the Casino grounds between 10 o'clock and 1 to watch the bathing. There are two establishments – one called the *petits bains*, open to the public; the other, the *grands bains*, reserved for members of the Casino. The two adjoin, but no attempt is made by the patrons of either establishment to mingle with those of the other. Attached to each is a set of cabins set apart for ladies only, but with this exception the baths are open to both sexes. The machine, so familiar a companion at an English seaside town, is unknown at Dieppe. Its place is taken by little tents or cabins arranged in double or treble lines at the summit of the narrow beach. If you want to bathe you hire one of these cabins. The price of a bath varies according to whether you go to the public or the Casino establishment...At the public baths the charges are about a third less than at the Casino, but then you have no pier from which to plunge into the sea, and chairs are not provided for the onlookers. The whole thing is a regular picnic without the eatables, and, as whole parties bathe together, the pastime is most popular. The costumes for men are generally tight combinations striped with red or blue, while those of the ladies are too numerous to name. Many women are neat and strong swimmers, and take their header off the pier with their male friends quite as a matter of course. On Sundays the scene is especially a gay one, for many come down after mass to see their friends in the water, and the scene on the beach reminds one of Sunday parade in the Park, even to the chairs...During the bathing hours the newsboys sell their papers, and the nougat man does a good trade. Beggars, however, are not permitted; and, as the place leads nowhere, there are no passers-by.[25]

5. The Bathing Beach at Dieppe

Anna Gruetzner Robins has observed that in paintings of this
scene "the casual groupings of a summer crowd also reveal
certain tensions between the clothed and semi-clothed women."[26]
In the canvases of Blanche, of Charles Conder, even of Sickert
himself, those tensions are both absorbed and redistributed,
sexual identities lost and found among the bright stripes of
umbrellas, swimsuits, and crested waves. In 1902 Sickert was
commissioned to paint murals for the Hôtel de la Plage:[27] in one
of them the striped suits of the bathers run parallel with the
lateral white bands of the waves, *à la julienne,* as if their bodies
almost meshed with the elements. Similarly Conder painted
Dieppe beach scenes with loose, liquid patches and blotches of
color which united the near-naked bodies with the diaphanous
garments that swirled about them. Helped by anachronism and
by erotic fantasy, Conder's Dieppe paintings escape identification
by scene or subject. This sexual Arcadia is both everywhere and
nowhere.[28]

In Symons's case the attempt to celebrate the body's freedom is
less easily sustained, for the "sentimental sensualist" feels a
prurient duty to record the sporadic ungainliness of the bathers'

which he finds unduly disturbing. There are times when the innocent artifice of beach fashion is threatened by the sight, neither purely artificial nor purely natural, of an all too female bather, in her "wet and dragging garments": "The lines of the grotesque and shapeless image, all in pits and protuberances for which Nature should be ashamed to accept responsibility" (230).

In paradise the grotesque should have no place. Yet flesh even obtrudes upon the sensibilities of Cynthia, the "Sea-side Flirt" of "John Winter's" novel:

A woman may look very smart indeed when she goes in, all black and red, and silk stockings and sham and bows and coquettish airs; but when a woman comes out, a sodden and bedraggled object, with her skin red, her complexion – well, entirely off – her eyes full of salt spray, her headgear entirely disarranged and awry – well it is a risk that Cynthia Willmot never sees the force of running.[29]

Safer perhaps to engage with the indoor thrills of the Casino. The second section of "Dieppe: 1895" closes in on its "many charms" and unique "fascination." The building Symons describes had been built in the mid 1880s and therefore counted as modern. It certainly offered "modern" experiences: a quickened sense of life, enhanced by the installation of electric light in 1894, an innovation that spread out on to the terrace the following year. It was also dreamily exotic, built in an Eastern style, peppermint brick iced with minarets and cupolas, "une mosquée en guise de casino," as Blanche put it.[30] Here on the famous terrace, sipping at milk and soda, Beardsley would indulge his own fantasies of elegance, by studying Denys Guibert's *Mémoirs pour servir à l'histoire de la ville de Dieppe*[31] along with *Mademoiselle de Maupin* and *Les Liaisons dangereuses*, period pieces which suited the surrounding architecture that he and Conder, who was working on lithographs of *La Fille aux yeux d'or*, called "Balzacian."[32] Prompted by Guibert, Beardsley imagined the exotic ballets that would feed into *Under the Hill*, dreamed of lavish pageants that would reenact the town's history.

Authentic "sentimental sensualists" also appear in "Winter's" *A Summer Jaunt*, only lightly disguised: a philosopher, a novelist and, easiest to identify, a "youthful artist, whose principal fancy is three-cornered ladies, hideous specimens, something between modern Japanese art and the early English nursery period." To the female narrator, who views them very much from the outside, they were "all faultlessly dressed, all wore fresh and exquisite buttonholes, and all seemed profoundly dissatisfied with themselves and the company that they were in." It is in the Casino that Cynthia, the "Sea-side Flirt," meets a man who "often ran over to Dieppe from Friday night to Monday morning," and who looks for a moment like her downfall, Vivian Dermott, an Irish wit, a kind of heterosexual Wilde. Cynthia describes him as "a dangerous person to know. He plays with fire, and he never gets burned himself." Dermott is much given to epigram ("the difference between women and men: women like what borders on the forbidden, men like best what goes well beyond"), and, very like Wilde, is obsessed with names: "Robert, John, Henry, Richard and Augustus – they are all fatal names...I would give every boy of mine a name to live up to." With his white suit, white homburg, and scarlet tie, Dermott is "a synonym for the frivolity of life" – though in the end it is he who rescues Cynthia from a far more dangerous entanglement with a Russian prince. Dermott is Cynthia's "admirer in a a purely artistic sense," which may be Winter's delicate tribute to the sexuality of the man she had in mind.

The Casino is the haunt of every kind of elegance, including "the most famous professional beauties of Paris," but gambling rules over all, and even Symons admits to temptation, stops lounging, opts for the deeper sensation: "I felt what I think must have been the intoxication of abandoning oneself to Fate, with an astonishing sense of superiority over ordinary mortals, from whom I was almost more absolutely removed than if I had been moving in a hashisch dream" (233), he confesses. "The universal humanity of the gambling instinct" (234) ensured that "there was no really disillusioning shock, either when I lost or when I won," and that he "played for the sake of playing" (233). In the end the feeling of personal superiority offered by gambling still holds no real possibilities for the "sensitive and appreciative man."

At the Casino time is fated, prophetic, sorting the risk-taking sheep from the observing goats. Gambling is a challenge to the values of hard work and just reward, performed within the portals of capitalist investment and display. Here an aesthete might glimpse the driven man, a figure with whom he shared a certain amount, but with whom he could never finally identify. The point is made in a later story by Max Beerbohm, "James Pethel,"[33] in which the poised narrator, a professional writer, a version of Max himself, unexpectedly finds himself caught up in the destructive aura of a Dieppe gambler. A psychological contest grows up between them culminating in a manic automobile ride to Rouen, designed to test the narrator's nerve – which survives. In witnessing the gambler's self-determined battle against fate, the dandy–narrator comes to understand more fully his own rather different need to live on his own terms.

At the Casino distanced appreciation was always under threat. According to Symons, even the croupiers sat "with folded hands and intent eyes, impassive, supercilious, like little Eastern gods, raking in the money without satisfaction, and tossing you your winnings with an air of disdain" (234). If he allowed too many to win, a croupier would find himself dismissed. To underline that point, that real danger, Symons ends his second section with a jolting present tense: "And here is the most imposing of all the croupiers offering himself and his wife, as servants, to a lady who played there" (234).

The Casino offered other worldly sights. In Section III Symons records the "Bal des Enfants," in which over-dressed children, with "their fans, their sashes, their gloves" (234), mimic adults in the vigor of their dance as they "turn, turn, stop short, stamp their heels, and turn again" (236). The sexual marginality of the pubescent (obliquely registered in Symons's final comparison with their elder sisters: "how little they invite the wandering of even the vaguest emotion!" [236]) could help explain the inspiration behind the otherwise mysterious figures in Beardsley's *The Bathers*, published in the first number of the *Savoy*, who stand on the shingle in inappropriate costumes, half modern, half Renaissance, joining, once again, artifice with simplicity, innocence with experience.

The fourth section of "Dieppe: 1895" is about the church of St. Jacques, which dates from the thirteenth century. Symons,

6. The Dieppe Casino at the turn of the century

who in 1895 was staying along with Conder in a hotel in the Rue de l'Oranger nearby, sees at first only "an adorable old church" and "a somewhat flamboyant Gothic" (236), and couples his sense of the sublime – one "feels its immensity as one feels the immensity of the sea" (237) – first with an unexpected sense of "intimacy," finally with another disrupting glimpse of the grotesque: "the patron saint of fishermen, who leans upon his staff, is a sensual Jewish person with fleshy lips and a smile which is somewhat sneering in the arch of the doorway" (237), finally with a vision of transcendence.

In 1902 Camille Pissarro was to stay at the nearby Hôtel de Commerce, where he painted from an upper room a shimmering sequence showing the church in a number of natural lights. Sickert, too, painted St. Jacques again and again, often from the vantage point of a side-alley. For Impressionist artists St. Jacques meant time lost, evidence of an elapse so slow that it could be represented only by the hourly changes of color and light. Whereas the painters realized that the incalculable exchange of perception and effect could be rendered only in a series, Symons found in its blackened textures grounds for a Symbolist trance. "The Eternal Church," he writes, "rises out of the agitations and feverish coming-and-going of the world" (238). The contrast with painting goes further. For Sickert St. Jacques was a touchstone, but a paradoxical one. Gazing up at its immensity he once insisted, with deliberate perversity, that it hardly mattered to a painter where he was since he was always "obliged to go on painting."[34] That is a true Sickertism, aimed at the conventional pieties, designed to embody the larger truth that a painting comes from the painter not just from his subject, that even St. Jacques had to be worked upon: the creed of a practicing artist rather than a dreamy tourist.

Close by St. Jacques, in its dark shadow, there was held, every August, a small traveling fair. Symons records its visit in horror, recoils at the memory of this "oppression," this "nightmare" (237) of repetition and circularity, seeing in the transgressive carnival of its shows a threat to his own meditative mood. Somewhat uncharacteristically (elsewhere he is adulatory about gypsies and entertainers), he dismisses the fair people as "motley": "a crowd of insects, throwing up their little mounds in the earth" (238), a *mélange* of petty pleasures. Beerbohm, though, ever the wise child, claimed to prefer the rejuvenating horses of the merry-go-round to the more demandingly adult "petits chevaux" at the Casino.[35]

In Section V Symons turns to the street-market which filled (and still fills) the Place Nationale every week of the year, from the sacred and monolithic church to commodities and hetero-geneity: the world of the "bargain," of the "collection," and "assemblage." Clothes, last described on the beach as "a flower garden," reappear here as "cheap trousers, flannel shirts, heavy boots and carpet shoes, braces, foulards, handkerchiefs, stays, bright ribbons, veils, balls of worsted, shoe-laces, and, above all, dress-pieces of every sort of common and trumpery pattern" (238–39).

On the pavement aesthetics receive the cold shock of eco-nomics, the pleasures of appreciation momentarily crushed by necessity. Even the vegetables are "splashes of somewhat tawdry green" (238) – though the distaste lightens later to "the fruit all in pale yellows, with the vivid red of tomatoes: the flowers mainly white and red" (239). Not for Symons the pleasure that, according to Blanche, Jean Renoir had found in the Saturday market when, riding off home in a cart, he would "disappear amongst melons, the claws of lobsters, and choice fish, smoking his pipe and joyfully rubbing his nose."[36] For Symons all is mixed, and muddle is everywhere: the crowd is made up of dichotomous elements: "slow, staring country-people, the blither natives of the town, the indifferent visitors, and now and again a little lounging line of sailors or fishermen" (239–40). Even so, there are hidden corners, unsolved mysteries: "Beyond, where the Rue St. Cathérine narrows...Few people pass. I have never actually seen anything bought, though I would not take upon myself to say that it never happens" (240).

If the market is visceral, and repellent, spilling out to the streets, shops are internalized, and tempting. Symons's favorite shop, the subject of Section VI, is a bric-à-brac emporium in the Rue de la Barre presented as a "garden of antiquities," a ruined garden, naturally, with its creepers, dust, its romantic age. This shop has to be penetrated, in stages: "you look in...you go in a little way...you go in a little farther" (241). Once again a hint of danger: amongst the junk, "two battered wooden representations of the flames of hell (as I imagine), the red paint much worn from their artichoke-like shoots" (242). The effect is "rigmarole," an unexpected word which has its origins in formal rhetoric, but a precise one, because the discourse of these antiquities is mere succession without connection: the bad rhetoric of commerce. Symons's choice of shop belies the effort to maintain his own stylistic poise.

Dieppe was famous for its range of shops: from the "foreign import" place that Blanche remembered as a boy ("all kinds of chinese albums made out of rice paper, elephant's tusks, pieces of madrepore, trees of coral"),[37] to the Casino bazaar with its "Russian bowls, job-lots of Algerian trinkets, Chinese bric-a-brac and Japanese lanterns."[38] These outlets were the result of Dieppe the sea-port. The gentlemen's outfitters, "Old England," which to Reggie Turner's "Imperial Brown" recalls "with painful distinctness the Brixton Emporium,"[39] and the high fashion boutiques, patronized by the likes of the "Sea-side Flirt" who spends her days looking "into every shop window of the Grande Rue, including the boot-maker, and Léon's, where the wonderful wigs are":[40] these were the result of its growing status as a resort.

But for the serious consumer all shops retail the fashionably pictorial. Symons, anxious to sidestep the conventional, writes of the junk shop that with "its absurd and delightful romanticism... made up a picture which hardly needed to be painted, it was so obviously a picture already" (242).

When Symons turns, in Section VII, to Dieppe's pincer-shaped harbor, he begins with its most obviously romantic feature, the eighteenth-century Arcades that face the water. The Arcades, he says, are both "characteristic" and "unfashionable" (242). A single zeugmatic sentence makes the essential point about them: here "waiters and women stroll up and down continually, touting for customers" (243). That giveaway is fittingly framed by references to the two *Calvaires* that mark the entrance to the harbour and to the "green hill" of Le Pollet opposite.

At right angles to the Arcades are the *boîtes* and *cafés-chantants* of the Quai Henri IV. Symons mentions one particularly rough and tough drinking den, M. Jean's. This is surely the Dieppe of Wilde's brothel trip, famously recounted by Yeats in *Autobiographies* with a carefully timed double joke: first a bawdy aside (the experience has beeen like "cold mutton"), a pause, then the parting shot ("But tell it in England for it will entirely restore my character".)[41] As Ian Fletcher once observed of Yeats's narration, "It is thoroughly dramatic: Wilde disappearing with an exit-line that is both pathetic and funny."[42] But then, along the *quai*, sex was, more often than not, a branch of show business. Sickert's well-known etching, *Quai Henri IV*, evokes the whole *quartier* with a scrawny *chanteuse*, girlish but too thin, all expressive, beseeching arms.

To the north, on the other side of the harbor altogether, lay Le Pollet, the ancient fishermen's quarter. Symons says little about it, except that here "one sees women making nets, once an industry, now fallen into some disuse" (244) and, in a typical aside, pregnant with insider knowledge, that it was this *quartier* that Dowson loved "more than any part of Dieppe" (244). What that might imply we are left to imagine, though in his memoir of Dowson, published in 1900, Symons was to be more categoric. "At Dieppe," he wrote, Dowson "discovered strange, squalid haunts about the harbour, where he made friends with amazing innkeepers, and got into rows with the fishermen who came in to

7. Walter Sickert, *Quai Henri IV*

drink after midnight."[43] The facts, such as they are, contradict
this portrait of a conventional *maudit*, since Dowson is known to
have stayed in 1895 first at the respectable Hotel Sandwich,[44] and
soon to have left for the quiet inland town of Arques, fleeing his
too boisterous compatriots to get down to serious work, a truth
disappointingly plain for Symons, self-designated chronicler of
the *fin de siècle*.

8. "Le Pollet," Dieppe

VIII returns us to "The charm of Dieppe!" (244), to the theme of time, to the sea, and to the seedier side of the summer season, hinted at by Symons, both in this essay and in poems which chart the dark edges of twilight sexuality. With titles like "Remembrance" and "The Wanderers," these Dieppe poems are prematurely autumnal, colors "wither" or "fade," and the speaker is usually alone on the shingles at evening. The verse matches the limited tones of a painting like Whistler's *The Shore, Pourville* (1899), where sea and sky are joined by a band of absinthe green that could belong to either.[45]

That same mood recurs in prose. Close to the "placid" and "indulgent" tides, time itself becomes sensual – Dieppe "lets you have your way with it" – and meditative: "I have spent all night wandering about the beach" (245). Correspondingly, Symons's descriptive antitheses become more daring: "warm and cool," the "liquid coldness of stone arches." The panorama is restored via the Rue Aguado, "modern and fashionable," the Casino, colors, daylight, and the narrative moves out among individuals and friends "made, or found, or fancied" (246). Some, like Conder, are named, some anonymous but unmistakable, like Beardsley: "all that feverish brilliance, the boyish defiance of things, the frail and intense vitality" (247). The town's hinterland is now briefly acknowledged: the surrounding villages with their distinguished residents.

Symons's essay on the town of Dieppe in the year 1895 will end not with places, but with people, with "beautiful faces," with "people one never knew, and yet, meeting them at every hour, at dinner, on the terrace of the Casino, at the tables, in the sea, one seemed to know them almost better than one's friends, and to be known by them just as well" (247).

Even in the nineties Dieppe was the scene of unlikely, unlooked-for meetings, as it always had been. It was on the streets of Dieppe in 1885 that Sickert had first met Gauguin, "a sturdy man with a black moustache and a bowler," and told him that he would be imprudent to give up "his good berth in some administration" in order to become a painter.[46] A rather stagey pastel by Degas from 1887 shows Sickert, Ludovic Halévy, Blanche, and others all arranged in an awkward group.[47] Blanche was to say of the market: "On a Saturday I saw the same people I had encountered so often around Dieppe, exchanging furtive looks without ever being tempted to take relations any further."[48] Even in "Winter's" *A Summer Jaunt*, Dieppe is "a little place where everybody meets everybody else, morning, noon, and night. It is a place where it is not the least use trying to be exclusive, or stuck-up, or anything of that kind";[49] while on one of her shopping trips the "Sea-side Flirt" meets "every woman I knew, and a lot of women who knew me and whom I didn't know."[50]

Symons adds complication to contingency by hinting not just at confrontations between acquaintances but, much more excitingly, at inexplicable rendezvous with persons unknown. "Much of the charm of life," he confesses, "exists for me in the unspoken interest which forms a sort of electric current between onself and strangers" (257). The professional outsider, the privileged member of "our little society," has begun to unbend. The principle of separation with which he opened has shifted its reference, or rather has disclosed its depths. Neither entirely reconciled with others, nor entirely at peace with himself, this "sensitive and appreciative Englishman" is full of a metaphysical yearning prompted by the incompletenesss of social exchange. "The moment's vague immense...inexplicable satisfaction which broods and dawdles around Dieppe" has modified to this "real emotion to me, satisfying, in a sense, for the very reason that it leaves me unsatisfied" (247–48).

Not so much carnival then as pastoral: the Dieppe holiday is finally revealed to be as contaminated by its origins as was its classical prototype, its moods to belong with the tradition of pastoral ideas as William Empson understood them, ideas which "assume that it is sometimes a good thing to stand apart from your society so far as you can...assume that some people are more delicate and complex than others, and that if such people can keep this distinction from doing harm it is a good thing, though a small thing by comparison with our common humanity."[51]

At Dieppe, in 1895, Arthur Symons, the aesthetic holiday-maker, delicate and complex, met his doubles, his alter egos: French artists and English tourists, performers from the *demi-*

monde and neighbors from the *bourgeoisie,* all that common humanity. His sinuous and insinuating essay reenacts the delayed shock of those inevitable moments of recognition.

RETURN VISITS

RICHARD: Have you ever been abroad at all?
JACKIE: Oh, yes: I went to Dieppe once...

Noel Coward, *Hay Fever*[52]

KATH: That vase over there came from Bombay. Do you have any interest in that part of the world?
SLOANE: I like Dieppe.

Joe Orton, *Entertaining Mr. Sloane*[53]

Here, on this other coast, the motifs multiply.

Carol Ann Duffy, "Poem in Oils"[54]

Oscar Wilde was hardly new to Dieppe when he stepped down from the nightboat *La Tamise* at 4:30 A.M. on 20 May 1897, carrying the manuscript of *De Profundis,* to be greeted by Robert Ross and Reggie Turner. But even Wilde was, in some ways, behaving like any other tourist: hoping to find freedom in France. Indeed, for a time he was able to wander freely, to come in from Berneval, the nearby village where he had taken a house, to mix (when they would have him)[55] with Beardsley, with Conder, as well as with the stalwarts Reggie Turner and Robert Ross, free to take up position at his favourite Café Suisse, which looked directly on to the *quai.* Though not Wilde's first choice, Dieppe was a brave and optimistic place to go, part joke, part confrontation. In Dieppe, a town he had first visited in 1879, where he had spent a week of his honeymoon in 1884, he could look the English in the face again; though they, as it turned out, were not always prepared to look back. The Dieppe venture soon turned sour, the holiday place began to look remarkably like home, and the family, whether English or French, closed ranks. Family holidays are, after all, only a further contradiction in terms. By September Wilde had departed the area for good.

Beerbohm, and his friends Turner, William Nicholson, and

William Rothenstein, continued to visit Dieppe well into the twentieth century, though with a creeping sense of the distance of the past. "In Dieppe everything depends on the weather: if rain, Hell; if sun, Heaven," Beerbohm decided in 1904.[56] And later that same summer he wrote to Turner complaining: "I really did feel as if the place belonged to me, so long as my 'set' was here: *now* I am a pariah – uniform with the man who was turned out of the diplomatic service."[57]

By the end of first decade of the new century Dieppe had become an outpost of Camden Town, the art produced there self-consciously Post-Impressionist, less sensitive to the nuance of place: Harold Gilman and Charles Ginner painted the town in hot, Fauvish tones. Later, though, in the 1930s, English Neo-Cubism would discover a cool white *gesso* style exactly right for a mood now more ludic than theatrical. Ben Nicholson's *Au Chat Botté* offers a shop window on three planes: a display shelf inside; the window itself, marked by a painted inscription; the vague reflection of someone (no doubt Barbara Hepworth), peering in. At the same time, these planes are disrupted by the outline of a central jug, seemingly on the shelf, yet overlapping with its lip a word on the window. Two Dieppe paintings from 1932, *Bocque* and *Auberge de la sole Dieppoise*,[58] make use of similarly deconstructive techniques. The interrupted word on the window of *Au Chat Botté* is DIEPPE itself. Elsewhere AUBERGE is cut to AUBE. Nicholson's broken lettering suggests fragmented memories of childhood holidays spent in the town with his father William, friend of Sickert and Blanche, whose own paintings had been conventionally Impressionist in their use of light to reveal architectural values.[59]

As war approached the holiday mood again darkened. In 1937 Samuel Beckett took *fin-de-siècle* gloom and rendered it nearly terminal. His "Dieppe"[60] is a redaction of Symons's seaside impressionism to a mere four lines, seventeen spartan words:

> again the last ebb
> the dead shingle
> the turning then the steps
> towards the lights of old

Minimal but meaningful: although Beckett rejects the sea's temptation "again," and "then" turns back towards the town, the placing of the adverbs suggests that the movement of the body is as detached from volition as the movement of the sea, relentlessly re-recurring, as empty of significance as the pull on the "dead shingle" of the beach. Repetition as death in life is the true rhythm of Beckett's channel tide. It is fitting then that it should have been in Dieppe in September 1939 that the painter Gwen John, fleeing the Nazis, heading for the Newhaven boat, should have collapsed and died.

After the war the painters started to come back and they continue to do so. None has been so creatively conscious of Dieppe's past as Nicholas Horsfield. In her wonderfully empathic "Poem in Oils," written in 1984, Carol Ann Duffy has Horsfield confess: "What I have learnt I have learnt from the air, from infinite varieties of light."[61]

From the painters too. Born in 1917, trained at the Royal College of Art, even as a student Horsfield knew of Sickert's association with Dieppe, though he didn't begin visiting the town himself until the 1950s.[62] Conscious that it has always been a place of artistic engagement (he particularly enjoys recalling the story of Sickert's recommendation that Gauguin return to the bank) Horsfield has often painted the harbor alongside which so many auspicious meetings took place. Aware that the two most obvious vistas of Dieppe (the Arcades and the hotels along the Promenade) both face north, offering a challenge that Sickert resolved by working late in the day when the fading light lay obliquely across the buildings, he has chosen to paint the *falaises* of Le Pollet in bright sun, as they can be seen from the Quai Henri IV. In a liquid play of planes the sea fills with sky, the cliffs catch its jewels and those famously opaline clouds tremor with violet and purple. The power of Dieppe's past still dares the artist to be different.

CHAPTER 7

Wilde interpretations

We live in an age of interpretation, a fact that is constantly mentioned in the theatrical journals. Some think that it has always been this way, that there never has been representation without mediation; others, like the director Jonathan Miller, believe that the power of interpretation is a recent phenomenon with complex origins. "Historical change has accelerated so much in the last fifty years that the differences between 'now' and even a quite recent 'then' are much more noticeable," says Miller, "the bequests of the past arouse our interpretative energies as never before." "Besides," he goes on, "the life of the mind has now taken a distinctively 'interpretative turn,' and with the development of self-consciously hermeneutic interests the problem of meaning assumes a paramount importance."[1]

Hence, among many other things, the ascent of the theater director, the individual who gives meaning to texts. But Miller also believes that acts of theatrical interpretation must, if they are to be valid, respond to elements already in the work, inherent in the initial choice of genre, and that all interpretations, if only to that extent, are still part of the author's "intention."

From these theoretical principles it would follow that any account of recent productions of Oscar Wilde ought not only to identify trends currently in operation, but, in the course of analysis, to reveal meanings that were already present, though sometimes hidden or unacknowledged, within the texts themselves.

It is certainly true that since the early 1980s (since, say, Peter Hall's National Theatre *Importance of Being Earnest* in 1982), full-scale professional productions in London have shared a number of characteristics. An extreme adventurousness in design and costume, more lavish even than the efforts of Cecil Beaton in the 1940s, has tried to match Wilde's linguistic extravagance with visual images, with sets that expand far beyond the backcloths and box-sets with which the author himself was most familiar.[2] There have also been constant attempts to make theatrical capital out of biographical connections between the work and its author. And there has been consistent engagement with the mixed modes of the play-texts: attempts to make the best, if not the most, of the strong elements of melodrama they undoubtedly contain.

This last probably represents the greatest investment of directorial energy. Whereas the Wildean epigram invites an impassive delivery that distances speakers from the world they are commenting upon, in the simplified moral universe of melodrama important statements must be expressed in a highly emotional and pictorial manner that signifies sincerity. The mixed modes may seem contradictory, they demand our undivided attention. In today's theater, the contrasts are more than just stylistic: they seem to reflect issues of social and sexual ethics at the very heart of Wilde's plays.

What follows is an experiment in two parts, inspired by the ideas of Jonathan Miller. The first part takes as its primary material the reviews of four major London productions, sifted and sorted according to my own memories and impressions. The plays are taken in the order of their composition. The second part considers what this survey might tell us about the theater of a century ago. Backtracking from "now" we head for "then."

1990s

"Lady Windermere's Fan"

In the summer of 1994 a production of *Lady Windermere's Fan*, Wilde's first successful society drama, originally staged by George Alexander at the St. James's Theatre in 1892, arrived at the Albery Theatre in London after an extensive tour of the regions. Directed and designed by Philip Prowse, best known for his work at the Glasgow Citizens' Theatre (where he had first staged *Lady Windermere* in 1988),[3] the new production had originated at the

Birmingham Repertory Theatre in April. The London reception reflected widespread expectations.

Prowse is celebrated for the extraordinary opulence of his designs, so lavish that even describing them becomes a challenge to critical ingenuity. According to Benedict Nightingale of *The Times*, the set for the first, second, and fourth acts (which Prowse made the first and third parts of the evening), a room in the Windermeres' house, gave him "the opportunity to indulge his Kubla Khan complex by constructing bits of Mayfair Xanadu: a great gilded rotunda, with sky painted above the columns and the filigree" (27 July 1994). Robert Cushman of the *Independent on Sunday* thought it "a domestic cathedral...a great semi-circle in sky-blues and salmon-pinks, stretching up to embrace an invisible dome and an extremely visible chandelier" (31 July 1994). For Clive Hirschhorn of the *Sunday Express* it was "like the waiting room of a chic Parisienne boutique" (31 July 1994), while David Murray (*Financial Times*, 27 July 1994) thought it "a huge boudoir ...artfully off-centre and festooned in deeply unlikely hues for Victorian times."

Prowse's notion of Lord Darlington's rooms, in which the second part of his production took place, was in strict contrast, seen either as "black-and-gold chinoiserie and plush red velvets in the pleasure dome" (*The Times*, 27 July 1994), or as "butch gilt, red plush and Chinese lacquer in the bachelor pad" (Nick Curtis, *Evening Standard*, 26 July 1994).

Inevitably all this material extravagance created practical difficulties, not least for the audience, since two long intervals were required in which to strike and rebuild the huge sets. For the actors the problem was how to survive such palatial surroundings. "A camp, inhuman monumentality about the décor that threatens to turn the poor actors into mannequins," wrote Paul Taylor of the *Independent* (27 July 1994). The point was widely shared. Prowse's love of surface seemed to leave his actors with the narrowest of choices: mannequin or monster. "As a designer, Philip Prowse has created all the frocks and furniture the Harrods school of theatre-going might wish for," pronounced Robert Hewison of the *Sunday Times* (31 July 1994); "as director, he has allowed the cast to be scarcely less wooden and padded than the stuff they are sitting on." Nick Curtis was only slightly more generous: "As a director, he's been called a choreographer who merely manoeuvres actors round his glossy set. He's much more than that, but you wouldn't know it from the first act."

In the case of Francesca Annis's Mrs. Erlynne, the choice came down to puppet or pin-up. One comparison ruled above all others: "a bargain-basement Joan Collins" (Charles Spencer, *Daily Telegraph*, 27 July 1994); "the full Joan Collins treatment" (*Financial Times*); "within a safe Joan Collins range" (*Independent*). Admiration for this central performance hinged upon the degree to which the critic thought that the star had negotiated the basic conflict between the character's social assurance and the maternal feelings she couldn't afford to show. Taylor found this "wonderfully moving." Murray thought that Annis managed "some nice feelings in her anguished private confessions" but that overall she was "a perfect and fearsome representation of "an *édition de luxe* of a wicked French novel. Alas this *édition de luxe* is never really opened" (27 July 1994).

Several critics remarked upon Wilde's own involvement in the play. Charles Spencer proposed the idea that although Prowse's production may have failed because of the lack of "real feeling" in the acting, creating that absence may, in fact, have been part of his intention:

The play can be viewed as an attack on the rigid decorum, vicious gossip and heartless morality of high society. Wilde himself must often have had premonitions of his own expulsion from this charmed but charmless circle, and there are moments of real tenderness in his portrait of Lady Windermere, the oh-so-conventional heroine who learns compassion from her own averted encounter with social disgrace.

Wilde's presence was rather less subtly represented by David Foxxe's Cecil Graham: "a fat frog-faced dandy with a green carnation...He might be Wilde; and he conveys, as does the whole play, the sense of relishing and fearing his society simultaneously" (*Independent on Sunday*); "a middle-aged toad" (John Gross, *Sunday Telegraph*, 31 July 1994); "a poisonously entertaining old queen" (*Daily Telegraph*); "a pastiche Wilde auditioning for entry to Reading Gaol...complete with powdered looks, mincing voice, a green carnation and a tendency to fiddle with pretty boys' knees" (*The Times*); "looking like something you might have got if Beardsley had illustrated *Wind in the Willows*" (*Independent*). Michael Coveney suggested that Foxxe's Graham and Tristram Wymark's Dumby "approximate to Oscar and Bosie themselves" (*Observer*, 24 April 1994).

These were somewhat predictable responses to a predictable idea. One of Prowse's more radical innovations, less widely remarked upon, was to cut the soliloquies and asides. This had the effect of returning the play to something like Wilde's original intention, before George Alexander persuaded him otherwise, of keeping the relationship between Mrs. Erlynne and her daughter obscure for as long as possible.[4] Nevertheless Taylor, for one, found a leadenness about the production that "holding back the disclosure of Lady Windermere's relation to Mrs. Erlynne until the final act does nothing to ease." Coveney's insistence that "Wilde's main point, that women are as entitled to their emotional and sexual secrets as are men, is perfectly well made and still worth making" put him in the minority. David Murray was more typical:

If we relish Oscar's wit in the marginal chat, we cannot take Lord and Lady Windermere's lofty protestations about marriage very seriously; but if we cannot do that, the very hinges of the plot become quaint and ludicrous.

For Wilde's modern admirers, the concluding judgment of Charles Spencer was, if anything, even more wounding:

There are moments when one hopes that Wilde was sending up the theatrical conventions of his day. But he wasn't. *Lady Windermere's Fan* was Wilde's first West End success, and he was delighted with it. Its melodrama and its sentimentality were written with serious intent, as if Wilde genuinely believed in the importance of being earnest. (*Daily Telegraph*, 27 July 1994)

"A Woman of No Importance"

Prowse's production of Wilde's second society drama, *A Woman of No Importance*, first performed at the Haymarket in 1893, was seen at the Glasgow Citizens' Theatre in 1984, revived at the Royal

Shakespeare Company's Barbican home in October 1991. It offered another superbly high-handed solution to some basic problems. Prowse collapsed the play's four acts into three, and then demanded two twenty-minute intervals to allow for elaborate changes of the sets he had, as usual, designed himself. His production was unashamedly operatic in its scale, full of color, imported incident, and meta-theatrical devices. By keeping his actors always on the move, even in quite crowded scenes, by relying on formalized blocking, close to choreography, and a rhetorical delivery that often addressed lines directly at the audience, he overcame any risk of dramatic stasis.

With typical boldness Prowse opened his production with an addition to the text: the ominous appearance, before the lights were fully up, of a golden youth lazily, pointlessly, miming a game of croquet. (In appearance obviously reminiscent of Lord Alfred Douglas, this eventually turned out to be the excessively minor character Lord Alfred Rufford.) The critics responded with open-mouthed awe: "a staggering haven of gilded urns and a circular pond of daffodils, narcissi and bamboo reeds" (Michael Coveney, *Observer*, 6 October 1991); "breathtakingly ornate: a park, backing onto a gigantic gilt-framed Claude landscape, where everything from the masonry to the vegetation has changed to gold. Nature is painted out" (Irving Wardle, *Independent on Sunday*, 6 October 1991).

The nagging question was whether Prowse's fascination with seductive artifice could coexist with what appeared to be, in general, a toughly critical attitude to the play's characters. "Prowse invests the melodramatic revelations about Gerald's parentage and the caddishness of Lord Illingworth...with a reality and weight they may not have. But he thus releases the rhythms and vicious satire of the piece in a way no one else has ever imagined," was Coveney's verdict. Wardle shrugged his shoulders: "The main plot is irreclaimable; partly for the obvious reason of its sentimental contrivance (as Hugh Leonard said, it makes one 'long for the coruscating saltiness of *East Lynne*'); but also because everyone in it can get up and go. The moralising American, the 'fallen' woman and her bank-clerk son, all have a life elsewhere." "Melodrama all the way," judged John Gross

(*Sunday Telegraph*, 6 October 1991), though Prowse's production got away with it, "partly because he takes it seriously, with no suggestions of unease. As soon as it's over, you realise that it is the stilted period piece that you always thought it was; but it is oddly moving while it lasts."

Listen for Oscar Wilde in *A Woman of No Importance* and you are first of all likely to hear him in Lord Illingworth: "the vile seducer and Wildean philosopher," played with "the smirking poise of a replete crocodile" (Wardle). Animal images crept into several critical minds: "sleekly dangerous lounge-lizard" (Michael Billington, *Guardian*, 5 October 1991), "cold and hawklike, obnoxiously sophisticated and majestically corrupt" (John Peter, *Sunday Times*, 6 October 1991). For the *Times Literary Supplement* it became "unpleasant to hear him exercise his wit, rolling out his decadent paradoxes about life, or trying to win over a good woman with wry, elegant seductiveness" (Lindsay Duguid, 11 October 1991). Benedict Nightingale (*The Times*, 3 October 1991) found Carlisle's performance historically suggestive none the less:

He does, after all, espouse Wilde's own aestheticism. His professed philosophy is all about the virtues of insincerity, inconstancy, and well-tied neckties. His author called him "a figure of art. Indeed, if you can bear the truth, he is MYSELF", and yet made him the villain.

Is Lord Goring Wilde's attempt to impose himself on his public or an instance of genuine self-criticism? Michael Billington, for one, thought he knew the extent of Wilde's involvement with the character. Admitting that *A Woman* might look like a "proto-feminist play" Billington finally decided that "it doesn't play like that":

Wilde clearly poured his talent, if not his genius, into the aphoristic aristo modelled on *Dorian Gray*'s Lord Henry Wotton: the wronged woman on the other hand is a real pain in the Arbuthnot, ready to sacrifice her son's future to her stored-up revenge.

Lindsay Duguid spotted autobiographical connections as well:

The scene in which a virtuous woman tries to prevent her only son from being led astray by the man who ruined her, may echo scenes with Speranza or Constance Wilde. It is also a strange precursor to the letter which Wilde wrote to Lady Queensberry in November 1893 (seven months after the first performance of *A Woman of No Importance*), begging her to keep Bosie away from the dangers of society.

And Charles Spencer (*Daily Telegraph*, 4 October 1991) agreed: "In the fate of Mrs. Arbuthnot, whose whole life has been wrecked by a sexual indiscretion, it is impossible not to be reminded of Wilde's own tragic last years."

If Lord Illingworth isn't exactly the Wilde we hope for, then perhaps his voice sounds more convincing when it issues from a female body – from Mrs. Arbuthnot, for example, or from one of the play's several other important women. Like most of Wilde's plays this has quite a range of female characters. Gross distinguished distinctive notes in a well-balanced chorus – "the acidulous Mrs. Allonby (Nichola McAuliffe), the dragonish Lady Caroline (Cherry Morris), the empty-headed Lady Stutfield (Mary Chater)" – and enjoyed "the flutterings of the seemingly soft and scatterbrained but ultimately invulnerable Lady Hunstanton," a character Spencer found to be "charmingly forgetful, terrifying complacent and with a delivery that makes even commonplace lines irresistible."

Cataloging the varieties of female in a Wilde play can easily develop into a critical sport, played mainly by men. Billington had "the pearl-chokered Lady Hunstanton" and "the eternally vigilant Lady Pontefract who views her husband as a piece of permananently lost property." For Coveney, the women ranged from "the wronged Mrs. Arbuthnot (Carol Royle) as a pinched and vengefully pained salon outcast" and "Barbara Leigh Hunt's blinkingly impervious Lady Hunstanton" to Nichola McAuliffe's "splendidly butch and world-weary Mrs. Allonby" and Cherry Morris's "dragon-like Lady Caroline." Then there was Prowse's masterstroke, "the casting of a black actress, the admirable Julie Saunders, as the American woman of the future who witnesses the last exhalations of these social dinosaurs while assisting on the melodrama's poignant resolution."

Wardle began with Mrs. Allonby: "the boldest of them (Nichola McAuliffe in quasi-hunting kit, one hand permanently on her hip)...a Mme. de Montreuil to his [Lord Illingworth's]

9. Hester (Julie Saunders), Mrs. Arbuthnot (Carol Royle), and Gerald (Andrew
Havill) in the final act of Philip Prowse's 1991 production of
A Woman of No Importance

Valmont" and went on to "the hatchet-faced Lady Caroline
(Cherry Morris) whose one aim is to keep her husband away from
the youngest of the ladies; and whose distracted panic when he
finally escapes her clutches would do justice to a Racine heroine."
The list ended with Lady Hunstanton (Barbara Leigh Hunt),
"best of all...as the ineffably complaisant hostess, who excuses a
beating husband – 'it runs in the family' – as though he suffered
from asthma, and underscores her most mindless comments with
deliciously ironic ambiguity."

Finally Wardle judged this to be a woman's play not just
because it pleads equal sexual justice, but because the women's
"chatter" is its most dramatic element. For Lindsay Duguid too it
was the staging of the all-female set-pieces, the introductory scene
in particular, which showed Prowse's directorial skills at their
most incisive. These witty women are "practiced": their riddles
and paradoxes may be funny, but they are old-fashioned, con-
cealing an inner panic. "They say the first thing that comes into

their heads because they are very anxious to hold on to their position and their men."

"An Ideal Husband"

Philip Prowse directed the play in Glasgow in 1986 and it has been revived quite frequently in recent years, though never to the kind of full-scale critical attention accorded Peter Hall's production at the Globe in 1992.

Again the sets, though less strikingly so than those designed by Prowse, set up a strongly meaningful mood. But this time the emphasis was on solidly material matters. Carl Toms's gilded interiors were fronted by a huge Victorian golden sovereign displaying the profile of the monarch. Correspondingly Hall tended to deploy costumes as evidence of conspicuous wealth rather than as symbols of moral worth. Careful to keep all his effects both stylized and serious, he modified the clumsy melodrama of the eavesdropping scene by substituting an opening door for the notorious falling chair, yet ended each act with an emotional tableau in an authentically Victorian way.

In a newspaper article published on the morning of the London opening Peter Hall set out his basic principles:

All Wilde's characters are extravagantly emotional and are quite naturally eccentric. But they do not show their feelings or release their emotions; that would be un-English. They utter witticisms instead. The more emotional they become, the more extravagant the wit. It is a type of English stiff upper lip; and it informs all Wilde's theatre. Beneath the wit there is always an intense emotional reality. The actor must investigate it, know it, and create it every night. Then he must mask it completely with the wit. (*Guardian*, 11 November 1992)

Hall went on to identify areas of interest that would soon be taken up by his critics: the play's relevance to contemporary politics and to scandal-mongering journalism, its concern with a feminism based on femininity, its ultimately compassionate vision, and its autobiographical element. According to its director all this came from the play's personal origins, but resulted in a universal vision nevertheless, since Wilde was bisexual and "we are just beginning to come to accept that vast numbers of people are bisexual."

The critics seemed satisfied enough. Even Billington (*Guardian*, 13 November 1992) saw the play as a comprehensive attack on Victorian values: "the false idealisation of men by women, the worship of wealth, the gap between public morality and private behaviour." Few could resist extending the list in time to include the difficulties experienced by British cabinet ministers in 1992 (the Matrix Churchill affair which involved the selling of arms to Iraq was currently in the news). On the opening night, "the audience tittered, clearly sensing parallels with you-know-what and guess-who" (Benedict Nightingale, *The Times*, 13 November 1992). By insisting throughout that the melodrama lay in the public rather than the personal sphere, Hall's production became, surprisingly, all the more realistic.

Paul Taylor (*Independent*, 13 November 1992) quoted Wilde himself on the personal dimension. The subject of the play, Wilde had once said, was "the difference in the way in which a man loves a woman from that in which a woman loves a man." Aware that this reversed the more familiar belief that it is men who idealize women ("you don't hear much of Beatrice's Dante"), Taylor allowed that there might at least be a historical truth here, that "it isn't fanciful to discern a link between the heroine's behaviour in the play and the mentality that sent men off to the front to prove that they were heroes in the Great War."

With Mrs. Cheveley there were few problems, "a sleek carnivorous butterfly, poised and dangerous, with eyes that miss nothing and a voice of cream and prussic acid" (John Peter, *Sunday Times*, 15 November 1992). Lady Chiltern was more difficult. Billington, who saw the central pair as "a quasi-Ibsenite couple whose married life is founded on a lie," called her "fatuously adoring" and applauded the psychological realism that had Sir Robert almost strike his own wife. Peter nevertheless found in this "saintly female unicorn a touch of sensuality." Though the actress playing the role (Hannah Gordon) came in for some stiff criticism from the *Daily Telegraph* (13 November 1992) for "entirely missing the character's icy calculation and smug moral complacency," Taylor thought her "the Lady Macbeth of virtuous career-guidance...there's a voracity about her that seems just as ruthless in its way as Anna Carteret's captivatingly unscrupulous Mrs. Cheveley." This disturbing comparison gave some evidence that for Wilde, women would always be "second-class citizens." Nightingale too, had difficulty with the proposition (given in the play to Lady Chiltern) that women's "curves of emotion" do not compare with men's "wider scope and greater ambitions."

The more morally ambiguous the older women appear, the greater the weight that is likely to fall upon Mabel Chiltern. "Plain and feisty," Charles Spencer (*Daily Telegraph*, 13 November 1992) called Victoria Hasted's interpretation, but Alastair Macaulay (*Financial Times*, 13 November 1992) judged that "to play this role as a bespectacled, nasal, energetic hoyden is an amusing mistake. Wilde's stage directions compare her to both a flower and a Tanagra statuette." Billington thought that she could see "right through her future husband." Taylor said that "to make the marriage go, Lord G, you feel, would have to develop an improbable passion for lacrosse."

Once again there was the sense that Wilde himself was up on stage, palpably so this time in the figure of Lord Goring as played by Martin Shaw.

Boasting an Oscarish tummy, mournful eyes and an insolent languor, Mr. Shaw makes the character far more than a walking jokesmith: he suggests that the mask of flippancy conceals infinite reserves of charity and shrewdness. (Billington, *Guardian*, 13 November 1992)

John Gross (*Sunday Telegraph*, 15 November 1992) came right out with it – "a closet gay if ever there was one" – though Nightingale found that the physical identification with Wilde "sorts oddly with the robust heterosexuality the plot demands of the character." Spencer reflected that Shaw "gets to the heart of the play, touchingly suggesting a man who uses affected dandyism to disguise both personal hurt and an innate decency." Peter also related Goring to the essential schizophrenia of his creator: careless wit and moral arbiter at one and the same time.

10. Martin Shaw as Lord Goring in Peter Hall's 1992 production of
An Ideal Husband

What seems to have happened to Goring is that he began to find the answers that life was providing increasingly fatuous, and, as his waistline grew more ample, his manner grew more florid to screen his disappointment. The exquisite triviality of his conversation is only a cover for a fastidious disaste. (*Sunday Times*, 15 November 1992)

A few felt dissatisfied with Goring's distaste. Wardle (*Independent on Sunday*, 15 November 1992) concluded that "the transitions from cold-blooded epigrams to clammy declarations of feeling have become unplayable." Macaulay (*Financial Times*) applauded Martin Shaw because "he has the authority to convey the moral seriousness behind the dandy's facade. Yet he radiates not only self-satisfaction but also affectation." Taylor was reminded of "Noel Coward in his finger-wagging, mother-knows-best mood."

"The Importance of Being Earnest"

Time and again reviewers of the society plays refer to *The Importance of Being Earnest* as if it were the only logical direction for Wilde's theatrical career to take: a brilliantly self-concealing answer to the clash between overt melodrama and evasive wit. As Jane Edwardes put it in her review of Nicholas Hytner's production of the play, which opened at the Aldwych in March 1993:

If as I suspect, we are only just becoming acquainted with the true emotion, not the melodrama, behind Wilde's wit, then *The Importance of Being Earnest* may not be so pleasing. It was, after all, the play in which Wilde completely hid his feelings, concentrating instead, through the role playing of Jack and Algernon, on the deceptions that his sexuality forced him to play. (*Time Out*, 17 March 1993)

There was evidence, though, that Wilde's elegantly theatrical solution to his own problems now puts a director in a quandary. Perhaps Hytner's expensive, star-laden production raised expectations it never could fulfil. For each of the play's three acts the designer (Bob Crowley) produced sets that were not merely stunning, they seemed suggestive as well, though precisely of what, no one was quite sure. The first act, Algy's flat in Half

Moon Street, "a slant-roofed property with sinful crimson walls which melt into carnation green" (Paul Taylor, *Independent*, 12 March 1993) was overlooked by an enormous mock-up of Sargent's portrait of the designer W. Graham Robertson. The second act was "dominated by an extraordinary hedge of salmon pink roses excessively topiarised into the shape of a peacock with an enormous, expanding tail" (*Time Out*, 17 March 1993). The third act was a creamy curved interior "like a skew-whiff Heartbreak House" (*Observer*, 14 March 1993).

The extraordinary plethora of references in descriptions of these extraordinary sets testifies to a general bemusement: "surreal" (*Plays and Players*, May 1993), "expressionist" (*What's On*, 17 March 1993), "Odilon Redon" (John Peter, *Sunday Times*, 14 March 1993); "Lewis Carroll" (Sheridan Morley, *Spectator*, 20 March 1993), "post-modernist" (Jack Tinker, *Daily Mail*, 17 March 1993). Wardle felt obliged to construct a whole surrealist tradition: "This is Wilde as seen in the rear-view mirror of Orton and Stoppard...on nodding terms with Magritte: or, as Cecily might have put it, This is not a spade" (Wardle, *Independent on Sunday*, 14 March 1993).

Who could inhabit such a world? Only fantasists and narcissists. Cecily was "an almost terrifying study in fresh-cheeked single-mindedness, believing her own diary fantasies with a fundamentalist's unblinking literalism" (*Independent*, 12 March 1993); Algy "an ostentatious velvet dandy," "a peacock on heat, but one who seeks most especially to love himself" (*Sunday Times*), reminiscent to some of the young Wilde. But this is where the problems began, for some of the acting was judged too conventional by far for such louche surroundings. There were strong reservations about Gwendolen (Susan Harker) and about Richard E. Grant, too, when he had "to struggle, paradoxically, to be languid and debonair as the smugly smiling Algernon" (*Independent*). Of the four young leads, only Jack, played by Alex Jennings as "a petulant, opinionated cherub, pompous and mean" (*Sunday Times*) offered a really surprising and therefore successful interpretation.

Curiously, very few critics referred to the production's most provocative, and puzzling, moment: the kiss of greeting that Jack

11. Algie (Richard E. Grant) and Jack (Alex Jennings) in Nicholas Hytner's
1993 production of *The Importance of Being Earnest*

bestowed on Algy at his first entrance. Was this critical *pudeur*, or
did the actors simply forgo the gesture on some nights early in the
run? Even so, a color picture of the two men on the back of the
souvenir brochure made its own unmistakably homoerotic point.
Those who did refer to the kiss were cautious. Robert Tanitch
(*Plays and Players*, May 1993) thought it might suggest "that the
director...is about to explore a Victorian gay sub-text and that
the true meaning of being 'earnest' and 'bunburying' will be
revealed," though his fears proved to be unfounded: to Tanitch's
personal relief, that suggestion turned out to be false. Sheridan
Morley found the idea of "gay young things" intriguing, "but one
incapable of being sustained once the girls appear" (*Spectator*, 20
March 1993).

The main focus of attention, commercially and theatrically
inevitable, was upon Maggie Smith's Lady Bracknell. For many
critics, perhaps the majority, Smith offered an exact study in the
mores of the English class-system.

Replace that imperious feathered hat with a head-scarf and milady's
pursed moues and her air of pinched, almost predatory respectability

would start to look distinctly surburban...The titled monster may be dead set against her daughter forming an alliance with a parcel, but you could deduce, from this production, that her own lofty social position has come about only thanks to Lord Bracknell's willingness to form an alliance with a parvenue. In which case, his wife's tireless penchant for making dogmatic discriminations emerges as the compulsive behaviour of the arriviste turned beady-eyed expert at border-control. (*Independent*, 12 March 1993)

This is no haughty old dowager guarding a bank of magisterial put-downs, but a scheming whirlwind, body askance in dove-grey silks, flyaway hat and perfect coiffure, a figure of frightening elegance who is not to be tampered with...She certainly inspects the young people like a beaky, agitated adjutant on parade. (*Observer*, 14 March 1993)

When it came to animal imagery, Nightingale (*The Times*, 10 March 1993) went the whole hog, first invoking the human vultures, ravens, and crows of *Volpone*, then describing Maggie Smith as a "maybe a lady griffin." Jane Edwardes spotted an unexpected sexual alignment along with the ornithological:

Smith is an exotic bird, looking with hawk-like disdain on her prey, while Edith Evans was an immoveable tank. Smith's stare is accompanied by a fluttering of her wings and a quick turn of the head. Dressed in shimmering grey with a hat dramatically angled, she gives a definitive, hilarious performance which threatens to soar into a stratosphere all of its own. Such high camp almost puts her on the side of her decadent nephew rather than the forces of bourgeois authority. (*Time Out*)

For Jack the final irony will come when he realizes that Gwendolen, like all women, has grown up into her mother. Further bizarre comparisons cropped up in Wardle: "part suburban *parvenue*, part drag artist, part vigilantly suspicious rodent" (*Independent on Sunday*).

That Maggie Smith possesses rare theatrical power is a truth that usually goes unquestioned. Respectful to the point of reverence, most London critics gave her the kind of reception that a Dame might expect. There was a single, but important, exception: Michael Billington. "Dame Maggie," he pronounced, "is a bundle of fussiness forever fidgeting."

She also constantly seeks laughs instead of letting them come to her...When assessing Cecily's profile Dame Maggie indulges in an orgy

12. Maggie Smith as Lady Bracknell in Nicholas Hytner's 1993 production of
The Importance of Being Earnest

of wide-eyed moues and stares far removed from the character's patronising beneficence...in stealing the show, Dame Maggie's hyperactive performance subtly undermines it. (*Guardian*, 11 March 1993)

And in a later review for *Country Life* (18 March 1993) Billington took these strictures even further:

She gets huge laughs, on her first entrance, by shooting withering, disdainful glances at Mr. Worthing as if he is a piece of untidy refuse, which makes nonsense of her second entrance when she recognises him instantly. In the famous interview, she clutches her stomach in revulsion on learning that he was found in "the cloak-room at Victoria Station". Again, this gets a big laugh. But it runs clean counter to the aristocratic temperament which registers high-voltage shock with maximum economy. In short, there is a strenuousness about Dame Maggie's performance that violently contradicts Lady Bracknell's indomitable self-assurance.

Billington had some reason to feel vindicated when the London *Standard* in June ran a piece under the heading "The Importance of Being Maggie Smith" which reported disturbing developments down at the Aldwych:

The audience erupts into applause at the mere sight of her; she pauses, discreetly acknowledging the adulation, before launching into a performance of comic grotesquerie that is not so much Wilde as *wild*. For a moment, one is whisked from the seats of the Aldwych to the studio audience of *I Love Lucy*...Every classic line, every gesture, is stretched to infinity for laughs. If an eccentric gesture doesn't get a laugh, she repeats it until it does. If a movement gets a laugh straight away, she repeats it for another one. (*Standard*, 15 June 1993, with later correspondence 21 June 1993)

There were, then, two schools, though of very unequal size. There was the minority view, headed by Billington, for whom Smith had indulged her technical skills at the expense of the role, and there was the majority view which saw nothing but creative comedy of a high order.

1890s

The danger with Jonathan Miller's theory is that it may too easily assume the historical relevance of the interpretations it chooses to address. A form of hermeneutic circling can come into play through which desired meanings are merely ratified by production style, and the validating process of historical discovery is lost. To avoid false inferences we may need to be sparing with our conclusions.

Or what if a production is so visually attractive, so persuasively acted, that the text dissolves in performance, transformed into something entirely different, but of undoubted power? That is certainly possible, though none of the recent productions of Wilde go quite that far. Even the lavish sets, essential for the success of a modern West End show, serve a function. Design is a prime mediator between action and audience, and the best work (the sets for *The Importance*, for instance) registers the ambiguities that now surround the plays, as the comments of critics also testify.

Handbags and glad rags

Acting styles are produced by the cultural moment as well, not just individually, but in the relation between a single performer and the surrounding company. One of the lessons to be learnt from Maggie Smith's performance, and the varied responses to it, is that we are still living in a time, which probably originated in the later nineteenth century, when star performances and ensemble styles coexist rather uneasily.

What then of Lady Bracknell in 1895? In fact critics frequently praised Rose Leclercq's rendering for its adherence to type, one of them remarking that it was "in the right vein of grave extravagance."[5] At the St. James's it was George Alexander's Jack who received most of the comic attention, which was understandable because Alexander was the leading actor in his own theater. What Rose Leclercq brought to Lady Bracknell was an established expertise in rather similar parts, the prototypes of Lady Bracknell, which may well have directed some attention away from her performance.[6] When she appeared in Pinero's *The Benefit of the Doubt* later in the same year Shaw wrote, with relief, that she was "not condemned this time to play the usual caricature of herself."[7] It took time for Lady Bracknell to become everybody's favorite Wildean joke: when Alexander revived the play for a second time in 1909 Max Beerbohm didn't even bother to give the name of the actress playing the part (Helen Rous).

The rise of the dowager to become the foremost character in the play was a gradual process that depended upon the changing attitudes and widening constituency of the theater audience to the point where she was finally revealed as an extraordinary social product, both culturally remote and eerily familiar. Imitations there certainly were: Lady Britomart in Shaw's *Major Barbara* of 1905 for one. St. John Hankin, a great admirer of Wilde who had attempted his own Lady Bracknell with Lady Faringford in *The Return of the Prodigal* in the same year, later complained that the role was "brilliant surface only." "Wilde has seen her with absolute clearness," said Hankin, "but he has seen her, as it were, in two dimensions only, not in the round. That is the weak point of all Wilde's character drawing. It lacks solidity." What Hankin, a typical Edwardian proto-realist, was looking for, and felt Wilde to be incapable of delivering, were sympathetic "souls" – not "external manifestations," but people you could really understand.[8]

The Importance was revived again at the St. James's in 1911 and 1913 and then at the Haymarket in 1923. By the time of Nigel Playfair's black-and-white "Beardsleyesque" production at the Lyric Hammersmith in 1930 the burgeoning question – was Wilde's masterpiece to be treated as a species of naturalistic farce or as a period fantasy? – was about to come to a stylish head. The Lady Bracknell was Mabel Terry-Lewis, greatly overshadowed by her nephew John Gielgud as Jack. Terry-Lewis was fifty-eight years old, having retired from the stage in 1905 only to return in the early 1920s. Gielgud later described her as "an instinctive actress, with a grace and skill which she has inherited from her family" and said that she shared with Marie Tempest and Irene Vanbrugh "that rare distinction of style, deportment and carriage which is so seldom seen on the stage today."[9] Others praised her Lady Bracknell for her "dry, incisive, unforced wit; her proud carriage, the exquisite precision of her emphasis; above all, the personal dignity that preserves a great lady in one who might have been a butt" (*The Times*, 8 July 1930).[10] Yet Gielgud also says that his aunt had no idea at all why Lady Bracknell was so comical. "Why are they laughing?" she asked him, "This line isn't funny to me,"[11] which strongly suggests that her success derived from an unconscious familiarity with the type she was playing.[12]

Tyrone Guthrie's 1934 production at the Old Vic was also historic, though in other ways: a cast consisting of some of the most promising young actors around town (Roger Livesey as Jack, James Mason as Merriman, Flora Robson as Gwendolen, Ursula Jeans as Cecily, Charles Laughton as Chasuble), and the presence in the first-night audience of two members of the original 1895 production (Irene Vanbrugh and Alan Aynesworth). For all the general enthusiasm there was a repeated qualification: "If there is a fault in the production, it is in the tendency now and then to laugh at its own jokes" (*The Times*, 6 November 1934). Only one performance escaped this criticism: Athene Seyler's Lady Bracknell. Whereas other actors were castigated for seeming too anxious that Wilde should amuse, Seyler "gave a performance of such wit and gusto that every line was in danger of being lost through being drowned in the laughter greeting the one before. But Miss Seyler knows what she is about, and did not throw away a comma" (*Sunday Times*, 11 February 1934). As a result, "in the middle act, when she does not appear, there is nothing which quite makes up for her absence, and the play sags perceptibly" (*Daily Telegraph*, 6 February 1934).

In her greatly admired book on comedy, first published in 1943, Seyler stresses that *The Importance* "shows the absurdities of the well-bred, cynical, easy manner of the 'upper classes' with its levelling of all emotion and experience to apparent indifference."[13] Gradually through the 1930s Lady Bracknell moved to center stage and, as she did so, she came to be seen more clearly, that is to say more collectively, as representative of class attitudes. Guthrie was later to describe his production as "galumphing" and to concede that it had been eclipsed by John Gielgud's glittering revival in 1939.[14] Yet when Edith Evans seized command of that classic production, and later the extremely popular 1953 film, making Lady Bracknell a part of great importance, she did so by mining the inherent possibilities of Seyler's "apparent indifference" to the very full.

Whereas Terry-Lewis had been able to base her reading on personal familiarity, Evans, born in 1888 and from a quite different social background, would capitalize upon her act of recognition, and oblige her audiences to do the same. Evans's acting style perfectly matched this concept of the role because it was part of her special brilliance as an actress to seem to be unaware of the effect she was creating, almost daring her audiences to laugh. Her Lady Bracknell drew in part on the same skill that served her so well as an imperious Millamant in *The Way of the World*. As Gielgud observed, she had the "perfect timing and control"[15] that could conquer any theater, though there was more to it than that. Gielgud records their initial reading of Wilde's play at his country cottage:

> I took a copy from the bookshelf and we read the handbag scene together to the other guests. After the laughter had died down Edith handed me the book and remarked gravely, "I know those sort of women. They ring the bell and tell you to put a lump of coal on the fire." (72)

Within that anecdote lies Evans's ultimate secret: an immediate dislike of a class type, born of personal experience, which would be expressed not through outright exposure, caricature, but rather through the deliberate recreation of an inscrutable manner that would oblige an audience to relive their own perceptions of the real world, this time as farce.

Gielgud particularly admired "the sly look of suspicion. . .as she glanced at the armchair she had chosen for the interview with Worthing in the first act. In those few seconds she managed to convey both appraisal and approval, reassuring herself of the suitability of that particular piece of furniture as a throne for her corseted dignity before deigning to lower herself into the seat" (72). Continually testing the world to see if it matched up to her own strict demands and usually finding it wanting, Evans's Bracknell exuded a particular form of arrogance that made little distinction between people and things. That, too, is what the *Times* critic saw:

13. Edith Evans as Lady Bracknell

Her appearance is masterly – perfectly upholstered, with a feminine art now lost, before and behind; and her voice is correspondingly upholstered so that every phrase, harsh and drawling, comes from the comfortable heart of Lady Bracknell's arrogance. A woman, of course, for the earnest to hang on the first lamp-post, but what a dying speech and what a superb corpse she would make! (*The Times*, 1 February 1939)[16]

On this occasion the "earnest" would presumably have been socialist revolutionaries; not that, in 1939, they can have been present in the audience in very large numbers.

The reasons why Gielgud's production should have become the "classic" are several and, although on the surface they have little to do with 1895, they are essentially historical. In his memoirs Gielgud records his frustration at being unable to glean any information whatsoever from Lord Alfred Douglas about the first production: "how much it was caricatured, all the nuances which I longed to discuss with him" (137). In the end Gielgud had the theatrical wisdom to avoid caricature altogether and go entirely for nuance, "tongue in cheek, like a solemn charade" (158). The result was a production that matched the distant epoch of the play's creation with the present moment of its performance.

It was premièred in January at the Globe Theatre for eight charity matinées, and then revived at the same theater on 16 August for a run that came to a halt with the declaration of war on 3 September, when all West End theaters went dark. At the Golders Green Hippodrome, in the middle of a uniquely grim September, *The Importance* opened for a third time. "With this performance the London theatre may be said to have begun its war-time life. Like the Elizabethan theatre, it is kept waiting at the gate" said *The Times* (15 September 1939). At Golders Green, "Gas masks were more easily disposed of under seats than were silk hats, when the revival was first seen at the Globe." Already a backwards look was in place: "If the past theatrical decade had to be represented by a single production this is the one that many good judges would choose." Moreover, Wilde's wit, "because it plays about no moral question and is consistently and deliberately trivial, is of the very kind to purge war-time melancholy." When, in the interval, as the conversation turned away from the war and towards Edith Evans, so "everybody realised the importance of not being earnest every hour of the day of the war; and the realisation assuredly did no harm."

The production returned to the Globe for a further six weeks from 26 December and was later revived at the Phoenix Theatre from 14 October to 12 December 1942. In 1946 there was a special Royal Matinée.[17] It is as well to be reminded of what theater-going involved in wartime. "In the the event of an Air Raid Warning an announcement will be made from the stage," the Phoenix programme informed the audience. "Patrons are advised to remain in the Theatre, but those wishing to leave will be directed to the nearest official air raid shelter, after which the performance will be continued for as long as is practicable." That was offstage; on stage, miraculously, "All again is lightness, clearness, ease and the fun becomes absolute" (*The Times*, 15 August 1942) – which is exactly how the actor and film director Bryan Forbes remembers the experience too:

The contrast between the stylish, effortless elegance of performance on stage at the Phoenix and the sandbagged drabness of wartime Soho outside almost made me lose my reason. If this seems a remembered exaggeration, I must justify it by explaining that to be a student of acting during that grim period of war was, in itself, a kind of madness: one unreality superimposed upon another. Edith and Gielgud represented the two pinnacles and they splashed their talents in vivid colours across the backcloth of austerity: one queued for a few ounces of butter and a piece of horsemeat – caviar to the masses – but, as the house lights were lowered in the Phoenix and Wilde's epigrams drifted across the footlights, spoken by two of the most beautiful voices that ever graced the English stage, an artistic All Clear sounded; for a few brief hours one enjoyed a return to the world of style and calm and all thoughts of war and death were mercifully suspended.[18]

A true memory of a necessary and collective fantasy: Gielgud's *Importance* belongs with that other great wartime hit, *Blithe Spirit*, consoling and inspiring through its invocation of an English style that, as Forbes allows, seemed an antidote to death itself.[19] So powerful was its cultural impact that Gielgud would eventually be able to boast that no one had dared risk another full-scale professional production for ten years. His interpretation can even stand as an emblem of English post-war history as a whole, since it depends upon an upper-class manner most potent when it is being satirized. Gielgud's ineffable grace under circumstantial pressure, preserved on film and on record, partnered by Evans's imperturbably arrogant Bracknell, defied the very impulse for change it provoked.

In Wilde's theater, rather in the manner of Restoration comedy, there are, notoriously, conscious wits and there are unconscious wits, and there are some, the most interesting, who are hard to keep in either category because they keep jumping from one to the other. For many years the modern tradition has tended to believe that Lady Bracknell belongs with these. Edith Evans was the actress who brought the manner to perfection, and, ever since, we have looked on the part as the supreme opportunity for a comic actress, to the point where we have almost forgotten how the role came to the fore. Despite drag versions, despite Judi Dench's notably youthful and sexy interpretation in 1982, the tradition of appearing blind to effect has continued.

But by the time Maggie Smith came to the part in 1993 circumstances seem to have changed, perhaps radically. Smith's performance went in quite another direction, almost daring the audience *not* to laugh. This technique clearly has its admirers, although the worry remains that an actress who controls our response to the extent that we find ourselves laughing at the role they are playing can severely reduce the satirical force of an imperturbable face. Maggie Smith's *parvenue* was fearsome, yet coercive. Nor was she quite human – "a hawk," "a vulture," "a griffin" – a fabulous female creature. The pained protests from Michael Billington and others indicate the lasting power of an established idea of what Wilde's most typical roles ask from players: the self-effacing opacity that obliges an audience to respond with a mixture of bemused recognition and baffled surprise.

Wilde's witty women

It is all the more intriguing, then, that one or two critics should have referred to Smith as a "drag-artist". Perhaps they meant that she was pretending to be one (an actress imitating a man imitating a woman) or perhaps that, in some sense, Lady Bracknell really is male (the actress playing a woman with male characteristics). Though the latter seems the more likely, both possibilities are oddly plausible: some would certainly say that she is a woman as only a man could imagine a woman. Or is this a camp joke that is, as so often the case, really about class? Is it that the relative flexibility of gender, when represented on stage, undermines the seeming rigidities of class as they operate in the real world? Is the point that Lady Bracknell's maleness lies in her autocratic behaviour rather than in any fluke of biology? Jack does after all rebuke her for "her masculine mind."

Even in *The Importance*, with its relatively small cast, there are a number of rather different women with whom to compare the dowager duchess. What then does female behavior amount to in a Wilde play? That is the question that recent productions encourage us to ask.[20]

In their versions of the three society plays the directors Peter

Hall and Philip Prowse defused the moral melodrama of sexual relationships by playing the passionate scenes according to convention, which freed them to bring out the more interesting complexities created by wits, in particular by female wits. It is as if they set out to persuade their audiences that Wilde's interest in group female discourse could eclipse those elements of melodramatic idealization (and, just possibly, misogynistic fear) also active in his work.

In their various ways modern productions suggest that Wilde's most long-lasting, or prophetic, contribution to feminism was to allow his women to be articulate, and then to subject them to moral evaluation according to the ways in which they put their verbal dexterity to amusing and constructive use. Minor, but telling, examples of this puzzle might be Lady Plymdale in *Lady Windermere's Fan*, who thinks Mrs. Erlynne could relieve her of the burden of her own husband's attentions ("What a mystery you are!" comments Dumby); and Lady Caroline Pontefract in *A Woman of No Importance*, who bafflingly proclaims, "femininity is the quality I admire most in women." Then there is the contrasting trio of Mabel Chiltern, Mrs. Cheveley and Lady Markby in *An Ideal Husband*. Fondness for riddling female wit proves Wilde to be a true contemporary of at least one kind of New Woman.

He certainly enjoyed the company of some of the most famously amusing and independent women of his time: from his own mother to actresses like Lillie Langtry. Ada Leverson, "The Sphinx," perhaps his closest female friend, started off by writing dialogues for *Punch* that parodied his plays, and went on to write novels whose comic effects depend on a Wildean ear for group voices and a Wildean taste for paradox, particularly when applied to the sexes. "Feminine intuition," she once wrote, was "a quality perhaps even rarer in women than in men."[21]

Leverson probably contributed epigrams to *A Woman of No Importance*.[22] The exchange between Lord Illingworth and Mrs. Allonby is said to be one: "Nothing spoils a romance more than a sense of humour in the woman," announces Illingworth. "Or the want of it in the man," comes the reply (*Works*, 474). That might serve as a commentary upon Leverson's own marital life, as well

as an ironic reversal of a commonplace (and probably unfair)
view of Wilde's hidden domestic relations.[23] Even when "The
Sphinx" wrote a parody of Wilde called "The Minx," she was
still playing Wilde's feminist game. For though Wildean jokes
about the mystery of women are usually jokes against the
mystification of women, those "sphinxes without secrets," there is
no guarantee that men will necessarily have the insight to
appreciate them. Even Gwendolen and Cecily remain a continual
puzzle to their suitors, as to the audience as a whole. Who can say
how much they control their situation, or how much it controls
them? Unity at least they achieve: speaking at one point in unison
and, in an early draft of the play, even dividing up a single
sentence between their two voices.[24] The sisterly trust demanded
for this brilliant double act promises well for the future.

"Mr. Oscar Wilde is not in the house"

The final lesson to be drawn from these recent productions,
appropriately paradoxical, is that the plays are, more than ever,
inseparable from their author's experience, and depend greatly
upon our seeing that to be the case. Directors have few qualms
about allowing actors to impersonate Wilde through one of his
characters, whether it's Cecil Graham in *Lady Windermere*, Lord
Goring in *An Ideal Husband*, or even Algy in *The Importance*.

One undoubted reason why these new stagings have gone for
the autobiographical element has been the enormous popularity
of Ellmann's best-selling biography. We have also in recent years
experienced a new frankness and curiosity about gay history and
gay relationships. Yet the Wildean presence only works on stage
today because it makes manifest a quality endemic to the plays:
an interplay between performance, audience, and outside world
that was already active in the conditions of late Victorian theater,
though taken to new extremes by Wilde from the very start of his
career.[25]

An inveterate theater-goer, Wilde made a point in the 1880s of
supporting the premières of personal favorites such as Helena
Modjeska and Lillie Langtry. He knew too how important it was
for his own professional progress that he should be seen to be

there on grand theatrical occasions. The first night is a fine example of the kind of social spectacle orchestrated for marketing purposes that was developing rapidly in the late nineteenth century. As Regenia Gagnier and others have shown, Wilde immediately recognized, and was anxious to exploit, the possibilities of this new commercial culture.

Lyceum premières were particularly grand (it was Irving's manager, H. L. Bateman, who had first realized the full publicity potential of the first night) and Wilde rarely missed one. When *Othello* opened on 2 May 1881 with Booth as Othello and Irving as Iago, the audience were also entertained by "the ubiquity of Oscar Wilde who, combining elegance and agility, was seen now leaning languidly from a box, now chatting in the stalls, and a moment later figuring prominently in a box opposite to the first."[26] Together with Constance he was again highly visible when *Twelfth Night* opened at the Lyceum in 1884: "Mr. Oscar Wilde and his bride occupied two chairs close to the orchestra, the apostle of culture being greatly altered in appearance now that his ample locks are shorn and elaborately curled."[27]

Already, when he reviewed Irving's Hamlet in 1885, Wilde's reference to the audience betrayed a characteristic self-awareness:

It sometimes happens that at a *première* in London the least enjoyable part of the performance is the play. I have seen many audiences more interesting than the actors, and have often heard better dialogue in the *foyer* than I have on stage. At the Lyceum, however, this is rarely the case, and when the play is a play of Shakespeare's, and among its exponents are Mr. Irving and Miss Ellen Terry, we turn from the gods in the gallery and from the goddesses in the stalls, to enjoy the charm of the production, and to take delight in the art. The lions are before the foot-lights and not in front of them when we have a noble tragedy nobly enacted. (*Works*, 952)

Throughout the 1880s the papers regularly reported Wilde's presence among the fashionable throng. Attendant at the first night of *Faust* in 1885 were the Princess Louise, the Prince of Wales (officially in mourning, he overcame the problem by watching the play from behind), and "the once famous apostle of high art in dress, with hair cut short, quite bland and harmless, who has evidently renounced the vegetarian cult and dines on a

14. Wilde represented as a prominent member of the audience by
Maurice Greiffenhagen

diet more generous than lilies." With him was his wife, "Mrs. Oscar," wearing "a wonderful ruffle like an oyster shell standing on end."[28] When the author took to the stage and addressed the first-night audience for *Lady Windermere's Fan* with "I congratulate you on the *great* success of your performance" (*Ellmann*, 346), he was simply offering an elegant variation on what had become a very familiar theme. "With many writers," *The Court and Society Review* had announced in a feature on first-nights in 1886, "the audience is regarded as hardly second in importance to the play itself."[29]

Wilde could cross from audience to stage and back again, and always with such consummate assurance, because in the Victorian theater the gap between the two was already narrow, and he had closed it even further by making his presence so theatrically conspicuous within the auditorium itself. This established mode of exchange between two spectacles did more than just enable Wilde's own first-night wit – "Mr. Oscar Wilde is not in the house," he announced at the opening of *A Woman of No Importance* (*Ellmann*, 360) – it encouraged his audiences to see and hear him on stage, speaking through the characters of his plays. One reviewer of the first production of *The Importance* confessed that his own failure to say much about the acting was evidence of the way in which the author had dominated the play.[30]

Today that familiarity has been reduplicated many times over by films, documentaries, biographies, the whole myth-making machinery. In which case the surprise is less that directors should build Wilde into their shows, than that anyone other than Wilde should ever appear in them at all. The explanation for this singular achievement must surely be that, in time, the "Wildean" has come to stand for so much more than just one man.

That, in turn, may go some way in explaining why many recent reviews have had regular recourse to the notion of "bisexuality," as if the concept revealed the plays. An implicit acknowledgment of the all-embracing nature of Wildean sexuality may be involved here (the strongly homosexual tone that is brought to ostensibly heterosexual relationships, for instance), but paradox is at work as well. Until the final confrontation with authority in 1895 Wilde had managed to be provocative, and to survive, by making paradox his weapon and his shield. The reviewer in the *Times Literary Supplement* (19 March 1993) who complained that Hytner's production of *The Importance* failed to follow through the gay signposting of its first act was surely being obtuse. That a play should set down a premise in its first act, but come to an apparently different conclusion in its third, is wholly in line with Wilde's dramaturgy. The structure of *The Importance* is paradoxical in just this way: it zig-zags from start to finish. Men who fraternize with men turn out to like some women, and luckily some women turn out to like some men too; some men behave like women and some women behave like men. This is a bisexual drama in which "bisexuality" is not just a universal sexual condition (though it is, of course, exactly that), but a model for the sympathetic, if contrary, dramatic imagination.

ENVOI

In the 1890s Wilde was a public figure, in the 1990s he is the public itself: we want him to be a liberated gay-man and a witty feminist, a worried parent and a guilty husband. When the Dublin-based Rough Magic company staged *Lady Windermere* in the early 1990s,[31] it turned the play into a riotous drag show that had Wildean figures popping up everywhere, irrespective of gender, re-creating its author as a reflection of today's admiration for sexual free-spirits.

And as an Irish writer Wilde necessarily becomes multicultural. Announcing its comparatively low-budget *Importance* in London in 1989 the all-black Talawa Theatre Company insisted:

In producing *The Importance of Being Earnest*, Talawa set out to be as truthful to the text as it was humanly possible to be, bearing in mind that an all-black production of *The Importance of Being Earnest* was probably very far from Wilde's wildest imagination. We found great support in his attitude to English society: his commentary was all the clearer perhaps because he was Irish. We felt it was important to set the play in England in 1895, but not ever to disguise or trivialise the fact that we were black.[32]

That there was nothing trivial about this performance of Wilde's "trivial comedy" didn't mean that it wasn't wonderfully funny. Some differences have to be emphasized if others are to dissolve.

At which point we should remember that Wilde's favorite formula for jokes always was based on difference. "Women are never disarmed by compliments. Men always are. That is the difference between the two sexes" (*Works*, 565). Most of Wilde's jokes work through this kind of self-canceling comparison, the point being not only to suggest absurd oppositions but, in exemplary deconstructive fashion, to defer resolution by requiring reconsideration of the premise. They foreshadow those ideal modes of collective living that always lie just beyond us, and even now can only be glimpsed on stage.

Notes

INTRODUCTION

1 *Pall Mall Gazette*, 21 December 1889, p. 6.
2 Alex Owen, *The Darkened Room* (London: Virago, 1989), p. 27. Also see Judith R. Walkowitz, *City of Dreadful Delight: Narratives of Sexual Danger in Late-Victorian London* (London: Virago, 1992), pp. 171–91.
3 Cheiro, *Cheiro's Memoirs. The Reminiscences of a Society Palmist* (London: William Rider, 1912), pp. 56–61; *Works*, p. 31.
4 H. Montgomery Hyde, *The Trials of Oscar Wilde* (New York: Dover, 1973), p. 108.
5 Wilde's interest in the relationship of science to religion can already be seen in the notebooks he kept at Oxford: *Oscar Wilde's Oxford Notebooks*, ed. by Philip E. Smith and Michael S. Helfand (New York and Oxford: Oxford University Press, 1989). The widespread late Victorian concern with the topic is surveyed by Karl Beckson in chapter 14 of *London in the 1890s: A Cultural History* (New York and London: Norton, 1992).
6 *The Collected Poems of Lord Alfred Douglas* (London: Martin Secker, 1919), p. 88.
7 George Sylvester Viereck, "Is Oscar Wilde Living or Dead?," *The Critic*, 47 (July 1905), 86–88.
8 *News Chronicle*, 3 February 1934, p. 15.
9 Information about Cravan is available in Arthur Cravan, *Œuvres*, Edition établie par Jean-Pierre Begot (Paris: Editions Gerard Lebovici, 1987). Further references are given after quotations in the text. Also see Arthur Cravan, *Maintenant*, Textes présentés par Bernard Delvaille (Paris: Erik C. Losfeld, 1957).
10 *The Standard Edition of the Complete Psychological Works of Sigmund Freud*, vol. XVII, trans. and ed. by James Strachey (London: Hogarth Press, 1955), p. 252.
11 Hester Travers Smith, *Psychic Messages from Oscar Wilde* (London: T. Werner Laurie, 1924), pp. 37–38. Further references are given

after quotations in the text. Wilde's script was reproduced in this book and caused further controversy. See G. D. Cummins, "The Strange Case of Oscar Wilde," *Occult Review*, 34 (1924), 102–10; Herbert Thurston, "The 'Oscar Wilde' Script in its Bearing on Survival," *Studies. An Irish Quarterly Review of Letters, Philosophy and Science*, 13 (1924), 14–28; Karl Beckson, "Psychic Messages from Oscar Wilde: Some New A. Conan Doyle Letters," *English Language Notes*, 17 (1979), 39–42.

12 Lazar, *The Ghost Epigrams of Oscar Wilde* (New York: Covici-Friede, 1929).

13 John Furnell, *The Stringed Lute* (London: Rider and Company, 1955), pp. 1–2. Further references are given after quotations in the text.

14 *Who Was That Man? A Present for Mr. Oscar Wilde* (Harmondsworth: Penguin, 1988). Further references are given after quotations in the text. For a discussion and contextualization of Bartlett's work see Joseph Bristow, "Being Gay: Politics, Identity, Pleasure," *New Formations*, 9 (1989), 61–81.

15 Maureen Borland, *Wilde's Devoted Friend. A Life of Robert Ross, 1869–1918* (Oxford: Lennard Publishing, 1990), p. 113; Max Beerbohm, *Around Theatres* (London: Hart-Davis, 1953), p. 379. For further memories of Farquarson see Harold Acton, *More Memoirs of an Aesthete* (London: Methuen, 1970), pp. 20–26; John Gielgud, *Backward Glances* (London: Hodder and Stoughton, 1989), pp. 165–66.

16 *The Letters of W. B. Yeats* ed. by Allan Wade (London: Hart-Davis, 1954), p. 451.

17 Diana Devlin, *A Speaking Part. Lewis Casson and the Theatre of his Time* (London: Hodder and Stoughton, 1982), p. 133.

18 Wolfit in *The Times*, 20 January 1966, p. 14, Gielgud in *The Times*, 18 January 1966, p. 12.

19 Peter Quennell made this claim in *The Marble Foot. An Autobiography* (London: Collins, 1976), p. 115, and repeated it in his obituary of Acton in the *Guardian*, 28 February 1994, p. 12. A complete history of representations of Wilde remains to be written, although there are some initial findings in Ian Fletcher and John Stokes, "Oscar Wilde," *Anglo-Irish Literature: a Review of Research* (New York: MLA, 1976), pp. 46–137 and *Recent Research on Anglo-Irish Writers* (New York: MLA, 1983), pp. 21–47.

20 Much of the most important recent work on Wilde has attempted to historicize his life and works in terms of contemporary concepts and representations of homosexuality which, of course, include the "camp." In addition to *Who Was That Man?*, see Richard Dellamora, *Masculine Desire. The Politics of Victorian Aestheticism* (Chapel Hill and London: University of North Carolina Press, 1990); Eve Kosofsky

Sedgwick, *Epistemology of the Closet* (Berkeley and Los Angeles: University of California Press, 1990) and *Tendencies* (London: Routledge, 1994); Jonathan Dollimore, *Sexual Dissidence* (Oxford: Clarendon Press, 1991); Joseph Bristow, "Wilde, *Dorian Gray*, and Gross Indecency," in *Sexual Sameness. Textual Differences in Lesbian and Gay Writing*, ed. by J. Bristow (London: Routledge, 1992), pp. 44–63; Christopher Craft, *Another Kind of Love, Male Homosexual Desire in English Discourse, 1850–1920* (Berkeley: University of California Press, 1994); Linda Dowling, *Hellenism and Homosexuality in Victorian Oxford* (Ithaca and New York: Cornell University Press, 1994); Alan Sinfield, *The Wilde Century: Effeminacy, Oscar Wilde and the Queer Moment* (London: Cassell, 1994). The many-sidedness of Wilde's sexuality is subtly explored in a novel by Rohase Piercy which imagines the experience of Constance: *The Coward Does it with a Kiss* (London: GMP, 1990).

21 Harold Acton, *Memoirs of an Aesthete* (London: Methuen, 1948), p. 65.

22 Goronwy Rees in the *Spectator*, quoted in Sheridan Morley, *Robert, My Father* (London: Weidenfeld, 1993), p. 49. Also see Robert Morley, *Responsible Gentleman* (London: Longman, 1966), pp. 79–81.

23 Leslie and Sewell Stokes, *Oscar Wilde* (London: Secker and Warburg, 1937).

24 See Christopher Fitz-Simmon, *The Boys. A Biography of Michéal MacLiammoir and Hilton Edwards* (London: Nick Hern Books, 1994), especially pp. 236–46.

25 Michéal MacLiammoir, *The Importance of Being Oscar*, with an introduction by Hilton Edwards (Dublin: The Dolmen Press; London: Oxford University Press, 1963), p. 68. Further references are given after quotations in the text.

26 See Elaine Dundy, *Finch, Bloody Finch. A Biography of Peter Finch* (London: Michael Joseph, 1980) and Trader Faulkner, *Peter Finch. A Biography* (London: Angus Robertson, 1979).

27 *Peter Finch*, p. 241.

28 In the *Evening Standard* Alexander Walker wrote of Morley: "It is not an impression of a man we get, but an anthology of bon mots...he comes into his own as his Wilde wilts under the merciless examination of Sir Ralph Richardson's Carson" (19 May 1960, p. 12). Four days later Walker was hailing Finch because "he has nothing of the grotesque in his playing – nothing of Morley's beamish boy popping with epigrams. In age, uncannily in looks too, in the physical strength Wilde had and in the moral flaw that ruined him, Peter Finch is recognisably a man you can believe in" (23 May 1960, p. 5). For an alternative view of Morley's performance see *Robert, My Father*, pp. 152–54.

29 Jonathan Vickers and Peter Copeland, "The Voice of Oscar Wilde: An Investigation," *British Association of Sound Collections News*, 2 (1987), 21–26.
30 See Merlin Holland, "Wilde as Salomé?," *Times Literary Supplement*, 22 July 1994, p. 14.
31 Walter Benjamin, "The Work of Art in the Age of Mechanical Reproduction," *Illuminations* (London: Fontana, 1970), pp. 221–22.
32 *The Wilde Century*, p. 6.
33 See Patrick Brantlinger, "Mass Media and Culture in *Fin-de-Siècle* Europe," and Alison Hennigan, "Personalities and Principles: Aspects of Literature and Life in *Fin-de-siècle* England," in *Fin de Siècle and its Legacy*, ed. by Mikulas Teich and Roy Porter (Cambridge University Press, 1990), pp. 98–112 and 170–215.
34 See Regenia Gagnier, *Idylls of the Marketplace: Oscar Wilde and the Victorian Public* (Aldershot: Scolar Press, 1987); Ian Small, *Oscar Wilde Revalued: An Essay on New Materials and Methods of Research* (Greensboro, NC: ELT Press, 1993), "Oscar Wilde as a Professional Writer," *The Library Chronicle of the University of Texas at Austin*, 23 (1993), 33–49, and with Russell Jackson, "Oscar Wilde: A 'Writerly' Life," *Modern Drama*, 37 (1994), 3–11.
35 Julie Speedie, *Wonderful Sphinx* (London: Virago, 1993), pp. 105–6.

1 THE MAGIC BALL

1 Jean Paul Raymond and Charles Ricketts, *Oscar Wilde, Recollections* (Bloomsbury: The Nonesuch Press, 1933). Further references are given after quotations in the text. André Gide, *Oscar Wilde* (London: William Kimber, 1951); Laurence Housman, *Echo de Paris* (London: Jonathan Cape, 1923); W. B. Yeats, *Autobiographies* (London: Macmillan, 1966).
2 *Le Chant du cygne, contes parlés d'Oscar Wilde*, recueillis et rédigés par Guillot de Saix (Paris: Mercure de France, 1942). Reprinted in *The Decadent Consciousness. A Hidden Archive of Late Victorian Literature*, ed. by Ian Fletcher and John Stokes (New York: Garland, 1979). Further references are given after quotations in the text.
3 *Oscar Wilde*, p. 20; Ellmann, *Golden Codgers* (London: Oxford University Press, 1973), pp. 81–100.
4 *Le Chant du cygne*, p. 105.
5 *Oscar Wilde's Oxford Notebooks*, ed. by Philip E. Smith and Michael S. Helfand (New York and Oxford: Oxford University Press, 1989), p. 163.
6 *Vie de Jésus*, Seizième Edition (Paris: Calmann Lévy, 1879), pp. 265–80.

7 David Friedrich Strauss, *The Life of Jesus Critically Examined* (London: SCM Press, 1972), pp. 519–27. Further references are given after quotations in the text. Miracles were widely discussed as an aspect of the supernatural. Henry Maudsley, *Natural Causes and Supernatural Seemings* (London: Kegan Paul, Trench and Co., 1886, several times reprinted), pronounces that "Charms and prayers, auguries and omens, oracles, ordeals, exorcisms, incantations, and divinations are the natural resort and refuge, as they are, the exponents, of active imagination co-operating with defective observation and little-developed understanding" (p. 39). Maudsley includes stigmatics among the phenomena that should be subjected to rational explanation.

8 *Le Chant du cygne*, p. 299; *Recollections*, p. 34.

9 *Le Chant du cygne*, p. 124.

10 London: John Lane, The Bodley Head, 1913, pp. 3–27. Further references are given after quotations in the text.

11 *Autobiographies* (London: Macmillan, 1966), pp. 173–74.

12 Robert Hichens recalls being told a version of the story in what must have been 1893 or 1894. *Yesterday. The Autobiography of Robert Hichens* (London: Cassell, 1947), pp. 66–67.

13 Tzvetan Todorov, *The Fantastic. A Structural Approach to a Literary Genre* (Ithaca, NY: Cornell University Press, 1975) and Rosemary Jackson, *Fantasy: The Literature of Subversion* (London: Routledge, 1981).

14 W. T. Beckford, *Vathek*, ed. by Roger Lonsdale (Oxford University Press, 1970), pp. 18–20.

15 Robert Louis Stevenson, *"Dr. Jekyll and Mr. Hyde" and Other Stories* (Harmondsworth: Penguin, 1979), p. 95.

16 *The Fantastic*, pp. 50–51.

17 A. H. Kober, *Star Turns*, trans. by G. J. Rénier (London: Noel Douglas, 1928). Further references are given after quotations in the text. LaRoche appeared with Barnum and Bailey's circus in London in the 1890s. There are further accounts of his act in Paul Adrian, *Attractions Sensationelles* (Bourg-la-Reine: L'auteur Adrian, 1962), pp. 94–98; Anthony Hippisley Coxe, *A Seat at the Circus* (London: Macmillan, 1980), p. 67; Ricky Jay, *Learned Pigs and Fireproof Women* (London: Robert Hale, 1986), pp. 203–11; M. J. Renévy, *Le Grand Livre du cirque* (Geneva: Bibliothèque des Arts, 1977), 2 vols., vol. II, pp. 324–28; Henry Thétard, *La Merveilleuse Histoire du cirque* (Paris: Juillard, 1978). For information on J. R. Lepère see Signor Saltarino, *Fahrend Volk* (Leipzig: Verlagsbuchhandlung von J. J. Weber, 1895). The trick is explained in Walter B. Gibson, *The Book of Secrets. Miracles Ancient and Modern* (New York: Mason Publishing, 1927),

pp. 82–83 and A. de Vaulabelle and C. Hemardinquer, *La Science au théâtre* (Paris: Henry Paulin, 1908), pp. 250–51.

18 R. M. Manning-Sanders, *The Golden Ball* (London: Robert Hale, 1954), p. 228.

19 See Jim Brent, *At the Balance* (London: Jonathan Cape, 1958).

20 See Kerry Powell, *Oscar Wilde and the Theatre of the 1890s* (Cambridge University Press, 1990).

2 SOME GENTLE CRITICISMS OF BRITISH JUSTICE

1 "Réponse à quelques journalistes," *La Revue Blanche*, 10, 552–53, p. 553.

2 Taken from Christopher Millard's translation of Douglas's unpublished article, housed in the William Andrews Clark Memorial Library, UCLA.

3 William More Adey (1858–1942), a friend of Robert Ross who worked hard to protect Wilde's interests while he was in jail and after his release.

4 "A Late Victorian Love Affair," in *Oscar Wilde, Two Approaches* (Los Angeles: William Andrews Clark Memorial Library, 1977), p. 15.

5 The Clark Library has a copy and there is a set of proofs with handwritten additions in the Miller Library (Special Collections), Colby College, Maine. A letter by Christopher Millard, Wilde's first bibliographer, attached to the Colby proofs, states: "This pamphlet is so rare that I have not seen more than three copies in the last twenty years. I somewhat doubt that it was actually issued – certainly it was never in any sense published."

6 The *Star* printed a letter of support for Wilde on 20 April 1895 under the heading "LORD ALFRED DOUGLAS APPEALS FOR FAIR PLAY" (p. 3). In *De Profundis* (*Works*, 1003, 1044) Wilde was twice to complain about the phrase, saying that it was "patronising and Philistine." In fact, Douglas appears not to have used it in print himself, though it does appear in an accompanying letter from Robert Buchanan.

7 Stead had contributed an editorial on the subject of Wilde's sentence to his new periodical *The Review of Reviews*. Douglas responded with a passionate letter in defense of homosexuality which Stead declined to publish. See H. Montgomery Hyde, *The Trials of Oscar Wilde* (New York: Dover, 1973), pp. 339–48.

8 Henry Du Pré Labouchère (1831–1912), MP for Northampton, founder of *Truth*. Labouchère was responsible for the clause that became section 11 of the Criminal Law Amendment Act under which Wilde was charged and found guilty. For an analysis of this moment see Richard Dellamora, *Masculine Desire. The Politics of*

Victorian Aestheticism (Chapel Hill and London: University of North Carolina Press, 1990), p. 201, and F. B. Smith, "Labouchère's Amendment to the Criminal Law Amendment Bill," *Historical Studies*, 17, 165–73.

9 Playfair originally referred to this man as "Hades" but later changed the disguise to "Hermes" (letter of 10 October).

10 Burton's name was raised in the course of the second trial, see Hyde, *Trials*, pp. 187–92.

11 A penciled note by Mason identifies this man as "Bernard Abrahams."

12 Mason identifies this as Lillie Langtry. The dead man was presumably George Alexander Baird, a rich lover of the actress, who had died in 1893.

13 Mason identifies this as "Bobbie Peel," probably William Robert Wellesley Peel (1867–1937), 4th Baronet.

14 Mason identifies one of these men as the actor Charles Brookfield. The other is said to have been the actor Charles Hawtrey.

15 Hyde, *Trials*, p. 269.

16 London: Elliot Stock. Further references are given after quotations in the text.

17 London: Headley Brothers, 1912, p. 68.

18 The correspondence between Wilson and Adey, on which the following account is based, is divided between the William Andrews Clark Memorial Library, Los Angeles and the Miller Library, Colby College, Maine. Unless otherwise stated, all my quotations are from the Clark collection. Spelling and punctuation have been corrected where necessary.

19 Dalhousie Young (1866–1921), an English musician who, although at that time unknown to Wilde, had in 1895 published a pamphlet in his defense entitled *Apologia pro Oscar Wilde*. Wilson may have seen this as a precedent, but the mood had changed.

20 Presumably the Rev. Stewart Headlam (1847–1924). Headlam, well known for his work supporting and defending members of the theatrical profession, particularly female dancers, had gone bail for Wilde in 1895. On Wilde's release in 1897 he was to offer his house as a refuge.

21 Charles Chaddock's translation of *Psychopathia Sexualis* had appeared in 1892 (Philadelphia and London: F. A. Davis), although on the evidence of the translations in *Zalmoxis* it would seem that Wilson could read German. Douglas certainly knew about Krafft-Ebing and may have directed him to it.

22 H. R. Fox Bourne, *English Newspapers. Chapters in the History of Journalism*, vol. II (London: Chatto and Windus, 1887), described

Reynolds' as "a formidable spokesman for the most irreconcilable portions of the community" (p. 348). *Reynolds'* celebrated its centenary in May 1950 with articles describing the importance that it had always had in the lives of working-class readers. For further history of *Reynolds'* see Virginia Berridge (née Cook), "Popular Journalism and Working Class Attitudes, 1854–86: A Study of *Reynolds' Newspaper, Lloyd's Weekly Newspaper* and the *Weekly Times,*" PhD thesis, University of London, 1976; V. Berridge, "The Language of Popular and Radical Journalism: The Case of *Reynolds' Newspaper,*" *Bulletin of the Society for the Study of Labour History*, 44 (1982), 6–7; V. Berridge, "Popular Sunday Papers and Mid-Victorian Society," in *Newspaper History from the Seventeenth Century to the Present Day*, ed. by George Boyce et al. (London: Constable, 1978), pp. 247–64; A. Humpherys, "G. W. M. Reynolds: Popular Literature and Popular Politics," in Joel H. Wiener, *Innovators and Preachers. The Role of the Editor in Victorian England* (Westport and London: Greenwood Press, 1985), pp. 3–21; A. Humpherys, "Popular Narrative and Political Discourse in *Reynolds' Weekly Newspaper,*" in *Investigating Victorian Journalism*, ed. by Laurel Brake et al. (London: Macmillan, 1990), pp. 33–47.

23 Interview with the Editor, 27 January 1895, p. 5.

24 See in particular Ed. Cohen, *Talk on the Wilde Side* (New York and London: Routledge, 1993).

25 I have discussed this phenomenon at greater length in *In the Nineties* (Hemel Hempstead: Harvester-Wheatsheaf, 1989).

26 *The Wilde Century: Effeminacy, Oscar Wilde and the Queer Moment*, (London: Cassell, 1994), pp. 64–65.

27 "Radical and/or Respectable," in *The Press We Deserve*, ed. by Richard Boston (London: Routledge and Kegan Paul, 1970), pp. 14–26, pp. 21–22.

28 Robert Harborough Sherard, *The Life of Oscar Wilde* (London: T. Werner Laurie, 1905), p. 390. Further references are given after quotations in the text.

3 WILDE AT BAY: THE DIARY OF GEORGE IVES

1 The diary and a great deal more Ives material is held by the Humanities Research Center, Austin, Texas. Since the numbering of folios in the diary is sometimes erratic, my quotations are identified by date of entry only. Portions are virtually illiterate and I have frequently corrected punctuation and spelling, while attempting to preserve Ives's idiosyncrasies. Occasionally Ives uses a variety of alphabetical codes, although none of the passages quoted

here make use of them. The W. A. Clark Library in Los Angeles also has Ives correspondence.

A fascinating selection from Ives's scrapbooks was published in 1980: *Man Bites Man. The Scrapbook of an Edwardian Eccentric*, ed. by Paul Sieveking (London: Jay Landesman, 1980). It was given an informative review by E. S. Turner in the *Times Literary Supplement*, 19 December 1980, p. 1434.

There are also accounts of Ives in Timothy d'Arch Smith, *Love in Earnest* (London: Routledge and Kegan Paul, 1970), Brian Reade, *Sexual Heretics* (London: Routledge and Kegan Paul, 1970), and Jeffrey Weeks's *Coming Out* (London: Quartet, 1977).

2 Ives was brought up by the Hon. Emma Ives, daughter of the 3rd Viscount Maynard. See *The Times* obituary, 5 June 1950, p. 6.

3 *Cambridge Review*, 8 May 1890, 312, records that in a debate about "stump oratory" Ives said that he "thought people should be allowed to say what they liked, and be looked up to for actions only. He longed for the times when voters would use their instrument conscientiously, and refuse to be cajoled."

4 Rothschild, Sir Lionel Walter, 3rd Baronet and second Baron Rothschild of Tring (1868–1937). Walter Rothschild, as he was known, later declined to make banking his metier and became a famous naturalist.

5 In December 1892 Ives addressed a London debating society on the subject of birth control, arguing not only that increased population brought disease and famine, but that overcrowded communities bred "morbid competition" and added to the "aggregate of human sorrow". See "The Struggle for Existence," *Malthusian*, 17 (1893), 5–6.

6 The best, fullest treatment is in Weeks's *Coming Out*.

7 According to a note made much later, Wilde said "I have the kiss of Walt Whitman still on my lip" (16 January 1900).

8 Ives kept in contact with Carpenter and visited him in April 1897. See *Love in Earnest*, p. 113; *Coming Out*, pp. 119–20.

9 Ives's first book of verse, published under the pseudonym "C. Branco" (London: Swann Sonnenschein, 1892).

10 André Raffalovich (1864–1934), a rich poet of Russian origin, who later developed a close friendship with the poet John Gray. His relationship with Wilde was always uneasy and culminated in a hostile account of homosexuality, published after Wilde's imprisonment.

11 Sir Egbert Sebright, 10th Baronet, born 1871, died off Batavia, Japan, in 1897.

12 London: Macmillan, 1893.

13 "The Evolution of Our Race. A Reply," *Fortnightly Review*, 54 (1893), 29–41.

14 *Contemporary Review*, 63 (1893), 153–66 and March 1893, 439–56.

15 See *Love in Earnest*, pp. 110–11; *Coming Out*, p. 120.

16 The attacks on Allen for his regression to "Phallic Worship" were summarized by W. T. Stead in *Review of Reviews*, 9: 398 and 490.

17 See *Sexual Heretics*, pp. 52–53: "1894 could be described as a golden year for homosexuals in England, for the very reason that it was the last year for a long time in which they could take shelter in public ignorance or tolerance to propagate a non-hostile climate of taste and opinion."

18 In 1889 Ives wrote to *Reynolds' Newspaper* complaining that "Those detestable drawers have crept in, even upon our quiet rivers, to hide our self-made shame from the unspotted swans, and are enforced at closed and high-walled swimming baths. I begin to feel more and more Walt Whitman's respect for the animals who never reach our depths of degradation" (17 September, p. 4). In the *Saturday Review* in 1905 Ives reviewed a history of swimming, again protesting against the modern insistence that the body should be covered (4 January, pp. 85–86).

19 *Man Bites Man*, p. 139.

20 *The Artist*, 15: 55.

21 *Book of Chains* (London: Swan Sonnenschein), pp. vii–viii. Reprinted in *Degeneration and Regeneration. Texts of the PreModern Era*, ed. by Ian Fletcher and John Stokes (New York: Garland, 1984).

22 More than fifty years later Ives was to record: "If only I had been there, I believe I could have stopped that insane law-suit. But I had had rather a tiff with Wilde at the time, and did not go to see him until I saw the newspaper posters" (23 May 1946).

23 "Moral Effects of Imprisonment," 28 May 1896.

24 *Eros' Throne* has a poem, presumably objecting to the Boer War, titled "The War," dated February 1900.

25 I can find only one conscious joke in the whole diary: Ives's comment to Lord Ronald Gower that the death of Queen Victoria was "not quite so dismally depressing as the Jubilee" (no date, 1901). Elsewhere Ives was more charitable, remarking that, although the Queen was "surrounded by a great army of liars, she meant well, and was very stern in her ideas of duty...It is said that she personally abolished the chimney sweep boys, and I hope for her sake, this is true" (23 January 1901).

4 ROMANTIC REINCARNATIONS

1 (London: Archibald Constable, 1909). Further references are given after quotations in the text.

2 Symons's most recent and authoritative biographer observes that "As a study of the English Romantics, it is disappointing, for its form is problematic...a source book for students and researchers rather than an organic work of criticism" Karl Beckson, *Arthur Symons: A Life* (Oxford: Clarendon Press, 1987), p. 270.

3 For many years the standard account of the relation of Modernism to the Romantics was Frank Kermode's *Romantic Image* (London: Routledge and Kegan Paul, 1957). Kermode argued that the ease with which connections were made between Romanticism and French Symbolism was the result of Symons's unique ability to synthesize what was already in the air. Because the Romantic inheritance was essentially a mood of isolation ("Empedocles is Arnold's Leech Gatherer"), the contempt for action, and the espousal of mysticism, felt first by the Decadents and then by Yeats, was a natural progression. The "transition" was, in fact, continuity. I have commented upon Kermode's influential version of literary history in "*Romantic Image* Revisited," in *Addressing Frank Kermode*, ed. by Margaret Tudeau-Clayton and Martin Warner (London: Macmillan, 1991), pp. 5–11. A brilliant essay by John Goode which attempts a materialist analysis of the "transition" has greatly influenced my own account. See "The Decadent Writer as Producer," in *Decadence and the 1890s*, Stratford-upon-Avon Studies 17 (London: Edward Arnold, 1979), pp. 110–29.

4 *The Renaissance: Studies in Art and Poetry* (Berkeley and Los Angeles: University of California Press, 1980), p. xxi.

5 M. H. Abrams, *Natural Supernaturalism* (London: Oxford University Press, 1971), pp. 34–35. Abrams's explanation of Romanticism as an inspirational force has not gone unchallenged. Jerome McGann's *Romantic Ideology* (Chicago and London: University of Chicago Press, 1983) argues for a continual re-reading of Romantic texts according to subsequent critical conditions. This, of course, was the practice of late nineteenth-century critics who most certainly read Romanticism in the light of what they felt to be their own changed circumstances.

6 Matthew Arnold, *Essays in Criticism. Second Series* (London: Macmillan, 1888), pp. 203–4.

7 *The Poems of Matthew Arnold*, ed. by Kenneth Allott (London: Longmans, 1965), p. 226.

8 *Essays in Criticism*, p. 202.

9 *Swinburne as Critic*, ed. by Clyde K. Hyder (London: Routledge, 1972), p. 38.

10 "Wordsworth and Byron," *Miscellanies* (London: Chatto and Windus, 1886).

11 I discuss Victorian readings of Wordsworth in "Aestheticism," in *Encyclopedia of Literature and Criticism*, ed. by Martin Coyle et al. (London: Routledge, 1990), pp. 1055–67.

12 *Swinburne as Critic*, p. 41.

13 *Miscellanies*, pp. 142–43.

14 *Poems of Matthew Arnold*, p. 208.

15 *Appreciations* (London: Macmillan, 1889), p. 56.

16 *The Poetical Works of William Wordsworth*, vol. III ed. by de Selincourt (Oxford: Clarendon Press, 1952), p. 82.

17 *Autobiography*, ed. by Jack Stillinger (Oxford University Press, 1971), p. 89.

18 *Appreciations*, p. 51.

19 *Reviews* (London: Methuen, 1908), p. 544, taken from Pater, *Appreciations*, pp. 62–63.

20 "Coleridge's Writings," in *Walter Pater: Essays on Literature and Art*, ed. by Jennifer Uglow (London: Dent, 1973), p. 1. This edition prints the 1866 version, but indicates the passages that were later dropped. Further references are given after quotation in the text.

21 Letter to J. Dykes Campbell, 11 December 1888, in *Arthur Symons. Selected letters, 1880–1935* ed. by Karl Beckson and John M. Munro (London: Macmillan, 1989), p. 40.

22 *The Savoy*, 8, p. 41. Reprinted in *Studies in Two Literatures* (London: Leonard Smithers), 1897.

23 *Reviews*, pp. 542–43.

24 "The Philosophy of Shelley's Poetry," *Essays and Introductions* (London: Macmillan, 1969), p. 95.

25 The best account of the cult of Keats, and of Wilde's involvement in it, is Estelle Jussim, *Slave to Beauty: the Eccentric and Controversial Career of F. Holland Day, Photographer, Publisher, Aesthete* (Boston: Godine, 1981).

26 "The Tomb of Keats," *Reviews*, p. 4. Keats also appears in an emotional passage in the early poem "Glikipikros Eros" where, in an echo of Keats's own "This Living Hand," Wilde imagines clasping "the noble hand of love in mine" (*Works*, 843).

27 *Miscellanies* (London: Methuen, 1908), p. 261.

28 *William Blake* (London: Archibald Constable, 1907).

29 See Deborah Dorfman, *Blake in the Nineteenth Century* (New Haven: Yale University Press, 1969), and *William Blake: The Critical Heritage*, ed. by G. E. Bentley Jr. (London and Boston: Routledge and Kegan Paul, 1975).

30 *Reviews*, p. 166.

31 *Miscellanies*, p. 261.

5 BEARDSLEY/JARRY: THE ART OF DEFORMATION

1 *Le Théâtre et son double* (Paris: Gallimard, 1964), p. 115.
2 *Aubrey Beardsley* (London: John Lane, 1909), p. 52.
3 It is the French journalist who says this, and he goes on to say that when he wrote the occasion up for his column he was punished with the lifelong enmity of the hostess. But a search through his paper reveals no such item and elsewhere he confuses Beardsley with Lord Alfred Douglas. It looks as if the journalist (he later became an impresario) found it necessary to invent a punishment to match an imaginary indiscretion that, however unfounded in fact, sounded in its details exactly right. See Jacques-Charles, *La Revue de ma vie* (Paris: Librarie Arthème Fayard, 1958), pp. 28–29.
4 *The Letters of Aubrey Beardsley*, ed. by Henry Maas et al. (London: Cassell, 1970), p. 47. Also see *Letters*, p. 339.
5 Diaghilev commissioned an article on Beardsley from the critic D. S. MacColl for his Symbolist magazine. It was later reprinted in R. A. Walker, *A Beardsley Miscellany* (London: The Bodley Head, 1949), pp. 17–32.
6 This is revealed by the comments that Craig wrote in the margin of his own copy, now in my possession.
7 *The Empty Space* (Harmondsworth: Penguin Books, 1972), p. 48.
8 Beardsley, *Letters*, p. 308.
9 "L'idée ne nous est venue à aucun d'entre nous de nous renseigner sur la signification des mots que nous prononcions. Ce qui nous plaisait c'est justement que nous ne les comprenions pas." Jacques Robichez, *Le Symbolisme au théâtre* (Paris: L'Arche, 1957), p. 370.
10 Alfred Jarry, *Œuvres complètes* (Paris: Gallimard, 1972), I, p. 399. Further references to *Œuvres I* and *II* (Paris: Gallimard, 1987) are given after quotations in the text. The best critical biography of Jarry is Keith Beaumont, *Alfred Jarry* (Leicester University Press, 1984).
11 Stanley Weintraub, *Beardsley* (Harmondsworth: Penguin Books, 1972), p. 208.
12 In an early French tribute to Beardsley, Henry Davray writes of "La déformation voulue de certains traits...cette laideur voulue, obtenue par des déformations savantes et précises." "L'Art d'Aubrey Beardsley," *L'Ermitage*, 8: 256.
13 See Ian Fletcher, "A Grammar of Monsters: Beardsley's Images and their Sources," *English Literature in Transition*, 30 (1987), 141–63.
14 Brigid Brophy, *Beardsley and His World* (London: Thames and Hudson, 1976), p. 41.
15 For Beardsley's treatment of Réjane, see my "A Kind of Beauty: Réjane in London," *Themes in Drama*, 6 (1984), 97–119; Brigid J.

Elliott, "Beardsley's Images of Actresses," in *Reconsidering Aubrey Beardsley*, ed. by Robert Langenfeld (Ann Arbor and London: UMI Research Press, 1989), pp. 71–101.

16 *Studio*, 13 (1898), p. 261. The obituarist was probably Gleeson White.

17 *The Memoirs of Arthur Symons*, ed. by Karl Beckson (University Park and London: Pennsylvania State University Press, 1977), p. 175.

18 *Beardsley Miscellany*, pp. 87–88.

19 This was Lewis Hind. See Brian Reade and Frank Dickinson, *Aubrey Beardsley. Exhibition at the Victoria and Albert Museum* (London, 1966), no.149.

20 Another of Beardsley's pictures actually represents Craig, who acted in the production, so Craig would hardly have missed this particular issue of the *Pall Mall Gazette*.

21 By Armand Silvestre and Isidore de Lara. Lautrec saw it in Bordeaux in 1900.

22 *Messalina: A Novel of Imperial Rome*, trans. by John Harman (London: Atlas Press, 1988), p. 19. Further references to this translation are given after the quotations in the text.

23 In *Aubrey Beardsley and Victorian Sexual Politics* (Oxford: Clarendon Press, 1990), Linda Gertner Zatlin points out that Beardsley's picture is of *Messalina Returning from the Bath*, an event that does not occur in Juvenal. "She is stout, less lusty than determined, and unhappy. Her breasts are naked, her pointed nipples suggesting either continued excitement or exposure to cold air, but Messalina does not licentiously stare at the viewer...Her breasts allude to her adulterous activities; along with her clenched fists, they suggest an open defiance of Claudius" (p. 57). It seems likely that Beardsley's picture evokes the notorious line cited both in Jarry's *Le surmâle* (*Œuvres II*, 306) and in the pornographic novel, *Teleny* (London: GMP, 1986), p. 166 in which Wilde is said to have had a hand: "Et lassat viris nec dum satiata recessit." In the version said to be Beardsley's favourite, Barten Holyday translates this as "Weary she did retire, not satisfied" (*Decimus Junius Juvenalis and Aulus Perfius Flaccus*, Translated and Illustrated as Well with Sculpture as Notes [Oxford: Printed by W. Downing, 1673]), p. 93.

24 "Beardsley's sexual fantasies are realistic in so far as they are really possible – they do not demand unflagging virility, impossible acrobatics, or absurd combinations" (Zatlin, *Beardsley*, p. 195). These are precisely the aspects of the erotic that interest Jarry most.

25 *Beardsley Miscellany*, p. 93.

26 For a list of obituaries in French newspapers, see Henry D. Davray in *La Plume*, 246: 449–51.

27 Weintraub, *Beardsley*, p. 205.

28 *Professionelles beautés* (Paris: Librairie Félix Juvan, 1905), p. 104.
29 *Selected Works of Alfred Jarry*, ed. by Roger Shattuck and Simon Watson Taylor (New York: Grove Press, 1965), p. 202. Further references to this translation are given after quotations in the text.
30 (London: Macmillan, 1891), vol. I, p. 317. In 1903 Jarry was to write apropos Wells's *Time Machine*: "On comprend mieux Wells et son admirable sang-froid dans la description non pas de l'absurde, mais du *possible* au sens mathématique, si l'on réfléchit qu'il écrit dans la langue ou professa Lord Kelvin." "De quelques romans scientifiques" in *Œuvres II*, p. 520.
31 J. E. Chamberlin, "Whose Spirit is This?" in *Fin de Siècle/Fin du Globe*, ed. by John Stokes (Basingstoke: Macmillan, 1992), pp. 220–39. Chamberlin observes that "even Hopkins, to take just one unlikely example, proposed to write what he referred to as 'a sort of popular account of Light and the Ether,' in order to counter the materialist tendencies of the time by demonstrating the essentially spiritual character of the discourses of the physical sciences" (p. 228). From a more historical perpective: "Lots of the scientists of the Fin de Siècle cheerfully went along, hand in hand with artists, sharing their conviction that knowledge of the real world was essentially subjective and figurative, a convenient imaginative construction" (p. 230).
32 Norman and Jeanne Mackenzie, *The Time Traveller. The Life of H. G. Wells* (London: Weidenfeld, 1973), pp. 84–85.
33 "The Rediscovery of the Unique," *Fortnightly Review*, 50: 106–11 (p. 106).

6 DIEPPE: 1895 AND AFTER

1 *Portraits of a Lifetime* (London: Dent, 1937), p. 52.
2 Jean Paul Raymond and Charles Ricketts, *Oscar Wilde, Recollections*, (Bloomsbury: the Nonesuch Press, 1933), p. 52.
3 See Mikhail Bakhtin, *Rabelais and his World* (Bloomington: Indiana University Press, 1984). For an alternative view of the holiday spirit see Peter Stallybrass and Allon White, *The Politics and Poetics of Transgression* (London: Methuen, 1986).
4 Basic information on the history of Dieppe can be found in Charles Merk, *A History of Dieppe* (Paris: Herbert Clarke, 1909); Gabriel Désert, *La Vie quotidienne sur les plages Normandes du second empire aux années folles* (Paris: Hachette, 1983); and two books by Simona Pakenham, *Pigtails and Pernod* (London: Macmillan, 1962) and *Sixty Miles from England* (London: Macmillan, 1967).
5 "About Dieppe," *Pall Mall Gazette*, 16 October 1893, p. 11.

6 See *The Dieppe Connection*, ed. by Caroline Collier and Julia Mac-
   Kenzie (London: Herbert Press, 1992) and the extremely informative
   catalog to the exhibition *Rendez-Vous à Dieppe. The Town and its Artists
   from Turner to Braque*, organized by John Willett at the Brighton
   Museum and Art Gallery, 1992.

7 *Savoy*, 1 (1896), 84–102, rpt. in *Cities and Sea Coasts and Islands*
   (London: Collins, 1918), pp. 227–48. Further references to the 1918
   edition are given after quotations in the text. *Punch*, 1 February 1896,
   p. 49, printed a parody of the essay, "Margate, 1895. By Simple
   Symons," the joke being that the mystique of foreignness was
   Symons's snobbish invention.

8 "The hotels make their harvest during the summer season," "About
   Dieppe" reported in 1893, "since at other times visitors are few. But
   there are plenty of good apartments to be had, and I should
   recommend those not prepared to spend thirty francs a day on their
   board and lodging to try them. Flats, too, can be obtained, and look
   exceedingly comfortable. Many are taken by Parisians who like to
   spend the weekend with their family. At the best hotels prices are
   high..."

9 *A Free House!* (London: Macmillan, 1947), p. 44. More information
   on Sickert's Dieppe paintings can be found in exhibition catalogs,
   for instance *Sickert in Dieppe* (Turner Gallery, Eastbourne, n.d.), and
   Walter Sickert and Jacques-Emile Blanche and Friends in Dieppe (London:
   Parkin Gallery, 1982) and, above all, in *Sickert Paintings*, ed. by
   Wendy Baron and Richard Shone (New Haven and London: Yale
   University Press), 1992.

10 *Imperial Brown of Brixton* (London: Chapman and Hall, 1908), pp. 1–2.

11 *A Summer Jaunt* (London: F. V. White, 1899), p. 36.

12 Denys Sutton, *Walter Sickert* (London: Michael Joseph, 1976), p. 123.

13 Reggie Turner, *Castles in Kensington* (London: Greening, 1904), p. 10.
   In Turner's *Imperial Brown* it appears as the "Hôtel des Deux
   Globes." Beerbohm's essay "The Maison Lefèvre" is included as an
   appendix to   *Letters to Reggie Turner*, ed. by Rupert Hart-Davis
   (London: Hart-Davis, 1964), pp. 302–4.

14 Evelyn Sharp, *Unfinished Adventure* (London: John Lane, Bodley
   Head, 1933), p. 65.

15 *A Sea-side Flirt* (London: F. V. White, 1897), p. 19.

16 *Summer Jaunt*, p. 210.

17 *Letters to Reggie Turner*, p. 203.

18 For a description of this area see *Portraits of a Lifetime*. Blanche
   produced several other autobiographical accounts of his life on the
   Normandy coast including *Essais et portraits* (Paris: Les Bibliophiles
   Fantaisistes, 1912); *Aymeris* (Paris: Plon, 1930); *Les Arts plastiques* (Paris:

Les Editions de France, 1931); *La Pêche aux souvenirs* (Paris: Flam-marion, 1949); and, the most comprehensive, *Dieppe* (Paris: Emile-Paul Frères, 1927).

19 At other times Diaghilev, Strindberg, Grieg, Coquelin, and Bern-hardt all came to visit Thaulow (see Blanche, *Dieppe*, p. 88). Blanche later took a manor house at Offranville where he entertained guests from André Gide to Virginia Woolf.

20 *Summer Jaunt*, pp. 41–42. Not everyone agreed with this. According to "About Dieppe," the esplanade was in a poor state: "The energy of the old Dieppois seems to have departed, or to be working itself out in building shipyards and improving the harbour, since it presents a most forlorn appearance...If only this space were laid out in gardens, and the sea walk railed in, the effect would be very pretty. In its present state, except for the sea, the look-out from the hotel windows is anything but attractive."

21 Bonington, Richard Parkes (1802–28). English painter and friend of Delacroix who frequently painted Dieppe.

22 Symons later reminisced that Cléo de Mérode "was to be seen every day on the sands of Dieppe" (*Star*, 3 June 1902, p. 1).

23 It is certainly very different from the introductory vignette of Dieppe offered by Jacques-Emile Blanche. For Blanche it is the view from the station that triggers childhood memory, a visual impression curiously impregnated with smells, Proustian in effect, if hardly in kind: "La première fois que l'on me conduisit à Dieppe, je crains que la nourrice qui me portait dans ses bras ne soit écriée, si l'on se préoccupait alors d'hygiène et puériculture: 'Quelle odeur!'. La gare puait l'eau saumâtre égouttée des mannes de poisson; elle était noire de charbon" (*Dieppe*, pp. 6–7).

24 See Laurel Brake, "*The Savoy*: 1896. Gender in Crisis?" *Subjugated Knowledges. Journalism, Gender and Literature* (London: Macmillan, 1994), pp. 148–65. Brake offers a powerful critique of the "reiterated misogyny" that characterized the *Savoy* as a whole.

25 "About Dieppe."

26 *Dieppe Connection*, p. 38.

27 See *Sickert Paintings*, pp. 128–29.

28 A study of Dieppe faces p. 129 of John Rothenstein, *The Life and Death of Conder* (London: Dent, 1938).

29 *Sea-side Flirt*, p. 48.

30 *Dieppe*, p. 55.

31 Dieppe: Bibliothèque Dieppoise, 1878, 2 vols.

32 *More Portraits of a Lifetime* (London: Dent, 1939), p. 105.

33 *Seven Men* (London: William Heinemann, 1919), pp. 107–35.

34 *More Portraits*, pp. 106–8.

35 *Letters of Max Beerbohm*, ed. by Rupert Hart-Davis (London: John Murray, 1988), p. 46.

36 *Portraits of a Lifetime*, p. 38.

37 *Dieppe*, p. 33.

38 *Aymeris*, p. 14.

39 *Imperial Brown*, p. 53.

40 *Sea-side Flirt*, p. 21.

41 *Autobiographies* (London: Macmillan, 1966), p. 328.

42 Ian Fletcher, *W. B. Yeats and his Contemporaries* (Brighton: Harvester, 1987), p. 146.

43 *The Memoirs of Arthur Symons*, ed. by Karl Beckson (University Park: Pennsylvania State University Press, 1971), p. 86.

44 See Mark Longaker, *Ernest Dowson* (Philadelphia: University of Pennsylvania Press, 1945).

45 See *W. B. Yeats and his Contemporaries*, pp. 257–58.

46 *A Free House!*, p. 105.

47 See *Portraits of a Lifetime*, p. 47.

48 *Dieppe*, p. 106.

49 *Summer Jaunt*, p. 130.

50 *Sea-side Flirt*, p. 130.

51 William Empson, *Some Versions of Pastoral* (Harmondsworth: Penguin, 1966), p. 23.

52 *Plays: One* (London: Methuen, 1976), p. 35.

53 *Complete Plays* (London: Methuen, 1976), p. 93.

54 *Standing Female Nude* (London: Anvil Press, 1985), p. 47.

55 See Oscar Wilde, *Berneval: An Unpublished Letter*, ed. by Jeremy Mason (Edinburgh: privately printed, 1981).

56 *Letters of Max Beerbohm* (London: Murray, 1988), p. 42.

57 *Letters to Reggie Turner*, p. 154.

58 See *Dieppe Connection*, pp. 44–52.

59 See Marguerite Steen, *William Nicholson* (London: Collins), 1943.

60 *Collected Poems. 1930–1978* (London: John Calder, 1984), p. 50.

61 *Standing Female Nude*, p. 47.

62 Information is taken from correspondence with the artist, drafts of a catalog essay to an exhibition to be held at the Walker Art Gallery in Liverpool in 1996, and the catalog notes by Pierre Bazin to the exhibition held at the Château Musée de Dieppe in September 1984.

7 WILDE INTERPRETATIONS

1 *Subsequent Performances* (London: Faber and Faber, 1986), p. 70.

2 The case that Wilde had an innovative sense of scenic design has

been strongly argued by Richard Allen Cave in "Wilde Designs: Some Thoughts about Recent British Productions of His Plays," *Modern Drama*, 37 (1994), 175–91.

3 For an informative interview with Prowse see Joel H. Kaplan, "Staging Wilde's Society Plays: A Conversation with Philip Prowse (Glasgow Citizens' Theatre)," *Modern Drama*, 37 (1994), 192–205. Also see Michael Coveney, *The Citz. 21 Years of the Glasgow Citizens' Theatre* (London: Nick Hern Books, 1990) and Joel H. Kaplan, "Wilde in the Gorbals: Society Drama and Citizens' Theatre," in *Rediscovering Oscar Wilde*, ed. by G. Sandulescu (Gerard's Cross: Colin Smythe, 1994). Before Prowse the most celebrated modern revivals were John Gielgud's production in 1945, designed by Cecil Beaton; a London revival in 1966, also designed by Cecil Beaton, directed by Anthony Quayle; and an admired production at the Bristol Old Vic in 1990. See J. C. Trewin, "Wilde: *Lady Windermere's Fan*," *Plays and Players*, 14: 56–58.

4 See Joel H. Kaplan, "A Puppet's Power: George Alexander, Clement Scott, and the Replotting of *Lady Windermere's Fan*," *Theatre Notebook*, 46, 59–73.

5 Unidentified cutting, Theatre Museum, London.

6 Rose Leclercq's obituary in *The Stage*, 6 April 1899, p. 11, said that "For some years she had been unrivalled in the depiction of the *grande dame* in modern drama, a depiction tempered by a sympathetic charm, which was part of her style," citing Lady Bellaston in *Sophia* (1886), Lady Bawtry in *The Dancing Girl* (1891), the Marchioness of Castle Jordan in *The Amazons* (1893), Hon. Mrs Fretwell in *Sowing the Wind* (1893), Lady Wargrave in *The New Woman* (1894), and Lady Ringstead in *The Princess and the Butterfly* (1897). Neither this, nor the the obituary in the *Era*, 8 April 1899, p. 13, so much as mentioned Lady Bracknell.

7 *Our Theatres in the Nineties* (London: Constable, 1932), vol. i, p. 221. Shaw had, by chance, seen an understudy as Lady Bracknell.

8 *The Dramatic Works of St. John Hankin*, vol. iii (London: Martin Secker, 1912), p. 194.

9 *Early Stages* (London: Macmillan, 1939), pp. 180–81.

10 The *Observer*, 13 July 1930, p. 13, thought her delivery realistic and called her a "plausible dragon." The *Daily Telegraph*, 8 July 1930, p. 8, said that her performance was "beautifully conceived."

11 *Backward Glances* (London: Hodder and Stoughton, 1989), p. 43.

12 "She was not, in the pure sense of the word, an 'actress', for all she did was to carry *herself* on to the stage. She was quite incapable of realising any character of any class apart from that with which she was acquainted, but, within a narrow range, she was impeccable."

Marguerite Steen, *A Pride of Terrys* (London: Longman, 1962), p. 287.

13 *The Craft of Comedy* (London: Nick Hern Books, 1990), p. 68.

14 Tyrone Guthrie, *A Life in the Theatre* (London: Hamish Hamilton, 1960), pp. 113–14.

15 *An Actor and His Time* (London: Sidgwick and Jackson, 1979), p. 72. Further references are given after quotations in the text.

16 "For her to say 'A handbag' is to to bring all the heavens of Mayfair crashing in one thunderbolt" (*Observer*, 20 August 1939, p. 9); "she gets over the dowager duchess of that stage-period perfectly" (*Illustrated London News*, 26 August 1939, p. 358); "a striking portrait – highly caricatured – of the latter-day grande dame" (*Bystander*, 23 August 1939, p. 273).

17 When the production toured Canada and the USA in 1947 the role was taken by Margaret Rutherford.

18 *Ned's Girl* (London: Hamish Hamilton, 1977), pp. 202–3.

19 The success of Gielgud's *Importance* is analyzed by Michael Billington in *Peggy Ashcroft* (London: John Murray, 1988), pp. 100–3.

20 The issue is pursued in two notable articles in *Modern Drama*, 37 (1994): Alan Sinfield, " 'Effeminacy' and 'Feminity': Sexual Politics in Wilde's Comedies," 34–52, and Joseph Bristow, "Dowdies and Dandies: Oscar Wilde's Refashioning of Society Comedy," 53–70.

21 *The Little Ottleys* (London: Virago, 1982), p. 460.

22 Julie Speedie, *Wonderful Sphinx* (London: Virago, 1993), p. 36.

23 There are signs that the much maligned Constance was encouraged to keep up with her husband, even if this then led to her being criticized for publicly giggling at her own jokes. See Anne Clark Amor, *Mrs. Oscar Wilde. A Woman of Some Importance* (London: Sidgwick and Jackson, 1983), p. 73.

24 *The Importance of Being Earnest*, ed. by Russell Jackson (London: Benn, 1980), p. 85.

25 See Joel H. Kaplan and Sheila Stowell, *Theatre and Fashion. Oscar Wilde to the Suffragettes* (Cambridge University Press, 1994).

26 Laurence Irving, *Henry Irving* (London: Faber and Faber, 1961), p. 375.

27 *Lady's Pictorial*, 19 July 1884, p. 45.

28 Report of the first night of *Faust*, *Pall Mall Gazette*, 21 December 1885, pp. 4–5.

29 " 'First Nights' at the Play," 7 October 1886, p. 931.

30 *Oscar Wilde: The Critical Heritage*, ed. by Karl Beckson (London: Routledge, 1970), p. 193. Of course Wilde's physical appearance had been mimicked on the London stage many times in his own lifetime. See *Ellmann*, pp. 128–29.

31 First staged in Dublin in 1991, subsequently revived in England and Ireland in 1991 and 1994.
32 From the programme notes to the Talawa Theatre Company production, directed by Yvonne Brewster, at the Bloomsbury Theatre, 15–27 May.

Select bibliography

Neil Bartlett, *Who Was That Man? A Present for Mr. Oscar Wilde* (Harmondsworth: Penguin, 1993).
Karl Beckson, *Arthur Symons: A Life* (Oxford: Clarendon Press, 1987).
  London in the 1890s: A Cultural History (New York and London: Norton, 1992).
  Oscar Wilde: The Critical Heritage (London: Routledge, 1970).
Laurel Brake, *Subjugated Knowledges* (Basingstoke and London: Macmillan, 1994).
J. Edward Chamberlin, *Ripe was the Drowsy Hour: The Age of Oscar Wilde* (New York: The Seabury Press, 1977).
J. Edward Chamberlin and Sander L. Gilman (eds.), *Degeneration: The Dark Side of Progress* (New York: Columbia University Press, 1985).
Ed. Cohen, *Talk on the Wilde Side* (New York and London: Routledge, 1993).
Christopher Craft, *Another Kind of Love: Male Homosexual Desire in English Discourse, 1850–1920* (Berkeley: University of California Press, 1994).
Richard Dellamora, *Masculine Desire. The Politics of Victorian Aestheticism* (Chapel Hill and London: University of North Carolina Press, 1990).
Jonathan Dollimore, *Sexual Dissidence* (Oxford: Clarendon, 1991).
Linda Dowling, *Hellenism and Homosexuality in Victorian Oxford* (Ithaca and New York: Cornell University Press, 1994).
  Language and Decadence in the Victorian Fin de Siècle (Princeton University Press, 1986).
Terry Eagleton, *Saint Oscar* (Derry: Field Day, 1989).
Richard Ellmann, *Golden Codgers* (Oxford University Press, 1973).
  Oscar Wilde (London: Hamish Hamilton, 1987).
Regenia Gagnier, *Idylls of the Marketplace* (Aldershot: Scolar Press, 1987).
H. Montgomery Hyde, *The Trials of Oscar Wilde* (New York: Dover, 1973).

Joel H. Kaplan and Sheila Stowell, *Theatre and Fashion: Oscar Wilde to the Suffragettes* (Cambridge University Press, 1994).

Robert Langenfeld (ed.), *Mr. Aubrey Beardsley Reconsidered: Essays and An Annotated Secondary Bibliography* (Ann Arbor and London: UMI Research Press, 1989).

Sally Ledger and Scott McCracken (eds.), *Cultural Politics at the Fin de Siècle* (Cambridge University Press, 1995).

E. H. Mikhail, *Oscar Wilde: An Annotated Bibliography of Criticism* (London and Basingstoke: Macmillan, 1978).

E. H. Mikhail (ed.), *Oscar Wilde: Interviews and Recollections*, 2 vols. (London and Basingstoke: Macmillan, 1979).

Murray Pittock, *The Decadent Spectrum: The Literature of the 1890s* (London: Routledge, 1993).

Kerry Powell, *Oscar Wilde and the Theatre of the 1890s* (Cambridge University Press, 1990).

Peter Raby, *Oscar Wilde* (Cambridge University Press, 1988).

Guillot de Saix, *Le Chant du cygne, contes parlés d'Oscar Wilde* (Paris: Mercure de France, 1942); Reprinted in Ian Fletcher and John Stokes (eds.), *The Decadent Consciousness. A Hidden Archive of Late Victorian Literature* (New York: Garland, 1979).

Gary Schmidgall, *The Stranger Wilde: Interpreting Oscar* (London: Abacus, 1994).

Eve Kosofsky Sedgwick, *Between Men. English Literature and Male Homosexual Desire* (New York: Columbia University Press, 1985).

Epistemology of the Closet (Berkeley and Los Angeles: University of California Press, 1990).

Tendencies (London: Routledge, 1994).

Elaine Showalter, *Sexual Anarchy: Gender and Culture in the Fin de Siècle* (London: Bloomsbury, 1991).

Alan Sinfield, *The Wilde Century: Effeminacy, Oscar Wilde and the Queer Moment* (London: Cassell, 1994).

Ian Small, *Conditions for Criticism*, (Oxford University Press, 1991).

Oscar Wilde Revalued: An Essay on New Materials and Methods of Research (Greensboro, NC: ELT Press, 1993).

John Stokes, *In the Nineties* (Hemel Hempstead: Harvester-Wheatsheaf, 1989; University of Chicago Press, 1989).

John Stokes (ed.), *Fin de Siècle/Fin du Globe* (London and Basingstoke: Macmillan, 1992).

Mikulas Teich and Roy Porter (eds.), *Fin de Siècle and its Legacy* (Cambridge University Press, 1990).

Judith R. Walkowitz, *City of Dreadful Delight: Narratives of Sexual Danger in Late-Victorian London* (London: Virago, 1992).

Oscar Wilde, *Complete Works of Oscar Wilde*, ed. by Merlin Holland (Glasgow: HarperCollins, 1994).

"The Importance of Being Earnest" and Related Writings, ed. by Joseph Bristow (London: Routledge, 1992).

The Importance of Being Earnest, ed. by Russell Jackson (London: Ernest Benn, 1980).

Lady Windermere's Fan, ed. by Ian Small (London: Ernest Benn, 1980).

The Letters of Oscar Wilde, ed. by Rupert Hart-Davis (London: Hart-Davis, 1962).

More Letters of Oscar Wilde, ed. by Rupert Hart-Davis (London: John Murray, 1985).

Oscar Wilde's Oxford Notebooks: A Portrait of Mind in the Making ed. by Philip E. Smith and Michael S. Helfand (Oxford University Press, 1989).

Two Society Comedies: "A Woman of No Importance" and *"An Ideal Husband"* ed. by Ian Small and Russell Jackson (London: Ernest Benn, 1983).

Katharine Worth, *Oscar Wilde* (London and Basingstoke: Macmillan, 1983).

Linda Gertner Zatlin, *Aubrey Beardsley and Victorian Sexual Politics* (Oxford: Clarendon Press, 1990).

Index